DIACHRONIC DIVERSITY IN CLASSICAL BIBLICAL HEBREW

Diachronic Diversity in Classical Biblical Hebrew

Aaron D. Hornkohl

https://www.openbookpublishers.com

©2024 Aaron D. Hornkohl

This work is licensed under an Attribution-NonCommercial 4.0 International (CC BY-NC 4.0). This license allows you to share, copy, distribute, and transmit the text; to adapt the text for non-commercial purposes of the text providing attribution is made to the authors (but not in any way that suggests that they endorse you or your use of the work). Attribution should include the following information:

Aaron D. Hornkohl, *Diachronic Diversity in Classical Biblical Hebrew*. Cambridge, UK: Open Book Publishers, 2024, https://doi.org/10.11647/OBP.0433

Further details about CC BY-NC licenses are available at http://creativecommons.org/licenses/by-nc/4.0/

All external links were active at the time of publication unless otherwise stated and have been archived via the Internet Archive Wayback Machine at https://archive.org/web

Any digital material and resources associated with this volume will be available at https://doi.org/10.11647/OBP.0433#resources

Semitic Languages and Cultures 29

ISSN (print): 2632-6906
ISSN (digital): 2632-6914

ISBN Paperback: 978-1-80511-435-2
ISBN Hardback: 978-1-80511-436-9
ISBN Digital (PDF): 978-1-80511-437-6

DOI: 10.11647/OBP.0433

Cover image (clockwise from top left): Leningrad Codex (Firkovich B 19 A), f. 8r, Gen. 14.12b–15.13a, https://commons.wikimedia.org/wiki/File:Page_from_the_Leningrad_Codex_01.jpg; Cambridge University Library Mosseri IX.224, detail of Gen. 32.30b–32a (courtesy of the Syndics of Cambridge University Library); The Great Isaiah Scroll (1QIsaa), cols I–IV, Isa. 1.1–5.14a, https://commons.wikimedia.org/wiki/File:The_Great_Isaiah_Scroll_MS_A_(1QIsa)_-_Google_Art_Project-x4-y0.jpg; 4QGeng (4Q7), Gen. 1.1–11a, https://commons.wikimedia.org/wiki/File:Genesis_1_Dead_Sea_Scroll_(Cropped).jpg; Aleppo Codex fol. 130r, Isa. 66.20–Jer. 1.17, https://commons.wikimedia.org/wiki/File:Aleppo-HighRes2-Neviim6-Jeremiah_(page_1_crop).jpg
Cover design: Jeevanjot Kaur Nagpal

The fonts used in this volume are Charis SIL, SBL Hebrew, SBL Greek, Estrangelo Edessa and Scheherazade New.

CONTENTS

Acknowledgements vii

Abbreviations ix

Preface xi

Introduction 1

Part I: Variation Perceptible in the Combined
Tiberian biblical Reading-Written tradition 25

1. The Onomasticon with and without *yahu* Names 27

2. 1st-person *wayyiqtol* Morphology 39

3. *Qal* versus *hifʿil* Forms of יס"ף 57

4. Construct מְאַת versus Absolute מֵאָה 89

5. *Qal* Internal Passive versus *nifʿal* Morphology 107

6. צֵע"ק versus זֵע"ק 127

7. 1CPL נַחְנוּ versus אֲנַחְנוּ 139

Part II: Variation Limited to the Written Component
of the Tiberian Biblical Tradition 143

8. FS הוא versus היא 145

9. FPL ן- versus -נָה 155

10. נער versus נערה with Feminine Singular Referent 167

11. Abstract Nouns Ending in -*ūt* 177

12. Orthography 183

Conclusion 203

References.. 209

Passage Index... 229

Subject Index 249

ACKNOWLEDGEMENTS

A great deal of the data and argumentation that inspired this book was gathered in the process of writing two previous works, so much of the gratitude expressed in the acknowledgement sections there remains relevant here. More specifically, I wish to recognise the various contributions of colleagues and students in the Cambridge, Middlebury, and SBL contexts where I enjoy so much engagement, collegiality, and encouragement, including such local coffee shops as Cambridge's Harvey's and Middlebury's Haymaker Bun Co., Little Seed Coffee Roasters, Royal Oak Coffee, and Otter Creek Bakery. Many thanks to Prof. Geoffrey Khan for years of friendship, generous support, and, along with Open Book Publishers, for acceptance into the Cambridge Semitic Languages and Cultures Series. My gratitude to the series reviewers for their insightful comments and to Anne Burberry for copyediting. And, of course, love and thanks to Anna, Emily, Yoel, and Moses (the bulldog), at home, and to Yoni and Adeline, farther afield, as well as to the American and Italian branches of our extended family.

ABBREVIATIONS

1	1st-person
2	2nd-person
3	3rd-person
A	Aleppo Codex
ABH	Archaic Biblical Hebrew
b.	Talmud Bavli
BA	Biblical Aramaic
BCE	Before the Common Era
BDSS	Biblical Dead Sea Scrolls
BH	Biblical Hebrew
c.	circa
C	common (gender)
CBH	Classical Biblical Hebrew
CE	Common Era
ch.	chapter
chs	chapters
DSS	Dead Sea Scrolls
DSSBH	Dead Sea Scrolls Biblical Hebrew
F	feminine
fn.	footnote
JDA	Judaean Desert Aramaic
JDH	Judaean Desert Hebrew
L	Leningrad Codex
LBH	Late Biblical Hebrew (Esther; Daniel; Ezra–Nehemiah; Chronicles)
LBH+	Late Biblical Hebrew+ (LBH; Ps. 119; Job 1–2; 42.7–17)

l.	line
ll.	lines
LXX	Septuagint
m.	Mishna
M	masculine
MT	Masoretic Textual Tradition
NBDSS	Non-biblical Dead Sea Scrolls
NENA	North-eastern Neo-Aramaic
NT	New Testament
OA	Old Aramaic
PL	plural
PS	proto-Semitic
QA	Qumran Aramaic
QH	Qumran Hebrew
RH	Rabbinic Hebrew
S	singular
SH	Samaritan Hebrew
SP	Samaritan Pentateuch
TA	Targumic Aramaic
TBH	Transitional Biblical Hebrew
y.	Talmud Yerushalmi

PREFACE

This study is offered with a healthy mixture of hope and fear. The hope is that readers might find the individual arguments regarding the relevant linguistic features as significant as the author finds them and their cumulative strength sufficiently convincing to warrant reassessment of certain entrenched views. If so, the research will have had the desired corrective result.

The fear is that the arguments here will be deemed too narrow and focused on linguistic and orthographic details to be of broad interest to biblical scholars and that the suggested implications will be considered too extreme to merit due consideration. As formulated, the proposals do not necessarily contradict long-held and cherished views, like scholarly consensus (such as it is) on the fundamentals of the Documentary Hypothesis or accepted theory and methods concerning ancient Hebrew diachrony and BH periodisation. They do, however, challenge certain extreme and simplistic notions associated with the relevant dominant paradigms. It is left to others to utilise the arguments and conclusions presented here for the further support, refinement, construction, and/or demolition of hypotheses and approaches.

The impetus for this book crystallised gradually in the course of previous research, including courses, lectures, articles, and, especially, my two previous monographs (Hornkohl 2014a; 2023). Each of the two books focuses, in its own way, on collections of linguistic features characterised by diachronically significant distributions—whether they distinguish the late pre-exilic, exilic, and early post-exilic TBH of Jeremiah from more standard pre-exilic CBH and post-Restoration LBH (Hornkohl 2014a) or, where the two are dissonant, the typologically early written component of Tiberian CBH from the sometimes later and secondary corresponding pronunciation component (Hornkohl 2023). Those studies largely accepted as axiomatic the regnant dichotomous view of BH, which divides it into pre-exilic CBH and post-Restoration LBH. Such an approach is adequate to explain the vast majority of the data. Even so, during examination of the linguistic phenomena highlighted in those studies, there came to light a minority of features characterised by distributional patterns that seemed to warrant a more finely tuned paradigm, specifically, one capable of comprehending a linguistic distinction between the CBH of the Pentateuch and the CBH of the relevant Prophets and Writings. The present book collects and examines in detail a series of such features, weighing possible explanations in light of the dominant approaches and considering the relevant theoretical ramifications.

Having expended the effort to write the book, it should be obvious that I believe there is something of value here for biblical and language scholars alike. Yet it bears mentioning that years of hesitation in writing up these results were only rather recently overcome by the cumulative weight of the evidence, which had the effect of transforming a hunch based on a few intriguing examples into a full-fledged hypothesis supported by a series of case studies.

Even so, the potentially far-reaching ramifications, which some may find troubling—if not downright objectionable—are not lost on the writer. Indeed, I have at times, and for various reasons, felt uneasy with the interpretation of the data and the implications. All I can say is that I was not pursuing this line of inquiry when I initially stumbled on the data. Rather, it flowed organically out of the honest (or honestly self-deluded) work of collecting, examining, and interpreting the data. This, in turn, led to the steadily growing conviction, notwithstanding some reluctance, that 'there is actually something to this' worth sharing with fellow members of the guild—whatever they end up thinking about it.

Aaron D. Hornkohl
October 2024

INTRODUCTION

Despite notable objections (especially Young, Rezetko, and Ehrensvärd 2008; Rezetko and Young 2014), the dominant paradigm of BH periodisation remains fundamentally dichotomous: Iron Age II CBH versus post-Restoration LBH (Hornkohl 2013; Hurvitz 2013). Additional strata are sometimes postulated: pre-classical ABH, ostensibly reflected in a few cases of biblical poetry (see, e.g., Mandell 2013), and late pre-exilic, exilic, and early post-exilic TBH, considered by some an intermediate stage between CBH and LBH proper (see, e.g., Hornkohl 2014a, 14–15, fn. 39; 2016a). But if recent critiques have eroded confidence in linguistic methods for periodisation of pre- versus post-exilic texts, they have drastically reduced optimism regarding finer-grain chronolectal distinctions. The problematic nature of the evidence—limited, fragmentary, ambiguous, multivalent, textually fluid, etc.—make for a daunting evidentiary situation, leading some to doubt the real-world temporal associations of the relevant periods, in favour of a paradigm according to which all apparent chronolects are deemed contemporary styles (Young, Rezetko, and Ehrensvärd 2008; Rezetko and Young 2014).

Against such an epistemologically fraught background, the topic of the present volume may seem at best ill advised, at worst a fool's errand. The main question is *Can CBH be divided into chronological sub-chronolects?* Certain preliminary considerations seem to militate against even entertaining such a question.

For one, scholars with expertise in ancient Hebrew diachrony have heretofore been content with a unified CBH chronolect sufficiently broad to encompass the Torah, the Former Prophets, and the pre-exilic Latter Prophets and Writings, declining to venture more granular chronological distinctions.[1] CBH is broadly associated with the four hundred years of the Iron Age II period, 1000–600 BCE—approximately the monarchic period, according to biblical historiography. Since, however, CBH includes traditions of content that predate that period, the reason for categorising so much material as a single chronolect must be due to linguistic similarity. And this is indeed the case. Allowing for expected language variety reflecting such factors as geography, register, genre, and group or personal style, CBH is remarkably uniform, especially the narrative sections in the Torah and Former Prophets. Based on this stylistic affinity alone, it is heuristically valid to lump the lot together as CBH.

Assuming the above association between the CBH portions of the Bible and the monarchic period, it seems likely that their production involved both the incorporation of earlier sources and the composition of new material. It is also clear that CBH material was later subjected to further literary and textual treatment. At issue here is the linguistic character of early sources in the hands of later writer-editors. However the linguistic profile of pre-monarchic sources may have differed from that of material composed in the monarchic period, the differences seem largely to have been levelled during the process of compilation, as CBH's broad linguistic homogeneity leaves very few traces of chrono-

---

[1] Exceptional in this regard are several studies by Elitzur (2015; 2018a; 2018b; 2019; 2022), which, though not limited to linguistic features, nevertheless propose diachronic diversity within CBH.

lectal distinctions. Further levelling may have occurred as a result of Second Temple editorial and textual activity.

Even so, CBH is not completely homogenous. This is hardly surprising. Notwithstanding the effects of secondary levelling, scholars discern non-chronological linguistic diversity in the Bible's constituent works, noting differences related to such factors as genre, source, sociolect, regional dialect, register, and literary device (e.g., Rendsburg 1990a; 1990b; 2002a; 2002b; 2006; Young 1993). Given its apparent historiographical range, it is not unreasonable to entertain the possibility that one might also discern diachronic variation within CBH. Even if detectable in only a minority of features, so as to pose no real challenge to the standard CBH–LBH dichotomy, the existence of meaningful patterns might entail reconsideration of our understanding of periodisation. The purpose of this study is precisely to investigate cases of perceptible patterns of diachronic variation within CBH and to assess their broader implications.

And, indeed, apparently meaningful patterns of language variation within CBH are discernible, with the clearest variations in usage patterns distinguishing the Pentateuch from the remaining CBH works of the Prophets and Writings.

But neither the evidence nor the explanation for the apparent distinction is straightforward. For this reason, methodology is of paramount importance. The following sections detail methodological strictures, obstacles that must be overcome, and responses to various criticisms of approach.

1.0. Methodology

Diachronic analysis and linguistic periodisation in any language are predicated on the known chronological status of control texts. In the case of ancient Hebrew, securely dated material is limited and is datable within only approximate ranges. For this reason, rigorous methodological strictures are required.

1.1. External Controls

Securely dated texts relevant to BH divide into two groups, early and late. The early evidence consists of a comparatively limited assemblage of Iron Age II Hebrew (and cognate) inscriptional material (from roughly 1000–600 BCE). Representing a later timespan is a much more extensive collection of biblical and extrabiblical Hebrew (and cognate) material from the Second Temple period (roughly 600 BCE–300 CE). Undisputed LBH sources include Esther, Daniel, Ezra–Nehemiah, and Chronicles. Late extrabiblical Hebrew material includes the DSS and other material from the Judaean Desert; Persian, Hellenistic, and Roman era epigraphy; Ben Sira; and Rabbinic material. Late extrabiblical non-Hebrew material includes various Aramaic corpora, the Syriac Peshiṭta, and Greek and Latin transcriptional material. The BA of Ezra and Daniel represents late non-Hebrew biblical evidence.

The linguistic evidence of these control groups can be utilised to assess the diachronic status of the Hebrew of biblical (and extrabiblical) texts of unknown date. Since, however, the cache of early comparative data is relatively small, disproportionate evidentiary significance necessarily attaches to the Second Temple material. In effect, the question becomes *Based on concentrations of late linguistic features distinctive of Second Temple texts, can a composition of unknown date be affirmatively proven late based on its inclusion of such a concentration?*

1.2. Isolating Diagnostically Late Linguistic Features

To avoid impressionistic arguments grounded in mere intuition, the gold-standard methodology employed by Hebraists consists of a three-pronged procedure to isolate late linguistic features for inclusion in an inventory of language elements positively diagnostic of Second Temple Hebrew. The three criteria are (1) late biblical distribution, (2) classical biblical opposition, and (3) extrabiblical confirmation (Hurvitz 2013, 334–35; 2014, 9–10). While these criteria may be applied to features from any domain of the language—phonology, morphology, syntax, lexicon, onomastics, pragmatics, semantics, sociolinguistics—for purposes of illustration, an onomastic example will suffice: the proper name יֵשׁוּעַ 'Yeshuaʿ', a late contraction (involving elision of *heh* and dissimilation of *o*- and *u*-vowels) of יְהוֹשֻׁעַ 'Joshua' (Hurvitz 2014, 130–32).

1.2.1. Late Biblical Hebrew Distribution

For consideration as potentially diagnostic of LBH, a given linguistic feature must satisfy the criterion of exclusive or predominate late distribution. For example, use of the form יֵשׁוּעַ in BH (29×) is restricted to late texts: Ezra (10×); Nehemiah (17×); Chronicles (2×). On this basis, one may proceed to the next criterion.

1.2.2. Classical Biblical Hebrew Opposition

Having established a given feature's late biblical distribution (see §1.2.1, above), the criterion of classical biblical opposition helps to ensure that its absence from CBH material is meaningful, and not an accident of the Bible's limited linguistic coverage. Returning, then, to the example יֵשׁוּעַ, its alternative יְהוֹשֻׁעַ is frequent in CBH texts (217×; it also occurs in LBH 1 Chron. 7.26), demonstrating ample opportunity for use of יֵשׁוּעַ outside LBH. Its absence from CBH is thus shown not to be a chance result of the narrow confines of the biblical corpus, but diachronically significant—apparently indicating that the late form יֵשׁוּעַ was not yet available when CBH writers composed their works.

The relevant distinction between CBH and LBH is especially conspicuous when comparing (1) and (2):

(1) '...according to the word of the LORD, which he spoke by Joshua the son of Nun (יְהוֹשֻׁעַ בִּן־נוּן)' (1 Kgs 16.34).
(2) '...for from the days of Yeshua the son of Nun (יֵשׁוּעַ בִּן־נוּן) to that day the people of Israel had not done so.' (Neh. 8.17)

1.2.3. Extrabiblical Confirmation

Especially relevant in the case of rare biblical features, satisfying the criterion of extrabiblical confirmation demonstrates that a given apparently late feature is not just narrowly characteristic of one or a few biblical writers, but broadly characteristic of the Second Temple linguistic milieu. One also verifies its absence from early inscriptions, confirming it to be uncharacteristic of Iron Age II. The form יֵשׁוּעַ is evidenced in late extrabiblical Hebrew (QH; JDH; DSSBH; Ben Sira), Second Temple Aramaic (BA;

JDA; Syriac), and ancient transcriptional material (LXX; NT; Vulgate), but missing from Iron Age II epigraphy. Its classical biblical absence and late biblical distribution are thus corroborated by similar situations, respectively, in pre- and post-exilic extrabiblical sources.

1.3. Linguistic Periodisation on the Basis of Accumulation

Since linguistic diversity in BH reflects diachronic as well as non-diachronic factors—both primary and secondary—such that certain features especially characteristic of LBH occasionally crop up elsewhere in BH, the linguistic periodisation of a composition may be established only on the basis of an *accumulation* of diagnostically late features relative to its length (Hurvitz 2013, 335; 2014, 10–11). The presence of late features in a text of unknown chronological provenance in anything less than a significant *concentration* is open to any number of non-diachronic explanations, whether linguistic (dialect, register), stylistic (genre, style switching), or secondary (redactional, textual).

2.0. The Problem of External Pre-Monarchic Hebrew Evidence

Adherence to the above methodological guidelines helps to compensate for the relative paucity of Iron Age II, i.e., monarchic era, data, but a more significant evidentiary gap faces researchers focusing on pre-monarchic Hebrew, as there is little to no extrabiblical Hebrew source material from before 1000 BCE to which ostensible early CBH may be compared.

Consider, by way of example, the onomastic distinctiveness of biblical sources depicting pre-monarchic historiography, as discussed below, ch. 1. The scarcity of theophoric names containing the morpheme *yahu* in the Pentateuch, Joshua, Judges, and Samuel distinguishes this material from both biblical material that deals with the monarchic age and Iron Age II epigraphy, not to mention later Hebrew (and cognate) sources. It is tempting to conclude that the onomasticon of Genesis–Samuel reliably preserves pre-monarchic naming traditions in which *yahu* names were yet to gain popularity. While this may indeed be the case, one must acknowledge that a lack of contemporary external control texts confirming a lack of *yahu* names in the pre-monarchic onomasticon, in the form of Bronze Age (pre-1200 BCE) or Iron Age I (1200–1000 BCE) Hebrew inscriptions, is an obstacle of considerable significance—though the existence of contemporary cognate evidence sometimes partially compensates for the absence of relevant Hebrew evidence (see, e.g., ch. 1, §3.0; ch. 2, §3.0).

Indeed, much of the evidence analysed in this volume shows the typological priority and/or special conservatism of the Hebrew of the Torah compared to other CBH works, but confirmatory external evidence of the antiquity of the Torah's language is often difficult, and sometimes impossible, to adduce.

3.0. The Polyvalence of the Linguistic Testimony of the Tiberian Biblical Tradition

Another challenge is the composite nature of the linguistic testimony presented by the Tiberian Masoretic tradition. In any given text, this may consist of associated, but potentially distinct, layers of tradition, including strictly consonantal form, partial marking of vowels via *matres lectionis*, vocalisation signs, cantillation accents, and paratextual Masora. Though interrelated, allowance must be made for the possibility that these components reflect dissonant layers of linguistic tradition. The *ketiv-qere* mechanism formally acknowledges hundreds of cases of divergence between the written and pronunciation components of the Tiberian tradition, Masoretic treatises note additional cases, and scholars have identified still more (many conveniently collected in Hornkohl 2023). Obviously, such polyphonic, and at times discordant, linguistic testimony, sometimes comprising diachronically distinct 'witness statements', complicates historical linguistic research. The proper response is neither to ignore the complexity nor summarily to abandon all hope of meaningful results, but to meet the challenge head on by disentangling the disparate strands of evidence and constructing a historical narrative that comprehends them.

4.0. Literary Development and Textual Fluidity

Some scholars, emphasising the complicated compositional development of biblical texts and the vagaries of their transmission as reconstructed on the basis of comparison with ancient textual witnesses, express extreme pessimism regarding the possibility of a diachronic approach to BH and of the linguistic periodisation of biblical texts (e.g., Young, Rezetko, and Ehrensvärd 2008, I:341–60; Carr 2011, 131–32; Rezetko and Young 2014, 59–116). There is no denying the reality of such complications nor the challenge that they constitute for diachronic approaches. If secondary interventions are so pervasive as to have obfuscated the original linguistic profile of biblical compositions, then diachronic linguistics is out of the question. But it is methodologically indefensible to prejudge the evidence as irremediably obscured without having first investigated it. The historical reliability of the data relative to each feature must be assessed on a case-by-case basis. As it turns out, and as diachronically sensitive Hebraists have repeatedly pointed out, extreme pessimism regarding the accessibility of solid historical linguistic data proves unwarranted, as it is contradicted by period-specific distribution patterns in the case of numerous linguistic features. Had the admittedly complex compositional and transmissional processes that biblical texts undoubtedly underwent irretrievably distorted their chronolectal profiles, one would not detect discernible diachronic accumulations (or absences) of diagnostically late features in specific texts. The fact that one does demonstrates that secondary developments, while not to be ignored, were not so extensive as to obliterate useful amounts of primary data. In sum, in pursuing the diachronic approach to BH and the linguistic periodisation of biblical compositions, one does not shy away from compositional and textual complexity, but neither does one make of it more than it is—a complication to be acknowledged and tackled feature-by-feature.

5.0. The Question of Late Imitation of Classical Style

On the basis of the unambiguously late linguistic profile of all compositions solidly dated to the Second Temple period on non-linguistic grounds, there is broad consensus among diachronically sensitive Hebraists that the ability to reproduce passable CBH was not common among Second Temple writers. Late writers consistently betray the linguistic milieu in which they wrote in the form of post-classicisms, not just occasionally, but in unmissable accumulations. This includes texts couched in biblical style, e.g., the Temple Scroll (11Q19), presented as the words of God revealed to Moses at Sinai (Qimron 1978a; 1980, 239ff; Yadin 1983, I:34; Hornkohl 2016b; 2021a), Ps. 151 (11Q5 28), pseudepigraphically ascribed to King David (Carmignac 1963, 377; Hurvitz 1967; Polzin 1967; Schuller 1986, 9; Smith 1997), and so-called Reworked Pentateuch/Rewritten Bible scrolls, e.g., 4QReworked Pentateuch (4Q158; 4Q364–367) and 4QCommentary Genesis A (4Q252), where even small additions and bridging material exhibit appreciable accumulations of late features (Hornkohl 2016b; 2021a).

Critics of linguistic approaches to periodisation question the assumption that late scribes could not produce good CBH. After all, Muslim scribes steeped in Qurʾanic Arabic could write flawless Classical Arabic long after the 7th century CE (Blau 1997, 28). Likewise, 19th-century Jewish writers composed works in passable BH during the *Haskala*. Might not Second Temple writers have been similarly possessed of such imitative powers?

The problem is one of historical context. The aforementioned late Muslim and Jewish writers worked in environments in which their respective scriptural chronolects had been canonised and were universally recognised and accepted. By most accounts, this was not the situation of Second Temple Judaism... especially if one holds that large portions of the Hebrew Bible, including the Pentateuch, were still in a process of composition in this period. And even if sizeable parts were in existence, neither their broad acceptance nor accessibility may be assumed.

As an extensive composition of disputed date, the Priestly source may serve as a useful example. Considered since Wellhausen's time a programmatic exilic or post-exilic account of Israelite history, legislation, polity, and cult, as a historical source, it has long been regarded with extreme suspicion, thought to project back into the Mosaic era ideological anachronisms reflecting much later times. The question is how much of P was newly composed in Second Temple times and how much pre-dated its purported fusion with other Pentateuchal sources. Having noted contemporary consensus on the pre-exilic provenance of other Pentateuchal sources, Wellhausen (1885, 9–10) remarks as follows on P:

> It is only in the case of the Priestly Code that opinions differ widely; for it tries hard to imitate the costume of the Mosaic period, and, with whatever success, to disguise its own.... The Priestly Code... guards itself against all reference to later times and settled life in Canaan...: it keeps itself carefully and strictly within the limits of the situation in the wilderness, for which in all seriousness it seeks to give the law. It has actually been successful, with its movable tabernacle, its wandering camp, and other archaic

> details, in so concealing the true date of its composition that its many serious inconsistencies with what we know, from other sources, of Hebrew antiquity previous to the exile, are only taken as proving that it lies far beyond all known history, and on account of its enormous antiquity can hardly be brought into any connection with it.

Wellhausen says precious little about language (cf. 1885, 390, ch.IX.III.2). By contrast, specialists who have focused on P's terminology often emphasise its antiquity (Grintz 1974–1975; Rendsburg 1980; Hurvitz 1974a; 1982; 1983; 1988; 2000; Zevit 1982; Paran 1983; Milgrom 1970; 1978; 1991–2001, 5–13 *et passim*; 1992, 458–59; 1999; 2007). For such experts, P's pre-exilic linguistic profile stands as insurmountable evidence of its early date. By contrast, for scholars convinced of P's late provenance, its language serves as a prime example of the possibility of successful linguistic archaising over long stretches of text (Cross 1973, 322–23; Young, Rezetko, and Ehrensvärd 2008, II: 15–16, and the scholarship mentioned there).

In this connection, a crucial question revolves around the nature of the exemplar(s) that P might have imitated. The obvious candidates are the other Pentateuchal sources. But the very fact that source critics can so easily distinguish P from J, E, D, and H implies that these were not P's models. Nor could it have been Ezekiel, Ezra–Nehemiah, or Chronicles, whose linguistic profiles P's chronolect typologically predates. One is left with the possibility that P imitated an early source or sources characterised by pre-exilic cultic concerns and phraseology. But is this not tantamount to affirming the existence of early Priestly material? Indeed, Young, Rezetko, and Ehrensvärd (2008, II:16–17) list several revisions of the Documentary Hypothesis that posit both a pre-exilic P and a lengthy period of Torah compositional development extending into the Persian Period. They reasonably conclude: "*Early material in P does not prove that the Priestly Source is early*" (17, italics in the original). Yet this surely depends on the extent of P's early material. The more substantial the proportion of early material in P, the less potentially flawless Persian Period CBH material it presents. The simplest explanation for its comparatively classical linguistic profile is that a significant majority of P is pre-exilic.

We face contradictory claims—on the one hand, that late writers could not compose flawless CBH; on the other, that CBH and LBH were contemporary styles, equally available to writers during the Second Temple period. The amount and nature of the data virtually preclude verification or falsification. Given the extant evidence, the approach adopted here is that CBH and LBH are literary reflections of genuine First and Second Temple chronolects and that certain exceptional late writers might, over short spans of text, passably simulate CBH. As exceptions, such cases do not disprove the general validity and viability of the framework.

6.0. Distributional Variety of Features Typical of the Classical Biblical Hebrew Sub-chronolects

In the majority of the cases discussed in this volume, linguistic diversity within pre-exilic Hebrew divides the CBH of the Pentateuch from that of the non-LBH Prophets and Writings. This applies to 1st-person *wayyiqtol* morphology (ch. 2), *qal* versus *hifʿil* forms of יס"ף (ch. 3) (but see below), construct מְאַת versus absolute מֵאָה 'hundred' (ch. 4), *qal* internal passive versus *nifʿal* morphology (ch. 5), צע"ק versus זע"ק (ch. 6), 1CPL נַחְנוּ versus אֲנַחְנוּ (ch. 7), FS הוא versus היא (ch. 8), FPL ן- versus -נָה (ch. 9), נער versus נערה with feminine singular referent (ch. 10), abstract nouns ending in *-ūt* (ch. 11), and orthography (ch. 12).

Exceptional in this regard is the onomasticon with and without *yahu* names (ch. 1), from the perspective of which the watershed appears to divide the pre-monarchic naming traditions seen in Genesis–Samuel and the monarchic traditions in such books as Kings, Isaiah, and Jeremiah.

In the specific case of *qal* versus *hifʿil* forms of יס"ף (ch. 3), though the shift to *hifʿil* had clearly taken place by the time of LBH, evidence of secondary orthographic development in the Prophets makes it difficult to pinpoint more precisely the historical depth of the development (see below, §8.0).

7.0. Early Variation versus Secondary Contemporisation

The prevalence of feature sets exhibiting inner-CBH diversity separating the Torah from the rest of CBH may seem to some suspicious. Since CBH as a whole, whatever its content, patterns as a chronolect of Iron Age II, approximately 1000–600 BCE, it is not immediately obvious that the Torah should necessarily be distinguished by typologically early features. The fact that it is *might* result from its incorporation of pre-monarchic traditions preserving facets of especially ancient linguistic profiles. Circumstantial evidence ostensibly indicating the early crystallisation of the

Torah's textual and linguistic traditions include, inter alia, its 3rd-century BCE translation into Greek, the comparatively infrequent incidence of *ketiv-qere* dissonances in the Pentateuch (Barr 1981, 32–33; Tov 2004a, 204, fn. 25); the disproportionate representation of Torah texts among the palaeo-Hebrew DSS (Tov 2004b, 246); and the occurrence at Qumran and in the Judaean Desert of long scrolls apparently containing multiple books of the Torah (Tov 2004b, 75). Tov (2004b, 252–53; 2012, 188–89) emphasises that the Torah in general did not escape levels of textual and linguistic fluidity seen in other biblical (and non-biblical) material. He also notes, however, that "[t]exts written in the paleo-Hebrew script were copied more carefully than most texts written in the square script…" and that "…these manuscripts were copied with equal care as the proto-Masoretic scrolls" (Tov 2004b, 253). Since Pentateuchal material is common in both groups, this comes as empirical evidence of the relative stability of the textual and linguistic tradition of the Torah in the proto-Masoretic tradition.

Yet, it is worth considering an alternative hypothesis: namely, that the CBH found in the Pentateuch, Prophets, and Writings was once more homogenous in regard to the features discussed in this volume and only secondarily diverged, in the course of redaction and transmission. Specifically, while the linguistic antiquity of the Torah was preserved thanks to its early consolidation and perceived sanctity, the CBH of the Prophets and Writings was treated less conservatively, being allowed to shift, even if only slightly, in the case of certain details, under the pressure of the conventions of a changing literary register, as seen in LBH and other late forms of classical Hebrew.

Such an alternative hypothesis is regularly entertained in the treatments of features included in this volume. In some cases, especially those in which differences are largely restricted to the written tradition, an explanation involving secondary contemporisation excluding the Pentateuch often seems as likely as one assuming more deeply rooted diversity. In others, though, the evidence seems to preclude such an explanation. A theory of secondary development fails to explain apparent diachronic variation involving onomastica with and without *yahu* (ch. 1), the trivalent character of 1st-person *wayyiqtol* morphology (ch. 2), construct מְאַת versus absolute מֵאָה 'hundred' (ch. 4), *qal* internal passive versus *nifʿal* morphology (ch. 5), and צע"ק versus זע"ק (ch. 6).

8.0. Linguistic versus Orthographic Explanations

Related to the question of whether the distinctiveness of the CBH of the Pentateuch vis-à-vis CBH outside the Pentateuch is rooted in the earliest layer of tradition or resulted from secondary development is the matter of truly linguistic versus merely orthographic diversity. The main problem is the vocalic opacity of defective orthography and the ambiguity of *plene* spelling, coupled with the possible secondary status of the pronunciation(s) reflected by *matres lectionis* and the vocalisation tradition.

For example, in the Pentateuch, when it comes to 1st-person *wayyiqtol* morphology, III-*y* verbs are regularly represented by short forms, e.g., ואעש (18 of 21 cases; see below, ch. 2, §1.0, Table 3). In the case of *hifʿil* and *qal* II-*w/y* forms, this is also true of 1CPL forms, where orthography and vocalisation regularly agree on short morphology, e.g., וַנֵּשֶׁב (Gen. 43.21) and וַנֵּסָב (Deut. 2.1) (7 of 8 relevant cases), but not of 1CS forms, where the orthography seems to presuppose short morphology, but the vocalisation reflects long morphology, e.g., וָאַשְׁלִךְ (Deut. 9.21) and וָאָקֻץ (Lev. 20.23) (6 of 8 relevant cases; see Hornkohl 2023, 431–33, for discussion). In the CBH Prophets and Writings, by contrast, long morphology is relatively common in all verb classes, comprising around half of all occurrences (see below, ch. 2, §3.0). In this volume and elsewhere (Hornkohl 2023, 397–99, 414–19), short and long 1st-person *wayyiqtol* spellings are, on the basis of such evidence, and notwithstanding a degree of uncertainty and a few 1CS counterexamples with apparent secondary vocalisation, construed as linguistic, rather than mere orthographic, variants. In other words, just as III-*y* short ואעש is assumed to differ morphologically from long ואעשה, so too are short ואשלך and ואקם considered morphologically distinct from long ואשליך and ואקום, respectively.

A measure of doubt similarly attaches to some defective and *plene (way)yiqtol* spellings of יס״ף, such as וי(ו)סף and וי(ו)ספו, which are variously interpretable as *qal* or *hifʿil*, the latter with long or short morphology (see below, ch. 3).

The degree of uncertainty only increases when it comes to the features discussed in chs. 8–11. Here, from the perspective of the combined written-reading Tiberian tradition, Pentateuchal and non-Pentateuchal forms differ only in terms of the written component, while, in terms of the pronunciation tradition, they are indistinguishable. Thus, in the case of FS הוא versus היא (ch.

8), FPL ךְ- versus ־כָה (ch. 9), and נער versus נַעֲרָה with feminine singular referent (ch. 10), a scholar might legitimately side with the vocalisation tradition and view the spellings as no more than unorthodox written representations of standard pronunciations.

According to the approach adopted in the present study, by contrast, a non-standard written form for which the traditional vocalisation demands the standard pronunciation is not uncritically dismissed as a mere spelling variant. Rather, the possibility that the written tradition reflects a distinct pronunciation tradition is seriously entertained. This means that the unorthodox Pentateuchal written forms of the features discussed in chs 8–11 are interpreted as linguistically divergent from the more standard forms found elsewhere in CBH, reflecting a pronunciation tradition different from that preserved in the received Tiberian pronunciation component—this notwithstanding the levelling effect of the Tiberian vocalisation, which has brought the written forms into phonological conformity with standard pronunciation.

9.0. Inner-Pentateuchal Diachronic Variation

It is instructive at this juncture to revisit the useful example of the Priestly source briefly explored above (§5.0). While there is broad agreement among Hebraists that P is not written in LBH, not all scholars consider it a manifestation of CBH proper. For instance, on the basis of various grammatical developments, Polzin (1976, 85–122, but cf. 168–69) sees the core Priestly material as transitional between the CBH of the combined JE material, D, and the Court History, on the one hand, and LBH Chronicles, on the other. Subsequent investigation of TBH, however, has helped to establish a more accurate diachronic contextualisation for P. Hurvitz (1982) shows that the Hebrew of P antedates that of Ezekiel, and Rooker (1990) and Hornkohl (2014a) show, respectively, that the Hebrew of Ezekiel and of Jeremiah are transitional between CBH, including P, and LBH. Shin (2007) convincingly does the same for Haggai, Zechariah, and Malachi; Dobbs-Allsopp (1998) does so for Lamentations; and Paul (2012) and Arentsen (2020) make a strong TBH case for Second Isaiah (chs 40–66). P may lie somewhere between more prototypical CBH and TBH compositions (but see below), but with the category of TBH so crowded with compositions presenting linguistic profiles typologically more advanced than P's, and with P's Hebrew more similar to that of the core CBH books than that of the TBH material, P is arguably better considered an instantiation of CBH than of TBH.

Even so, on the basis of the prevailing JEDP relative dating of the Documentary Hypothesis (Young, Rezetko, and Ehrensvärd 2008, II:12), one might expect P to pattern typologically later than the other Pentateuchal sources as well other CBH texts. To cite a rather famous example, some take P's nearly exclusive use of the 1CS independent subject pronoun אֲנִי instead of אָנֹכִי 'I' as evidence of the source's relative lateness—in line with LBH and other post-exilic forms of Hebrew and with Aramaic (Giesebrecht 1881, 251–58; S. R. Driver 1898, 155–56, n. †; cf. Hornkohl 2014a, 108–11, especially fn. 4, for counterarguments and bibliography).

Similarly, Hendel (2000) argues "the complementary distribution of *yālad* (*Qal*) for 'beget' in the J source and *hôlîd* (*Hiphil*) for 'beget' in the P source is attributable to a diachronic development in Classical Biblical Hebrew," i.e., not diachronic development between CBH and LBH. On the other hand, he dates P to the time of the Exile or the early Persian Period (Hendel 2000, 46).

To clarify this matter, the phenomena discussed in this volume were subjected to source-critical analysis, relying on the identification of sources given by Friedman (1989, 246–55). This seemed particularly appropriate in cases of features where typological alternants occurred within the Torah. The results of the source-critical analysis of the twelve phenomena treated herein are somewhat equivocal, but certainly do not point unambiguously to P's relative lateness, whether in the Pentateuch, specifically, or in CBH, more generally. In several instances, no discernible differences between sources could be detected. This applies to onomastica with and without *yahu* names (ch. 1), 1st-person *wayyiqtol* morphology (ch. 2), צע"ק versus זע"ק (ch. 6), 1CPL נַחְנוּ versus אֲנַחְנוּ (ch. 7), FS הוא versus הִיא (ch. 8), and נער versus נַעֲרָה with feminine singular referent (ch. 10).

In other instances, various typologically significant tendencies emerge, P patterning with a CBH profile slightly later than that of one or more of the other Pentateuchal sources. Thus, in the case of *qal* internal passive versus *nifʿal* morphology (ch. 5), J is typologically early in its preference for *qal* passive morphology, while P and E both show statistically similar patterns of mixed usage, while no Pentateuchal source conforms to the *nifʿal* dominance of key verbs seen in CBH outside the Pentateuch.

When it comes to FPL ןָ- versus נָה- (ch. 9), all sources with more than a single case show some degree of mixing vowel- and consonant-final morphology, J and E presenting more balanced usage, P exhibiting definite preference for -נה, though with widely divergent distributions depending on book (consistently ןָ- in Genesis–Exodus and -נה in Leviticus–Numbers).

In ch. 11, if lexemes ending in *-ūt* are to be deemed especially characteristic of late forms of ancient Hebrew, then their Pentateuchal concentration in P may be significant.

Finally, with regard to several features, P stands out as typologically early. This holds for *qal* versus *hifʿil* forms of יס״ף (ch. 3), construct מְאַת versus absolute מֵאָה 'hundred' (ch. 4), 1CPL נַחְנוּ versus אֲנַחְנוּ (ch. 7), and orthography (ch. 12).

10.0. Structure of the Monograph

The features discussed in this volume have been divided into two groups. The first group is presented in Part I, which consists of six chapters, each dedicated to a set of variants that reflect inner-CBH typological diversity perceptible in the combined Tiberian written and reading biblical tradition, i.e., in both its consonantal and pronunciation components. In practice, this means that the linguistic variation is sufficiently rooted in the consonantal text that divergences could not be levelled, or could be only partially levelled, in the pronunciation prescribed by the vocalic component. In some cases, orthographic intervention, in the form of the addition of internal *matres lectionis*, seems to indicate relatively early secondary linguistic development that obscured more ancient linguistic detail.

In Part II, the second group of features is represented by four chapters on sets of alternants that are here considered linguistic in nature, but could legitimately be deemed mere orthographic variants, as well as a final chapter on orthography. In these cases, inner-CBH variation is perceptible only at the level of the written component of the Tiberian biblical tradition, including consonants and *matres lectionis*, but is not manifest on the level of vocalisation. Indeed, from the perspective of the oral reading component, no variation obtains, the pronunciation tradition levelling all variants in line with the standard BH forms (see above, §8.0).

PART I:
VARIATION PERCEPTIBLE IN THE COMBINED TIBERIAN BIBLICAL READING-WRITTEN TRADITION

1. THE ONOMASTICON WITH AND WITHOUT *YAHU* NAMES

Biblical scholars through the years have pointed to patterns of diachronic significance in the selection of personal names. A preliminary observation was made by Wellhausen in his *Prolegomena*, in line with his argument for a late date for the Priestly source. Commenting on several personal names in the book of Numbers, he noted (1885, 390, ch.IX.III.2):

> The study of the history of language is still at a very elementary stage in Hebrew. In that which pertains to the lexicographer it would do well to include in its scope the proper names of the Old Testament; when it would probably appear that not only *Parnach* (Numbers xxxiv. 25) but also composite names such as *Peda-zur*, *Peda-el*, *Nathana-el*, *Pag'i-el*, *Eli-asaph*, point less to the Mosaic than to the Persian period, and have their analogies in the Chronicles.[1]

More recently, expanding on work by Meek (1936, 32; 1939), Hoffmeier (2005, 223–25) observes a noticeable concentration of

---

[1] The Hebrew forms of the names (and their references) are פַּרְנָךְ (Num. 34.25), פְּדָה צוּר/פְּדָה־צוּר/פְּדָהצוּר (Num. 1.10; 2.20; 7.54, 59; 10.23), פְּדָהאֵל (Num. 34.28), נְתַנְאֵל (Num. 1.8; 2.5; 7.18, 23; 10.15), פַּגְעִיאֵל (Num. 1.13; 2.27; 7.72, 77; 10.26), and אֱלִיָסָף (Num. 1.14; 2.14; 3.24; 7.42, 47; 10.20) (cf. Black and Menzies's English translation, where *Phag'i-el* of the original German edition is mistakenly given as *Pazi-el*). Since all these names appear in Numbers alone, the evidentiary support for Wellhausen's claim that they point to the Persian period is rather flimsy. Crucially, it is not based on evidence that holds up to the strictures of accepted modern procedures (see above, Introduction, §1.0).

Egyptian names in the Pentateuch, especially among Levites (see also Friedman 2017, 32–34, and the bibliography that he cites). Moving eastward, Noth (1968, 18) noted that the use of names with -*ṣūr*- and -*ammi*- in Numbers is paralleled in the Bronze Age Mari letters, which predate the late 19th century BCE.[2] See also the more recent and broader discussion of Rahkonen (2019) on the strong correlation between personal names in the Pentateuch and the 2nd-millennium BCE Northwest Semitic onomasticon, both of which differ palpably from the Iron Age II Hebrew onomasticon, as seen in biblical and extrabiblical sources alike.

1.0. Yahwistic Names in Biblical Hebrew and Beyond

Returning to the Graf-Wellhausen Documentary Hypothesis, one of the most conspicuous differences between the sources that purportedly comprise the Pentateuch involves designations of the Israelite deity. While the Yahwist uses *Yhwh* throughout his narrative sections, that name goes unused in the work of the Elohist until Exod. 3.13–15 and in the Priestly source until Exod. 6.2–3. Rounding out the picture, Deuteronomy employs *Yhwh*.

Mainstream critical scholarship interprets this diversity as inconsistency among the Pentateuch's sources concerning the timing of the Tetragrammaton's revelation. Yet, this should not overshadow significant points of agreement among the reputed sources. Beyond concurring on the specific name *Yhwh*, of primary significance for purposes of the present chapter is the fact that the sources jointly reflect a Hebrew onomasticon generally

---

[2] I am grateful to James Bejon for this citation.

devoid of Yahwistic names. This is remarkable given the ubiquity of such theophoric names in biblical and extrabiblical sources reflecting the period of the monarchy and later. Whatever the process of the Torah's literary development, whenever it began and finished, and however one is to interpret, literarily and historically, its complicated depiction of the name's explicit or implicit revelation, the sources are unanimous that knowledge of the name *Yhwh* had little effect on the pre-monarchic Hebrew onomasticon. Indeed, the Pentateuch includes just two names with any form of the Tetragrammaton, in both cases a prefix: יְהוֹשֻׁעַ 'Joshua' and יוֹכֶבֶד 'Jochebed' (see Hornkohl 2014a, 86, fn. 35). This dearth of *yahu* names also holds true for the books of Joshua, Judges, and Samuel. In sum, from the perspective of Yahwistic names, the onomastic tradition of the Torah, along with that of other biblical books depicting the pre- and early monarchic period (including Ruth), differs dramatically from the onomasticon of the monarchic period and beyond in terms of the presence or absence of *yahu* names.

2.0. Diachronic Trends

The anthroponymic trend with clearest diachronic import in BH involves the distinction between long and short forms of theophoric names with suffixes based on the Tetragrammaton. Iron Age inscriptions are matched by CBH texts in showing preference for the long form יָהוּ-, while post-exilic extrabiblical Hebrew and Aramaic, as well as LBH and BA, show strong partiality for the abbreviated form -יָה.[3] Hornkohl (2014a, 87) provides the following table of names ending in long -יָהוּ or short -יָה in the standard Tiberian biblical tradition.

Table 1: Masoretic biblical distribution of personal names ending in long and short forms of the theophoric suffix based on *Yhwh*

Book	long (%)	short (%)	Book	long (%)	short (%)
Judges	2 (100)	---	Zephaniah	1 (20)	4 (80)
Samuel	4 (33.3)	8 (66.7)	Zechariah	1 (7.1)	13 (92.9)
Kings	248 (76.3)	77 (23.7)	Malachi	---	1 (100)
(1 Kings	102 [85.7]	17 [14.3])	Proverbs	---	1 (100)
(2 Kings	146 [70.9]	60 [29.1])	Esther	---	1 (100)
Isaiah	62 (96.9)	1 (3.1)	Daniel	---	9 (100)
Jeremiah	241 (74.4)	83 (25.6)	Ezra	1 (1.3)	77 (98.7)
Ezekiel	4 (66.7)	2 (33.3)	Nehemiah	---	185 (100)
Hosea	---	2 (100)	Chronicles	275 (57.6)	202 (42.4)
Amos	---	4 (100)	(1 Chronicles	85 [33.5]	169 [66.5])
Obadiah	---	1 (100)	(2 Chronicles	190 [85.2]	33 [14.8])
Micah	---	1 (100)	Total	839 (55.5)	672 (44.5)

In line with what has already been said (§1.0), the biblical distribution of names bearing long and short theophoric suffixes based on *Yhwh* begins with the book of Judges, excluding entirely the Torah, as well as Joshua. To be sure, according to the figures, the book of Samuel also exhibits relatively limited use of the relevant names (just 12 total: 4 long, 8 short). Names ending in a form of the relevant suffix accumulate appreciably only in

---

[3] The two biblical corpora that buck these trends are the CBH books of the Twelve (Hosea, Amos, Obadiah, Micah, Zephaniah), on the one hand, and LBH Chronicles, on the other; for details, see Hornkohl (2014a, 88–89). On the predominantly (but not exclusively) northern use of names ending in -יו *-yaw*, with elision of the *heh*, see Hornkohl (2014a, 85 and n. 33) and the references there.

Kings, Isaiah, Jeremiah, the Twelve, Daniel, Ezra, Nehemiah, and Chronicles.

The situation of names with one of the corresponding theophoric prefixes, -יְהוֹ or -יוֹ, is somewhat more complex. This is due partially to a smaller pool of tokens, to lower frequency of forms, and to the exceptional preponderance of certain names in particular texts. For example, the names יְהוֹשֻׁעַ 'Joshua' in the Hexateuch and יוֹנָתָן/יְהוֹנָתָן 'Jonathan' in Samuel skew the data in the relevant books, where beyond these names, Yhwh-based anthroponyms are rare. For purposes of the present discussion, the most pertinent point is the aforementioned rarity of names prefixed by -יְהוֹ or -יוֹ in the Pentateuch compared to most of the rest of the Hebrew Bible.

Beyond the Pentateuch, as already stated, those books depicting the pre-monarchic period, i.e., Joshua and Judges, also display a dearth of Yhwh-based names, as does Samuel, focusing on the early monarchy. Literature focusing on the divided monarchy shows a dramatic uptick in use of Yhwh-based names. In the case of the pre-exilic books, the preference is for the long ending -יָהוּ, whereas post-exilic books show a strong predilection for the short -יָה form of the suffix. Crucially, the Masoretic biblical evidence is confirmed by non-Masoretic biblical sources and, more importantly, by extrabiblical material, both early and late. This latter material is of immense importance, because, unlike the biblical evidence, it was not subject to secondary changes in the course of scribal transmission. Thus, Iron Age epigraphy shows overwhelming dominance of the long יהו- suffix, whereas in Persian and Hellenistic inscriptions, NBDSS texts, 1QIsaᵃ, and RH, short יה- forms are the norm.

3.0. Interpreting the Data

The question is how to interpret the infrequency of theophoric names based on *Yhwh* in biblical texts that appear to reflect pre-monarchic naming practices, especially the Pentateuch. An argument based on the absence of these names is, by definition, an argument from silence. But is the silence historically meaningful?

According to what is perhaps the most straightforward interpretation of the evidence, the preserved anthroponymic usage patterns may be considered representative of different historical chronolects. Thus, working backwards, the LBH and late extrabiblical dominance of יָה- names reflects onomastic practices from the Restoration period, i.e., post-450 BCE, on; the books depicting the period of the divided monarchy reflect naming traditions of the period spanning approximately 900–450 BCE; and material recounting pre-monarchic events preserves onomastic conventions redolent of a time before 900 BCE.

The foregoing scheme raises numerous issues, apparently flying in the face of mainstream source critical and linguistic theories alike.

3.1. Source Criticism

In terms of compositional development, many scholars remain convinced of Wellhausen's exilic or post-exilic dating of the P source. As was shown in the quote from Wellhausen at the beginning of this chapter, however, he largely excluded linguistic evidence and argumentation, which has subsequently been exploited to challenge his view (Rendsburg 1980; Hurvitz 1974a; 1982; 1988; 2000).

Moreover, the significance of the apparent affinity he saw between a short list of compound names in Numbers and similar names in Chronicles pales in comparison to the significance of the onomastic disparity between the Torah, almost completely devoid of Yahwistic names, and those books dated securely to the exilic and post-exilic period on the basis of their language, which show regular use of such names. Whenever the P source may have been composed, from the perspective of Yahwistic names, its onomastic tradition can hardly be said to be that of exilic or post-exilic times.

Pre-empting the farfetched contention that the Torah's onomasticon was artificially fashioned, so as to avoid mention of Yahwistic names, one may point to the inconvenient presence of the two *yahu* names that do appear there. According to P, Moses's mother goes by the Yahwistic name יוֹכֶבֶד 'Jochebed' (Exod. 6.20) in the same chapter in which the name *Yhwh* is revealed (Exod. 6.2). Unless she is thought to have undergone an undisclosed name change, P's narrative implies that she bore her Yahwistic name prior to the revelation of the Tetragrammaton.[4] Had there been a conscious effort to expunge all Yahwistic names from the Torah, it is surely strange that this case should have been left as is.

---

[4] See Segal (1967, 4). The classification of the passage as belonging to P is according to Friedman (1989, 250).

Perhaps somewhat less problematic is the distribution of the name יְהוֹשֻׁעַ 'Joshua', as the relevant personage is not mentioned until after the Tetragrammaton has been revealed according to all sources and since use of the alternant name הוֹשֵׁעַ 'Hosea' (Num. 13.8, 16; Deut. 32.44) can be interpreted as evidence of Yahwistic renaming. At any rate, use of יְהוֹשֻׁעַ 'Joshua' is as prevalent in E as it is in P, the latter also employing הוֹשֵׁעַ 'Hosea'.[5]

3.2. Chronolects and Linguistic Periodisation

Turning to diachronic linguistics, scholars who deal with ancient Hebrew diachrony are generally content to distinguish between pre-exilic CBH and post-exilic LBH. Though pre-classical ABH is variously acknowledged in some biblical poetry (Mandell 2013) and TBH is recognised by some scholars as a viable chronolect linking CBH and LBH (Hornkohl 2014a, 14–15, fn. 39; 2016a), few attempt to divide CBH into monarchic and pre-monarchic sub-strata. However, this is precisely where a straightforward reading of the onomastic data seems to lead.

To be clear, the issue here is not, strictly speaking, the date of the Pentateuch's compilation, redaction, or even, necessarily, composition, but rather the historical depth of its linguistic traditions and the degree to which the historical representativeness of their naming patterns was kept intact as they were transmitted

---

[5] יְהוֹשֻׁעַ: E—Exod. 17.9, 10, 13, 14; 24.13; 32.17; 33.11; Num. 11.28; Deut. 31.14, 14, 23; P—Num. 13.16; 14.6, 30, 38; 26.65; 27.18, 22; 32.12, 28; 34.17; Deut. 34.9; Dtr$_1$—Deut. 1.38; 3.21, 28; 31.3, 7. הוֹשֵׁעַ: P—Num. 13.8, 16; Dtr$_2$—Deut. 32.44.

orally, written down, and retransmitted.⁶ It would seem that the Torah (along with the rest of biblical literature depicting pre- and early monarchic historiography) reflects naming traditions that differ from those of the rest of CBH and of LBH. This is presumably because the *Yhwh*-based patterns shown by extrabiblical inscriptions to be popular from the 8th century BCE on had not yet become entrenched in earlier centuries, and that the books of the Pentateuch (and Joshua, Judges, and Samuel) preserve such earlier anthroponymic traditions.

Even if the language of the Pentateuch saw significant historical development, it should not be particularly surprising that its onomastic tradition should prove especially resistant to change. According to Anderson (2007, 92–93), "Names tend to institutionalize…. Institutionalized naming traditions in general tend to be or become very conservative, whatever the original source of the names." No matter the exact compositional process that produced the Torah and other biblical material reflecting pre-monarchic historiography, their onomastic tradition seems characteristic of a historical reality different from that of CBH material depicting the monarchic period and of LBH and late extrabiblical sources.

---

⁶ For differential treatment of diachronically significant detail among ancient writers, see Steiner (2005, 240–43) on Josephus's treatment of names with gutturals and Hornkohl (2014a, 85) on Ben Sira's treatment of *-yahu* suffixed names.

3.3. The Absence of Extrabiblical Pre-monarchic Hebrew Sources

Despite the plausibility, perhaps even probability, of the arguments advanced, evidence sufficient for their verification remains tantalisingly lacking. This is due to gaps in chronologically contemporary extrabiblical evidence.

The characteristic use of pre-exilic monarchic יהו- and post-exilic יה- is firmly corroborated by extrabiblical sources in Hebrew and Aramaic, and even farther afield in Akkadian (Abraham 2024, esp. 149–51), but for the apparent pre-monarchic onomasticon of Genesis–Samuel, no such direct extrabiblical Hebrew corroboration is available. True, the aforementioned study by Rahkonen (2019) shows similarity between names in the Pentateuch and those used more broadly in 2nd-millennium BCE Mesopotamia. For Akkadian specifically, Abraham (2024, 139) says explicitly that "[t]here are no… attestations of Yahwistic names in Babylonian records from pre-exilic times" beyond a single possible case from the late 7th century BCE. This concords with Hess's (1993) findings on Amarna personal names and with Van Soldt's (2016) on Ugaritic theophoric names, which lists include no Yahwistic forms. While consistent with the general absence of Yahwistic names in Genesis–Samuel, this evidence is mainly negative and circumstantial—a resounding silence in contemporary sources in related languages. More direct extrabiblical onomastic evidence, in the form of Hebrew (or Canaanite) inscriptions from the pre-monarchic period, remains a desideratum, in the absence of which we are left with a narrative that fits the facts, but remains without extrabiblical corroboration.

Even so, the likelihood that the Torah's onomasticon (and that of other biblical material containing pre-monarchic traditions) reliably portrays pre-monarchic anthroponymic patterns may be strengthened if the onomasticon proves to be just one of several features distinguishing pre-monarchic CBH from monarchic CBH, as the rest of this book seeks to substantiate.

2. 1ST-PERSON *WAYYIQṬOL* MORPHOLOGY

Depending on verb class, 1st-person *wayyiqṭol* verbs in Tiberian BH may exhibit up to three alternative patterns: short (< PS *aq-tul*), long (< PS *aqtulu/a*), and augmented (< PS *aqtulan[na]*) (also known as 'pseudo-cohortative').[1] See Table 1.

Table 1: Short, long, and augmented 1st-person *wayyiqṭol* forms in the Tiberian tradition[2]

	Strong	**III-y**	*hifʿil*	*qal* II-w/y
1CS	וָאֶשְׁלַח, וָאֶשְׁלְחָה	וָאַעַשׂ, וָאֶעֱשֶׂה	וָאָעֵד, וָאָעִיד, וָאָעִידָה	*וָאָקָם, וָאָקוּם, וָאָקוּמָה
1CPL	וַנִּשְׁלַח, וַנִּשְׁלְחָה	וַנַּעַשׂ, וַנַּעֲשֶׂה	*וַנָּעֵד, *וַנָּעִיד, *וַנָּעִידָה	*וַנָּקָם, וַנָּקוּם, וַנָּקוּמָה

Though each of the morphological patterns finds representation throughout the biblical text, their respective distributions exhibit discernible diachronic correlations. These distinguish not just LBH from CBH, but also the CBH of the Torah from the rest of CBH.[3]

---

[1] For various opinions on the proto-Semitic antecedents to the various forms, see, among others, Rainey (1986, 4, 8–10); Talshir (1987, 589); JM (§§114a–f, 116a–c); Bloch (2007, 143); Blau (2010, §4.3.3.3.4 and the note there); Dallaire (2014, 108–11); Khan (2021, 322–23); Sjörs (2021a; 2021b).

[2] For the sake of convenient comparison, the table includes both documented and reconstructed forms. See Hornkohl (2023, 386, fn. 4, 426–34) on the reconstructions.

[3] Recent discussions include Talshir (1986; 1987); Revell (1988, 423); Qimron (1997, 177; 2008, 153–54); Bloch (2007); Hornkohl (2014a, 159–71; 2023, 385–439); Gzella (2018, 29–35); Khan (2021, 319–40); Sjörs (2021a; 2021b).

1.0. Late Biblical Hebrew and Post-Exilic Sources

LBH 1st-person *wayyiqtol* morphology is distinctively characterised by high incidence of long and augmented forms, which each come at the expense of shorter alternatives. Hornkohl (2023, 388, 392) presents the following tables, Table 2 showing the incidence of augmented 1st-person *wayyiqtol* morphology, which excludes III-*y* forms, and Table 3 showing the incidence of long III-*y* 1st-person *wayyiqtol* morphology.

Table 2: Incidence of augmented 1st-person *wayyiqtol* (ואקטלה, ואעידה, ואקומה) forms across representative ancient Hebrew corpora

	MT			BDSS	NBDSS	SP	Ben Sira
Torah	Proph.	Non-LBH+ Writings	LBH+				
4/105	19/254	8/26	69/127	21/55	23/31	34/106	4/7
(3.8%)	(7.5%)	(30.8)	(53.9%)	(38.2%)	(73.3%)	(32.4%)	(57.1%)

Table 3: Incidence of long 1st-person III-*y* forms (e.g., ואעשה) across representative ancient Hebrew traditions

	MT			BDSS	NBDSS	SP	Ben Sira
Torah	Proph.	Non-LBH+ Writings	LBH+				
3/21	38/66	7/13	18/25	7/10	10/11	21/22	2/2
(14.3%)	(57.6%)	(53.8%)	(72%)	(70%)	(90.9%)	(95.5%)	(100%)

In both categories, the statistics show that LBH+ opts for the longer alternative—augmented forms in the case of non-III-*y* verbs, long forms in the case of III-*y* verbs—far more frequently than other parts of the Bible.[4]

---

[4] Hornkohl's (2023, 385–439) study compares CBH to LBH+, the latter a broader category than the core LBH corpus of Esther, Daniel, Ezra–Nehemiah, and Chronicles, that also includes Ps. 119 (Hurvitz 1972, 130–52); Job 1–2; 42.7–17 (Hurvitz 1974b; cf. Young 2009; Joosten 2013); and Qohelet (Delitzsch 1877, 190–99 *et passim*; Driver 1898, 474–75; Hurvitz 1990; 2007; Schoors 1992–2004; Seow 1996; cf.

The LBH+ predilection for long 1st-person *wayyiqtol* morphological alternatives also obtains beyond III-*y* verbs, i.e., in the case of *hifʿil* and *qal* II-*w/y* verbs (see Hornkohl 2023, 393–96, for detailed discussion). Table 4, which focuses on consonantal morphology alone (see below on the pronunciation tradition), is reproduced from Hornkohl (2023, 394).

Table 4: Incidence of long 1st-person III-*y* (ואעשה), *hifʿil* (ואעיד), and *qal* II-*w/y* (ואקום) *wayyiqtol* forms: number of long forms out of number of combined short, long, and augmented forms (percentage long)

	Verb Class	MT Torah	MT Proph.	MT Non-LBH+ Writings	MT LBH+	BDSS	NBDSS	SP	Ben Sira
	III-*y*	3/21 (14.3%)	38/66 (57.6%)	7/13 (53.8%)	18/25 (72%)	7/10 (70%)	10/11 (90.9%)	21/22 (95.5%)	2/2 (100%)
hifʿil	*hifʿil* long	1/12 (8.3%)	14/33 (42.4%)	—	9/21 (42.9%)	0/2 (0%)	2/5 (40%)	10/13 (76.9%)	2/2 (100%)
	hifʿil aug.	0/12 (0%)	3/33 (9.1%)	—	10/21 (47.6%)	2/2 (100%)	3/5 (60%)	3/13 (23.1%)	—
	hifʿil long + aug.	1/12 (8.3%)	17/33 (51.5%)	—	19/21 (90.4%)	2/2 (100%)	5/5 (100%)	13/13 (100%)	2/2 (100%)
qal	II-*w/y* long	0/6 (0%)	9/15 (60%)	1/3 (33.3)	14/21 (66.7%)	0/3 (0%)	0/3 (0%)	4/5 (80%)	—
	II-*w/y* aug.	0/6 (0%)	1/15 (6.7%)	2/3 (66.7%)	7/21 (33.3%)	1/3 (33.3%)	3/3 (100%)	1/5 (20%)	—
	II-*w/y* long + aug.	0/6 (0%)	10/15 (66.7%)	3/3 (100%)	21/21 (100%)	1/3 (33.3%)	3/3 (100%)	5/5 (100%)	—
total	long	4/39 (10.3%)	61/114 (53.5%)	8/16 (50%)	41/67 (61.2%)	7/15 (46.7%)	12/19 (63.2%)	35/40 (87.5%)	4/4 (100%)
	long + aug.	4/39 (10.3%)	65/114 (57%)	10/16 (62.5%)	58/67 (86.6%)	10/15 (66.7%)	18/19 (94.7%)	39/40 (97.5%)	4/4 (100%)

Fredericks 1988; Young 1993, 140–57)—all material of unknown date the linguistic profile of which dates them to the post-Restoration period.

Forestalling the objection that this corpus-centric presentation obscures inner-corpus variation of potential linguistic significance, Hornkohl (2023, 399–404) compares book by book, concluding—despite outliers—that these figures indeed give a representative picture of the linguistic profiles of the constituent compositions.

Crucially, the above data also demonstrate late non-Masoretic biblical and extrabiblical confirmation of the late tendencies seen in the Tiberian LBH+ distributions of augmented and long 1st-person *wayyiqtol* morphology. From this perspective, the evidence of the BDSS and NBDSS is especially important, as, once produced near the turn of the era, these corpora were subject to no further scribal transmission (see Hornkohl 2023, 404–7, for detailed discussion).

2.0. Classical Biblical Hebrew and Pre-Exilic Sources

Tiberian CBH texts display 1st-person *wayyiqtol* morphological unity, corporately contrasting with LBH+, as well as diversity, with some texts, but not all, showing significant commonalities with LBH+ and other late non-Masoretic and extrabiblical Hebrew sources.

Against the late predilection for lengthened augmented 1st-person *wayyiqtol* morphology with ־ָה, CBH corpora generally eschew forms of this type. Table 2, from above, is reproduced here as Table 5 (facing page) for the sake of convenience.

Table 5: Incidence of augmented 1st-person *wayyiqṭol* (ואקטלה, ואעידה, ואקומה) forms across representative ancient Hebrew corpora

Torah	Proph.	MT Non-LBH+ Writings	LBH+	BDSS	NBDSS	SP	Ben Sira
4/105	19/254	8/26	69/127	21/55	23/31	34/106	4/7
(3.8%)	(7.5%)	(30.8)	(53.9%)	(38.2%)	(73.3%)	(32.4%)	(57.1%)

While all the above corpora reveal some use of augmented 1st-person *wayyiqṭol* morphology, only those comprised of material composed in the Second Temple period—Masoretic LBH+, the NBDSS, and Ben Sira—reveal majority augmented morphology. The significant minorities seen in other corpora are also important, though they arguably reflect a variety of factors. The elevated percentage in non-LBH+ Writings evidently indicates a correlation between augmented 1st-person *wayyiqṭol* morphology and poetry (Hornkohl 2023, 401–2). Comparable proportions in the BDSS and the SP show the effects of late secondary developments in otherwise classical material, evidencing both classical and late features—though it should be noted that the fragmentary state of the BDSS renders their testimony somewhat challenging to interpret (Hornkohl 2023, 404–11).

In addition to the morphological similarity uniting CBH texts that has just been discussed, they also divide with respect to an important distinction, that is, incidence of short versus long 1st-person *wayyiqṭol* morphology in the case of III-*y*, *hifʿil*, and *qal* II-*w/y* verbs. Table 6 (overleaf) gives the totals of forms per corpora according to the relevant lines in Table 4 (above).

Table 6: Incidence of long 1st-person III-*y* (ואעשה), *hifʿil* (ואעיד), and *qal* II-*w/y* (ואקום) *wayyiqtol* forms across representative ancient Hebrew corpora

Verb Class	MT Torah	MT Proph.	MT Non-LBH+ Writings	LBH+	BDSS	NBDSS	SP	Ben Sira
III-*y* long	3/21 (14.3%)	38/66 (57.6%)	7/13 (53.8%)	18/25 (72%)	7/10 (70%)	10/11 (90.9%)	21/22 (95.5%)	2/2 (100%)
hifʿil long	1/12 (8.3%)	14/33 (42.4%)	—	9/21 (42.9%)	0/2 (0%)	2/5 (40%)	10/13 (76.9%)	2/2 (100%)
II-*w/y* long	0/6 (0%)	9/15 (60%)	1/3 (33.3)	14/21 (66.7%)	0/3 (0%)	0/3 (0%)	4/5 (80%)	—
total long	**4/39 (10.3%)**	**61/114 (53.5%)**	**8/16 (50%)**	**41/67 (61.2%)**	**7/15 (46.7%)**	**12/19 (63.2%)**	**35/40 (87.5%)**	**4/4 (100%)**

Conspicuous here is the Tiberian Torah, the only corpus in which long 1st-person *wayyiqtol* morphology is rare. Notably, other CBH corpora—the CBH Prophets and non-LBH+ Writings—display comparatively frequent use of long 1st-person *wayyiqtol* forms, similar to LBH+ and late non-Masoretic biblical and extrabiblical corpora.

Incidentally, the typological antiquity of the Tiberian Torah's preference for short 1st-person *wayyiqtol* morphology and general lack of augmented 1st-person *wayyiqtol* morphology find confirmation in the (admittedly foreign, but cognate) ancient Moabite of the Meshaʿ Stele. Here III-*y* 1st-person *wayyiqtol* forms are consistently short, e.g., ואעש 'and I made' (ll. 3, 9), וארא 'and I saw' (l. 7), ואבן 'and I built' (l. 9), ואשב 'and I captured' (l. 12). At the same time, forms eligible for augmented morphology show no indication thereof, e.g., ואהרג 'and I killed' (ll. 11, 16), ואהלך 'and I went' (ll. 14–15), ואקח 'and I took' (ll. 17, 19–20), ואסחב 'and I dragged' (l. 18), ואמר 'and I said' (l. 24), ואשא 'and I carried'

(l. 30), and וארד 'and I descended' (l. 31). Anticipating the possible objection that a final *a* might have been realised, but not orthographically represented (i.e., spelled defectively), it is relevant to note the apparent marking of final *a* in such forms as בללה 'at night' (l. 15) and בנה 'he built' (n. 18), which lead one to expect that similar orthography would have been employed in the case of augmented *wayyiqtol* morphology, had it been used.

To summarise, Tiberian CBH compositions unite when it comes to infrequency of the augmented 1st-person *wayyiqtol* morphology so typical of LBH+ and other later material, but divide when it comes to the use of long, rather than short, 1st-person *wayyiqtol* morphology in the case of III-*y* (ואעשה), *hifʿil* (ואעיד), and *qal* II-*w/y* (ואקום) verbs. The Masoretic Pentateuch is largely devoid of such forms, while in the CBH Prophets and non-LBH+ Writings they are common, appearing in proportions that approach those characteristic of LBH+ and additional late sources.

3.0. Interpreting the Data[5]

The Meshaʿ Stele's exclusive use of short III-*y* 1st-person *wayyiqtol* (ואעש) forms and lack of augmented *wayyiqtol* (ואקטלה, ואקומה, ואעידה) forms tally with the Masoretic Torah's preference for short 1st-person morphology. Likewise, the striking affinity for long and augmented 1st-person *wayyiqtol* forms among late non-Tiberian biblical traditions—the BDSS, the SP—and late extrabiblical sources—the NBDSS, Ben Sira—is strong evidence of

---

[5] The ensuing discussion is a slightly abridged version of Hornkohl (2023, 413–26).

the historical authenticity of the Masoretic LBH+ preference for long and augmented *wayyiqtol* morphology.

The argument advanced to this point is consistent with, but does not exhaust, the evidence. The data sustain more far-reaching conclusions. Not only are long 1st-person *wayyiqtol* forms—ואקום, ואעיד, ואעשה—the norm in Tiberian LBH+ and other late written traditions; they are also common in what is generally considered CBH material outside the Pentateuch, e.g., the CBH Prophets and non-LBH+ Writings, where their incidence is closer to that seen in MT LBH+ than to that of the MT Torah (Talshir 1986, 6–8; 1987).

Against the background of the associations already established—i.e., classical short, on the one hand, and late long and augmented, on the other—how are the specific profiles of the CBH Prophets and non-LBH+ Writings—characterised by the apparently early distribution of long 1st-person *wayyiqtol* morphology, but not augmented 1st-person *wayyiqtol* morphology—to be explained?

Since long morphological forms (ואקום, ואעיד, ואעשה) are absent from the Torah's written tradition, but common in the rest of the MT—again, not just in LBH+, but outside the Pentateuch more generally—one might venture the hypothesis that long forms were not originally characteristic of *any* CBH material and pin the difference between the CBH of the Torah (where short forms dominate) and CBH outside the Torah (where long forms are quite standard) on late scribes. These copyists—it seems reasonable to conjecture—might have more assiduously preserved the ancient morphological integrity of the Torah than that of the rest of CBH, which was contemporised in the direction of LBH+ under the influence of Second Temple morphology. If so, 1st-person *wayyiqṭol* morphology in the Torah's written tradition would be historically more pristine and authentic than its counterpart in the rest of CBH, which shows many signs of secondary development. The theory is attractive, but can be no more than partially correct, as it is contradicted by important data points.

Key in this connection is the unambiguous written evidence of long 1st-person III-y (ואעשה) and augmented (ואקטלה, ואעידה, ואקומה) forms. See Chart 1 (reproduced from Hornkohl 2023, 416).

Chart 1: Incidence of long 1st-person III-y (ואעשה) and augmented 1st-person (ואקטלה, ואע(י)דה, ואק(ו)מה) forms across representative ancient Hebrew traditions as percentage of potential cases

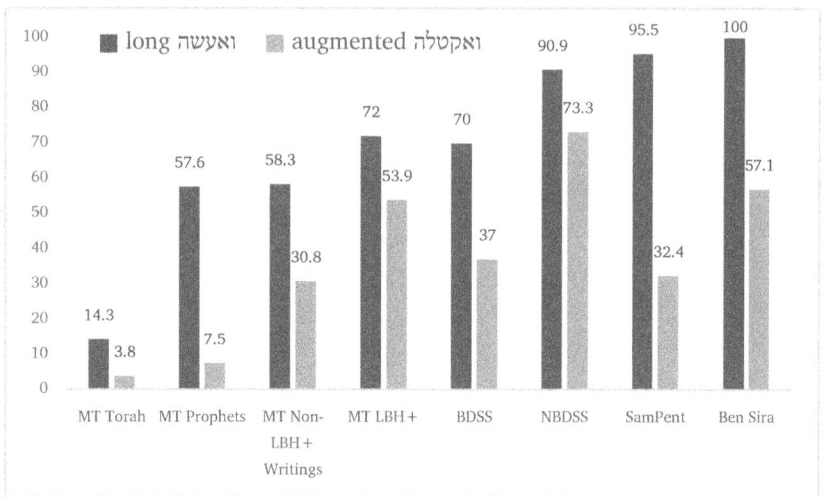

Generally speaking, the frequency of long (ואעשה) forms positively correlates with the frequency of augmented (ואקטלה, ואקומה, ואעידה) forms. That is, the use of one often goes hand in hand with the use of the other. Both are largely lacking in the MT Torah, but are common in MT LBH+ and in other late corpora, biblical and extrabiblical alike. The glaring exception in this regard is the MT Prophets, where long forms are comparatively frequent (57.6 percent), but augmented forms are rare (7.5 percent).

Returning to the speculative hypothesis proffered above, i.e., that 1st-person *wayyiqtol* forms may have been more or less uniformly short throughout CBH and only outside the Torah were contemporised in line with late linguistic customs—on this assumption, it would be reasonable to expect a marked increase in *both* long III-*y* forms *and* augmented forms in CBH outside the Torah. And this for the following reason: if late scribes appended final *heh* to originally short 1st-person III-*y wayyiqtol* forms according to Second Temple convention, i.e., changing ואעש to ואעשה, then it is reasonable to expect that they would do the same where necessary to expand the use of augmented forms, changing ואקטל to ואקטלה, etc., since these were no less characteristic of Second Temple Hebrew.

Crucially, this situation does not obtain. Against the norm in the MT Torah, and similarly to MT LBH+ and other late corpora, the CBH Prophets and non-LBH+ Writings show an affinity for long 1st-person III-*y wayyiqtol* (ואעשה) forms. At the same time, similar to the MT Torah and against the convention in MT LBH+ and other late texts, augmented (ואקומה, ואעידה, ואקטלה) forms are largely absent from the CBH of the Prophets. From the admittedly narrow perspective of 1st-person *wayyiqtol* forms, then, the written tradition of the MT CBH Prophets is that of *neither* the MT Torah *nor* MT LBH+, but reflects some sort of typologically transitional phase between Pentateuchal CBH and LBH+.

Less compelling is the explanation proffered by Talshir (1986, 5–8; 1987). On the basis of minority augmented 1st-person *wayyiqtol* morphology in the Torah and the Prophets, Talshir reasons that augmented 1st-person *wayyiqtol* morphology early on co-existed with short 1st-person *wayyiqtol* morphology, the latter dominant in the Torah, the former at one time more prevalent in the Prophets. Talshir speculates that, for unknown reasons, later scribes secondarily expunged and replaced augmented 1st-person *wayyiqtol* morphology in the Prophets with what he views as completely artificial long 1st-person *wayyiqtol* morphology. This arbitrary move was, in Talshir's view, based on analogy with the late merger of indicative long and volitive augmented 1st-person *yiqtol* seen in some Second Temple sources, whereby the formerly semantically distinct forms were no longer morphologically distinguished. With synonymous 1st-person *wayyiqtol* forms at their disposal, scribes opted for the morphologically simpler. Exactly why this should have happened when LBH and other late forms of Hebrew prefer the augmented 1st-person *wayyiqtol* form is unclear, especially as any secondary movement in the CBH Prophets may have been contemporary with the composition of LBH texts.

We appear to be left with three typological profiles involving 1st-person *wayyiqtol* morphology:

(1) nearly uniformly short (ואקם, ואעד, ואש) and standard (ואקטל) morphology (< PS *aqtul*) in the CBH of the Torah;

(2) commonly long (ואקום, ואעיד, ואעשה) and standard (ואקטל) morphology (< PS *aqtulu/a*), but rarely augmented morphology in the CBH of the Prophets;

(3) commonly long (ואקום, ואעיד, ואעשה) morphology (< PS *aqtulu/a*) and commonly augmented (ואעידה, ואקטלה, ואקומה) morphology (< PS *aqtulan[na]*) in LBH+.

A note on the MT non-LBH+ Writings: their incidence of long (ואקום, ואעיד, ואעשה) forms is similar to that of the MT Prophets, but Psalms especially shows a comparatively high incidence of augmented (ואקומה, ואעידה, ואקטלה) forms. Given the uncertainty inherent in the linguistic periodisation of poetry, it is difficult to determine whether this relatively frequent use of augmented forms is a function of chronolect, poetic genre, another factor or factors, or some combination thereof.

It bears explicit acknowledgment at this point that the proposed chronological interpretation of the typology is at odds with certain views common in biblical studies, not least those that see the Torah and other CBH biblical material as products of the post-exilic period and/or that reject language as a reliable diachronic indicator when it comes to an oral recitation tradition written down and transmitted over centuries. The position advocated here is not that alternative evidence should be deprivileged in favour of orthographic and linguistic evidence, but that the latter should receive due attention and be integrated with evidence gleaned from other approaches.

But these results also arguably necessitate a revision of the dominant dichotomous linguistic periodisation of BH. Most discussions of ancient Hebrew diachrony distinguish post-exilic (or, more accurately, post-Restoration) LBH from pre-exilic CBH, eschewing any finer sub-divisions (for overviews, see Hornkohl 2013; Hurvitz 2013). While this chronolectal division adequately comprehends most diachronic variety in BH, it leaves other data unexplained. Some scholars, therefore, also recognise pre-classical (i.e., pre-1000 BCE) poetic ABH (Mandell 2013)—though there is no consensus as to its significance for dating the relevant compositions. A number of scholars also support the notion of an intermediate category between CBH and LBH termed TBH (i.e., 600–450 BCE; for a list of such scholars, see Hornkohl 2014a, 14–15, fn. 39; 2016a). Differences of opinion revolve around such questions as the correlation between language style and date of composition; the heuristic value of positing more or fewer divisions; and the location of the boundaries between proposed chronolects and liminal cases. Whether they are accepted or not, the addition of ABH and TBH does not suffice to explain the inner-CBH diachronic diversity under discussion here.

Certain aspects of 1st-person *wayyiqtol* morphological diversity are consistent with the regnant bipartite CBH–LBH division, notably, the high frequency of short (ואקם, ואעד, ואעש) morphology in the written tradition of the Tiberian Torah and the Meshaʿ Stele, on the one hand, and, on the other, the rarity of short morphology and the concomitant accumulation of augmented (ואוקמה, ואעידה, ואקטלה) morphology in Tiberian LBH + and other biblical and extrabiblical sources that reflect Second Temple Hebrew.

Yet the proposed typology also arguably challenges at least one component of the regnant diachronic linguistic paradigm. In the distributions of the 1st-person *wayyiqtol* morphological variants in the Tiberian written tradition, one confronts a situation that calls for greater nuance than what typically characterises diachronic discussions. This is because the three-stage diachronic division of material based on the distribution of 1st-person *wayyiqtol* morphology can only with difficulty be squeezed into a dichotomous CBH–LBH framework. Nor, on the surface, is it consistent with the existing tripartite ABH–CBH–LBH paradigm, or even with the maximally nuanced ABH–CBH–TBH–LBH arrangement. This is because the pertinent distributional combinations of short, long, and augmented 1st-person morphology do not correspond to any of the proposed paradigms, instead respecting different boundaries. The distinction between the CBH of the Torah and the CBH of the relevant Prophets and Writings, on the one hand, and the unity of the non-LBH + Prophets and Writings, on the other, seem to indicate diachronic isoglosses that do not coincide with the borders of TBH, but land squarely within CBH, thereby calling for finer shading within what is conventionally termed CBH.

Preliminarily, two explanations suggest themselves. One option is that the Torah's written linguistic tradition is, as it seems, typologically older than that of the rest of CBH, in which case there may be some justification to distinguishing between chronological sub-strata within CBH, i.e., CBH_1 and CBH_2, both typologically prior to TBH and LBH (see Elitzur 2015; 2018a; 2018b; 2019; 2022).

One may, alternatively, envision a scenario in which original CBH short 1st-person *wayyiqtol* morphological dominance gave way to secondary diversity when material outside the Torah was contemporised—not according to LBH, but in line with norms typologically transitional between those of the MT Torah and LBH proper, that is, of a period when long (ואעיד, ואעשה, ואקום) forms were in wide use, but augmented (ואעידה, ואקטלה, ואקומה) were not yet in vogue. In this case, what appears to be CBH₂ would be a result of the contemporisation of CBH in line with post-CBH but pre-LBH conventions.

There is some concrete data supporting what otherwise remains quite theoretical conjecture. Hornkohl (2023, 401, Table 8) shows broadly similar proportions of long and augmented morphology in Joshua, Judges, Kings, and Isaiah compared to TBH Jeremiah and Ezekiel. However, the approach cannot account for Samuel's exclusive employment of long morphology (13/13 cases), but rare usage of augmented forms (7/25 cases). Finally, in the interests of methodological parsimony, one should suspend judgment on the notion that TBH influence on CBH best explains the emergence of the sub-chronolect CBH₂. If no other feature discussed in this volume necessitates such an explanation, it should be judged unlikely.

As for actual historical dates, the Meshaʿ Stele fortuitously furnishes chronologically fixed control data—albeit in a Canaanite language cognate, and geographically peripheral, to ancient Hebrew, rendering its relevance to the latter somewhat questionable. If the monument's consistent use of short instead of long or augmented (III-*y*, *hifʿil*, *qal* II-*w/y*) and standard instead of augmented (strong, *hifʿil*, *qal* II-*w/y* verbs) morphology can be construed as more or less representative of the situation in ancient Hebrew, then its 840 BCE date usefully serves as a solid historical data point for purposes of historical linguistic comparison. The Tiberian Torah's CBH₁ 1st-person *wayyiqtol* morphological tradition is consistent with mid-9th century BCE Moabite evidence, while the combination of forms found in LBH+, which is confirmed by late non-Masoretic and extrabiblical material, seems datable to post-450 BCE. This would seem to leave the period of the 8th–6th centuries BCE for the morphological combinations typical of CBH_2 and TBH texts from the Prophets and Writings. Interestingly, this diachronic division is largely consistent with that seen in the case of the BH onomasticon (above, ch. 1).

It also bears mentioning that there is no perceptible concentration of typologically late forms in any single Pentateuchal source. J has three forms; E has two; P has one; and Dtr_1 has two.[6]

Finally, one should mention a degree of dissonance between the linguistic traditions reflected in the consonantal text, on the one hand, and the vocalisation and accentuation, on the other. In the Pentateuch and the Prophets especially, many apparently short *hifʿil* and *qal* II-*w/y* written forms—which, according to the approach here, presuppose pronunciations associated with short morphology—are realised in the reading tradition with long morphology. See Table 7 (facing page). In this way the pronunciation tradition lines up more closely than the written tradition with Second Temple Hebrew—though it is important to note that (a) the Torah specifically preserves short morphology in the vocalisation of 1cpl *wayyiqtol* forms and (b) the development seen in the vocalisation of CBH beyond the Torah reflects the continuation of a developmental trend already underway in

---

[6] J: Gen. 24.48; 32.4; Num. 21.30 (?); E: Gen 41.11; 43.21; P: Num. 8.19; Dtr_1: Deut. 1.16, 18.

the corresponding written tradition (for detailed discussion, see Hornkohl 2023, 426–35).

Table 7: 1st-person short and long *hifʿil* and *qal* II-*w/y wayyiqṭol* morphology in the Masoretic reading tradition of the Torah

	Singular	Plural
Short	וָאוֹלֵךְ (Lev. 26.13; Deut. 29.4)	וַנַּגֶּד־לֹו (Gen. 43.7; Gen. 44.24)
		וַנֵּשֶׁב (Gen. 43.21)
		וַנַּקְרֵב (Num. 31.50)
		וַנֵּסָב (Deut. 2.1)
		וַנַּחֲרֵם (Deut. 2.34; 3.6)
Long	וָאָשִׂם (Gen. 24.47; Deut. 10.5)	וַנָּשִׁים (Num. 21.30)
	וָאָבִא (Exod. 19.4)	
	וָאָקִץ (Lev. 20.23)	
	וָאַבְדִּל (Lev. 20.26)	
	וָאַשְׁלִךְ (Deut. 9.21)	
Invariable	וָאָבֹא (Gen. 24.42)	וַנָּבֹא (Deut. 1.19)

3. *QAL* VERSUS *HIFʿIL* FORMS OF יס״ף

Throughout the Hebrew Bible, two verbs that share the root יס״ף compete in the meaning 'add, do again': *qal* יָסַף and *hifʿil* הוֹסִיף. Their synonymy is demonstrated by the example pairs in (1)–(8), with *qal* and *hifʿil* forms presented in odd- and even-numbered examples, respectively:

(1) וְלֹא־יָסַף שְׁמוּאֵל לִרְאוֹת אֶת־שָׁאוּל עַד־יוֹם מוֹתוֹ
'And Samuel did no more see Saul until the day of his death…' (1 Sam. 15.35)

(2) כִּי אֲשֶׁר רְאִיתֶם אֶת־מִצְרַיִם הַיּוֹם לֹא תֹסִיפוּ לִרְאֹתָם עוֹד עַד־עוֹלָם
'…For the Egyptians whom you see today—you shall no more see them again.' (Exod. 14.13)

(3) וְהִנֵּה לֹא הֻגַּד־לִי חֲצִי מַרְבִּית חָכְמָתֶךָ יָסַפְתָּ עַל־הַשְּׁמוּעָה אֲשֶׁר שָׁמָעְתִּי
'…And behold, half the greatness of your wisdom was not told me; you have surpassed the report that I heard. (2 Chron. 9.6)

(4) וְהִנֵּה לֹא־הֻגַּד־לִי הַחֵצִי הוֹסַפְתָּ חָכְמָה וָטוֹב אֶל־הַשְּׁמוּעָה אֲשֶׁר שָׁמָעְתִּי
'…And behold, the half was not told me. You have accumulated[1] wisdom and wealth beyond the report that I heard.' (1 Kgs 10.7)

(5) וַיְשַׁלַּח אֶת־הַיּוֹנָה וְלֹא־יָסְפָה שׁוּב־אֵלָיו עוֹד
'…and he sent forth the dove, and she did no more return to him again.' (Gen. 8.12)

---

[1] Or 'you have surpassed in wisdom and wealth'.

(6) נָפְלָה לֹא־תוֹסִיף קוּם בְּתוּלַת יִשְׂרָאֵל

'She has fallen. She will no more rise, the virgin of Israel.' (Amos 5.2)

(7) וְיָסַפְתָּ לְךָ עוֹד שָׁלֹשׁ עָרִים עַל הַשָּׁלֹשׁ הָאֵלֶּה

'...then you shall add three other cities to these three.' (Deut. 19.9)

(8) וְיוֹסִיפוּ לְךָ שְׁנוֹת חַיִּים

'and years of life will be added to you.' (Prov. 9.11)

As things stand in the extant combined Tiberian written-reading tradition, *hifʿil* forms outnumber *qal* forms.[2] Intriguingly, however, neither stem boasts a complete paradigm. Especially conspicuous is the apparent absence of the *qal* prefix conjugation (but cf. below), whether in *yiqtol* or *wayyiqtol* forms. Table 1 (facing page) summarises the paradigms.

The discussion that follows focuses on the distribution of the two stems, with particular sensitivity to diachronic trends. To avoid combining diachronically diverse layers of evidence, it is necessary to separate morphologically unambiguous written (i.e., purely consonantal) forms from ambiguous written forms, as the latter were amenable to secondary processes of morphological reinterpretation in the pronunciation tradition(s) reflected in orthographic developments (the addition of *matres lectionis*) and vocalisation and/or remain morphologically ambiguous.

---

[2] According to the Groves-Wheeler (1991–2016) electronic tagged database available with the Accordance software, the figures are *qal* 36 and *hifʿil* 173. Yet, since many forms, especially in the prefix conjugation, are morphologically ambiguous or have been wrongly classified as *hifʿil*, these figures ought to be viewed with suspicion.

Table 1: Summary paradigms of qal and hif'il י"סף

Form	qal	hif'il
suffix conjugation	יָסַף	הוֹסִיף
participle	יֹסְפִים	מוֹסִיפִים
prefix conjugation	—³	יוֹסִיף/יֹסֵף
wayyiqtol	—³	וַיּוֹסִיפוּ/וַיֹּסֶף
infinitive construct	לִסְפּוֹת/סְפוֹת⁴	לְהוֹסִיף
imperative	סְפוּ	—
external passive	נוֹסַף	—⁵

1.0. Unambiguous Written Evidence

1.1. The Tiberian Masoretic Tradition

Table 2 (overleaf) presents the statistics relevant to those forms with unequivocal consonantal shapes in qal and hif'il, i.e., suffix conjugation, participle, infinitive, and imperative. According to purely consonantal evidence—i.e., excluding evidence for stem differentiation based on *matres lectionis* and vocalisation—the picture is relatively clear. Qal forms—such as suffix conjugation יסף, participle יספים, and imperative ספו—dominate in CBH,[6] whereas LBH shows preference for consonantally unambiguous

---

[3] According to the standard I-y/w qal pattern, the expected Tiberian prefix conjugation form would be יִסַף*, *wayyiqtol* וַיִּסַף*; but see below.

[4] Cf. Moabite לספת (Meshaʿ [KAI 181] l. 21); see below, fn. 6.

[5] Cf. BA hof'al הוּסְפַת 'was added (FS)' (Dan. 4.33).

[6] These figures include the qal infinitival forms לִסְפּוֹת (Num. 32.14) and סְפוֹת (Isa. 30.1), despite the III-y (rather than I-y) morphology, on the grounds that their stem morphology is transparent. By contrast, the qal qere יֵסֵף (1 Sam. 27.4; ketiv יוסף) is excluded, since it is not part of the consonantal tradition, whereas the stem of the ketiv is ambiguous.

hif'il morphology—such as suffix conjugation הוֹסִיף, participle מוֹסִיפִים, and infinitive construct לְהוֹסִיף. The overall CBH *qal* to *hif'il* ratio is 33:5 (Pentateuch 16:1, Prophets 16:3, non-LBH + Writings 0:1), whereas LBH shows a reverse trend of 1:6.

Table 2: MT distribution of unequivocal forms of *qal* יָסַף and *hif'il* הוֹסִיף (see §4.1 for citations)

Book	qal	hif'il	Book/Corpus	qal	hif'il
Genesis	2	0	Ezra	0	1
Leviticus	7	1	Nehemiah	0	1
Numbers	3	0	Chronicles	1	1
Deuteronomy	4	0	**Pentateuch**	16	1
Judges	2	0	**Prophets**	16	3
Samuel	4	0	Former	8	3
Kings	2	3	Latter	8	0
Isaiah	5	0	**Writings**	1	7
Jeremiah	2	0	Non-LBH +	0	1
Psalms	0	1	LBH +	1	6
Qohelet	0	3	**TOTALS**	33	24

1.2. Extrabiblical, Non-Tiberian, and Cognate Sources

Maintaining the focus on unambiguous *qal* and *hif'il* consonantal forms (suffix conjugation, participle, infinitive construct, imperative), we find that the same diachronic pattern seen above in the case of the Tiberian consonantal evidence is discernible in extrabiblical and non-Tiberian biblical consonantal material. The incidence of unambiguous *qal* and *hif'il* forms in classical and post-classical corpora is summarised in Table 3 (facing page).

3. Qal versus hif'il Forms of יס"ף

Table 3: Distribution of unequivocal forms of qal יָסַף and hif'il הוֹסִיף in the MT, Extrabiblical Sources, and Non-Tiberian Biblical Material (see §4.2 for citations)

Corpus	qal	hif'il	Corpus	qal	hif'il
Mesha' (KAI 181)	2	0	NBDSS	2	16
Zakkur (KAI 202)	0	1	Ben Sira	0	3
BDSS	16	4	Mishna	1	75
SP	18	0			

Reflecting early patterns of stem usage outside Masoretic BH, the mid-9th-century Moabite of the Mesha' Stele, the BDSS, and the SP, show dominant use of qal forms. The BDSS and the SP, however, paint a mixed picture. As biblical traditions rooted in antiquity, they unsurprisingly exhibit persistence of early qal dominance. At the same time, as Second Temple manifestations of BH, they also show the effects of the influence of late linguistic conventions in stem distribution of יס"ף verbs. In the case of the BDSS, the fragmentary nature of the evidence permits only tentative observations. Even so, if the few relevant cases can be taken as more broadly representative, it is worth highlighting a noticeable trend of opting for hif'il rather than qal, which occurs in at least three (and possibly four) of six cases (all involving the participial form at Deut. 5.25):

אִם מֹ[וֹ]סִ'פִים (4Q37 3.7 || MT אִם־יֹסְפִים Deut. 5.25); וְהוֹסַפְתִּי (4Q83 f9ii.13 || MT וְהוֹסַפְתִּי Ps. 71.14); [וֹ]סִפִים] אם יֹ (4Q41 5.7 || MT אִם־יֹסְפִים Deut. 5.25); [וֹסִיפִים] כי מ (4Q129 f1R.13 || MT אִם־יֹסְפִים Deut. 5.25); אִם מֹ[וֹ]סִיפִים (4Q135 f1.4 || MT אִם־ יֹסְפִים Deut. 5.25); אִם מ/יסִפִים (4Q137 f1.31 || MT אִם־יֹסְפִים Deut. 5.25); אִם יֹסְפִים (XQ2 1.6 || MT אִם־יֹסְפִים Deut. 5.25).[7]

---

[7] Several instances of the participle corresponding to MT Deut. 5.25 may have been influenced by the presence of mem in the preceding word, but this obviously does not apply to [וֹסִיפִים] כי מ (4Q129 f1R.13).

As for the SP—despite superficial similarity between it and the MT concerning the preservation of *qal* יָסַף, there are significant differences, all pointing to SH's relative typological lateness. First, in the case of I-y verbs, the Samaritan tradition routinely replaces *wayyiqtol* with non-converted *we-qatal* forms: not only is ויסף read as *qal wyā̊saf* (cf. the unequivocally *hifʿil* ויוסיפו *wyūsīfu* Deut. 20.8), but so, too, is feminine ותסף *wtā̊saf* (Gen. 4.2; cf. תוסף *tūsaf* Gen. 4.12; תוסיפון *tūsīfon* Gen. 44.23). Second, against MT *qal*, the SP sometimes has *piʿʿel*, e.g., MT וְיָסַפְתִּי || SP ויספתי *wyassafti* 'and I will continue' (Lev. 26.18; see also Lev. 26.21; Deut. 19.9).[8] Third, as demonstrated below, in three of the eight instances in which old *qal yaqtel*[9] prefix conjugation forms are arguably preserved in the MT Pentateuch, the SP written and/or reading tradition evinces an unambiguous *hifʿil*; see תֹּסֶף || SP תוסף *tūsaf* (Gen. 4.12); תֹּסֵף || SP תוסיפו *tūsīfu* (Deut. 13.1); אֹסֵף || SP אוסיף *ūsaf* (Deut. 18.16).

Likewise, unequivocal *hifʿil* usage is frequent in late extrabiblical sources, e.g., the NBDSS, the Mishna, and Ben Sira. *Qal* usage, by contrast, is exceptional and conditioned, limited to

---

Though some apparently *qal* 3rd-person *weqatal* forms in the DSS are given to analysis as instances of *hifʿil* (or *qal*) *wayyiqtol* or *we-yiqtol*, e.g., ויספו (1QIsaᵃ 23.29 || וְיָסְפוּ MT Isa. 29.19; cf. the following paragraph on the SP), the prevalence of *mater waw* in I-w/y *hifʿil yiqtol* forms in the DSS (26 of 28 cases) makes it likely that the forms identified above as *weqatal* are indeed instances of the *qal* suffix conjugation.

[8] On pielisation as a feature of Second Temple Hebrew, see Hornkohl (2023, 253–88) and the references mentioned there.

[9] Alternatively, a form like Samaritan *tūsaf* can be analysed as an original *yaqtul*, whereby **tawsup* > **tōsup* > **tōsip* (due to dissimilation).

biblical citation and allusion. No unambiguous *qal* forms appear in Ben Sira. Notably, the two *qal* cases in QH come in the 'rewritten Bible' or 'reworked Pentateuch' material of 4QCommentary Genesis A (4Q252 1.18, 20), where the language was undoubtedly influenced by its CBH source (MT Gen. 8.12). In other cases, tellingly, QH has transparent *hifʿil* morphology against a more ambiguous MT form, e.g., לוא תוסיף עליהמה ולוא תגרע מהמה 'you will not add to them and you will not subtract from them' (11QTᵃ [11Q19] 54.6–7) || לֹא־תֹסֵף עָלָיו וְלֹא תִגְרַע מִמֶּנּוּ (MT Deut. 13.1), תוסיף לשוב בדרך הזואת עוד 'You shall no more again return that way' (11QTᵃ [11Q19] 56.17–18) || לֹא תֹסִפוּן לָשׁוּב בַּדֶּרֶךְ הַזֶּה עוֹד (MT Deut. 17.16), and ולוא יוסיפו עוד לעשות כדבר הזה בקרבכה 'and they will no more do that sort of thing among you again' (11QTᵃ [11Q19] 61.11) || וְלֹא־יֹסִפוּ לַעֲשׂוֹת עוֹד כַּדָּבָר הָרָע הַזֶּה בְּקִרְבֶּךָ (MT Deut. 19.20). Likewise, the sole case of *qal* morphology in the Mishna (Soṭa 9.5) was inherited from the Bible (MT Deut. 20.8).[10]

With specific reference to the incidence of indisputable *hifʿil* consonantal forms in non-Tiberian biblical material: the late-9th–early-8th-century Old Aramaic instance of הוספ[ת 'I added' (Zakkur [*KAI* 202] B.4–5) is solid evidence of early *hifʿil* usage. It may be seen as supporting evidence for the authenticity of the lone instance of unambiguous *hifʿil* in the Tiberian Torah, לְהוֹסִיף (Lev. 19.25), though textual and interpretive questions leave some doubt (see below).

---

[10] Note also the Mishna's combined written-reading testimony of בַּל תּוֹסַ(י)ף 'Thou shalt not add' (Zevaḥ. 8.10, 10, 10), where the vocalisation in Codex Kaufmann conforms to that of the Tiberian tradition לֹא־תֹסֵף (MT Deut. 13.1). Cf. בַּל תּוֹסִיף in printed editions.

2.0. Ambiguous Consonantal Evidence, Orthography, and Vocalisation

Conspicuously absent from the foregoing account are the prefix conjugation forms *yiqtol* and *wayyiqtol*. Exempting such forms from the initial survey is necessary, because purely consonantal prefix conjugation forms are morphologically ambiguous, disposed to both *qal* and *hifʻil* interpretations. The morphology is often clarified thanks to the inclusion of *mater yod* and via unequivocal vocalisation, but these might involve the imposition of secondary morphological interpretations. Moreover, even some vocalised forms are morphologically equivocal.

2.1. The Morphology of *(way)yiqtol* יס"ף Forms

2.1.1. Wholesale *(way)yiqtol* Hifilisation?

Given the unequivocal *qal* shapes of most of the suffix conjugation, imperatival, infinitival, and participial forms cited above, it would be reasonable to expect, with Ginsberg (1934, 223), that the corresponding *qal* prefix conjugation form would be of the typical I-*y/w* pattern, i.e., *yiqtol* יֵסֵף** and *wayyiqtol* וַיִּ֫סֶף**. From this perspective, a vocalised form such as תֹסֵף 'there will (not) be again' (Exod. 11.6) should be identified as an original *qal* form, which might be expected to yield Tiberian תֵסֵף**, that was secondarily realised with *hifʻil* pronunciation in line with Second Temple tendencies. Thus, in *plene* spellings such as יוסף, יסיף, and יוסיף, the *waw* and/or *yod matres* might reasonably be considered secondary. Even the apparently early consonantally unambiguous *hifʻil* infinitive לְהוֹסִיף (Lev. 19.25) arouses scepticism, the context more suited, in Ginsberg's opinion, to the Samaritan להאסיף, presumably 'to gather'.[11] On Ginsberg's view, then, the expected Tiberian CBH paradigm is *qal* (לְ)סְפֵת-סַף-*יֵסֶף-יָסַף*, with the *hifʿil* paradigm (לְ)הוֹסִיף-*הוֹסֵף-יוֹסִיף-מוֹסִיף-הוֹסִיף* late and secondary. If so, all apparently CBH *hifʿil* realisations, whether indicated by *matres lectionis*, by Tiberian vocalisation signs, or by a combination of the two, are anachronistic. To sum up: Ginsberg's view is that the mixed CBH paradigm is the result of the artificial extension of the post-exilic *hifʿil* paradigm to pre-exilic *qal* spellings amenable to *hifʿil* realisation.

One conspicuous upshot of the *hifʿil* reinterpretation of original *qal* forms is that the distribution of the two stems blurs the otherwise straightforward picture of diachronic development presented on the basis of purely consonantal evidence above (§1.0). Because a certain number of originally *qal yiqtol* forms were apparently recast as *hifʿil*, the rather tidy diachronic picture sketched above based on consonantally unambiguous forms is distorted due to apparent secondary *qal* > *hifʿil* shifts in the

---

[11] In the passage's context of harvesting, 'gather' is at least as apposite as 'add'. Vulgate *congregantes* reflects the former; LXX πρόσθεμα, Onqelos לְאוֹסְפָא, and the Syriac ܘܡܘܣܦܐ the latter. The Samaritan evidence is itself varied: the Targum has למכנשה 'gather', against Arabic ليضاعف 'multiply'. For the meaning 'gather' one expects *qal* לאסף in Samaritan as well as Tiberian Hebrew; indeed, the *hifʿil* is otherwise unknown. Also, as noted above, the Samaritan pronunciation *līsaf* reflects neither לאסף nor להאסיף, but seemingly להסיף 'bring to an end'. Cf. MT תֵּאָסְפוּן || SP תוסיפון *tūsifon* (Exod. 5.7), where, again, the context is amenable to both 'con-tinue' and 'gather'. Similar cases of possible conflation occur within the Tiberian tradition: אס"ף and סו"ף in Jer. 8.13 and Zeph. 1.2, אס"ף and יס"ף in 1 Sam. 18.29 and 2 Sam. 6.1 (see Ben-Ḥayyim 2000, 143, 213).

realisation of ambiguous spellings. The basically diachronic suppletion described above, consisting of classical *qal* and late *hifʿil*, is complicated by a situation of seeming synchronic suppletion within CBH, in which only those *qal* forms impervious to *hifʿil* reinterpretation—*(we)qatal*, participle, imperative, infinitives construct and absolute—preserved their original stem, while the remaining *(way)yiqtol* forms shifted to *hifʿil*. The suppletive nature of the paradigm is especially conspicuous in morphologically divergent forms in proximity. Consider the contrasting stems in the following examples of verses in close context:

(9a) ...וַיֹּ֣סֶף שַׁלַּ֔ח אֶת־הַיּוֹנָ֖ה מִן־הַתֵּבָֽה׃

'...and he again sent forth the dove from the ark.' (Gen. 8.10b)

(9b) ...וְלֹֽא־יָסְפָ֥ה שׁוּב־אֵלָ֖יו עֽוֹד׃

'...and (the dove) did not again return.' (Gen. 8.12b)

(10a) ...וְיָסַ֥ף חֲמִשִׁת֖וֹ עָלָֽיו׃

'...and he must add a fifth of it thereupon...' (Lev. 27.27b)

(10b) ...חֲמִשִׁית֖וֹ יֹסֵ֥ף עָלָֽיו׃

'...a fifth of it he must add thereupon.' (Lev. 27.31b)

(11a) ...וְלֹא־יָ֨סְפ֥וּ ע֛וֹד גְּדוּדֵ֥י אֲרָ֖ם לָב֣וֹא בְּאֶ֥רֶץ יִשְׂרָאֵֽל׃

'...and the bands of Arameans no longer came into the territory of Israel.' (2 Kgs 6.23b)

(11b) ...כֹּֽה־יַעֲשֶׂה־לִּ֤י אֱלֹהִים֙ וְכֹ֣ה יוֹסִ֔ף...

'...thus will God do to me and thus will he repeat...' (2 Kgs 6.31a)

(12a) ...סְפ֥וּ שָׁנָ֖ה עַל־שָׁנָ֑ה...

'...add year upon year...' (Isa. 29.1)

(12b) ...לָכֵ֣ן הִנְנִ֧י יוֹסִ֛ף לְהַפְלִ֥יא אֶת־הָֽעָם־הַזֶּ֖ה

'Therefore, behold, I will again do wonderful things with this people...' (Isa. 29.14)[12]

(12c) ...וְיָסְפ֧וּ עֲנָוִ֛ים בַּֽיהוָ֖ה שִׂמְחָ֑ה

'And the meek will increase joy in the LORD...' (Isa. 29.19)

2.1.2. An Alternative Approach

On the face of it, Ginsberg's view is straightforward and compelling, adequately explaining most of the evidence. It fails, however, to account for certain significant details. The specific constellation of spelling and vocalisation characteristic of the יס״ף prefix conjugation forms seems to reflect a situation more complex than the wholesale application of post-exilic *hifʿil* morphology and phonology wherever pre-exilic *qal* consonantal spelling made it possible.

One intriguing piece of evidence in this connection is the comparatively high incidence, especially in the Masoretic Pentateuch, of what look to be short *yiqtol* (< PS *yaqtul*), i.e., jussive, *hifʿil* forms in contexts better suited to full *yiqtol* (< PS *yaqtulu*) morphology and indicative semantics, e.g.,

(13) כִּ֤י תַֽעֲבֹד֙ אֶת־הָ֣אֲדָמָ֔ה לֹֽא־תֹסֵ֥ף תֵּת־כֹּחָ֖הּ לָ֑ךְ

'When you work the ground, it will no longer yield to you its strength.' (Gen. 4.12 || SP תוסף *tūsəf*)

---

[12] For more on this construction see the discussion below, §2.2, on examples (21)–(22).

(14) וְאֵת֩ אֲשֶׁ֨ר חָטָ֜א מִן־הַקֹּ֗דֶשׁ יְשַׁלֵּם֙ וְאֶת־חֲמִֽישִׁתוֹ֙ יוֹסֵ֣ף עָלָ֔יו וְנָתַ֥ן אֹת֖וֹ לַכֹּהֵ֑ן...

'And for what he has done amiss in the holy thing he must make restitution and a fifth of it he must add thereupon and he will give it to the priest...' (Lev. 5.16 || SP יסף *yåsəf*; see also Lev. 5.24; 27.31; Num. 5.7)

(15) וְעַתָּ֗ה שְׁב֨וּ נָ֥א בָזֶ֛ה גַּם־אַתֶּ֖ם הַלָּ֑יְלָה וְאֵ֣דְעָ֔ה מַה־יֹּסֵ֥ף יְהוָ֖ה דַּבֵּ֥ר עִמִּֽי:

'And now, stay here then tonight you, too, that I may know what more the LORD will say to me.' (Num. 22.19 || SP יסף *yåsəf*)

(16) אֵ֣ת כָּל־הַדָּבָ֗ר אֲשֶׁ֤ר אָֽנֹכִי֙ מְצַוֶּ֣ה אֶתְכֶ֔ם אֹת֥וֹ תִשְׁמְר֖וּ לַֽעֲשׂ֑וֹת לֹא־תֹסֵ֣ף עָלָ֔יו וְלֹ֥א תִגְרַ֖ע מִמֶּֽנּוּ: פ

'Everything that I command you, it you will be careful to do. You must not add to it or take from it.' (Deut. 13.1 || SP תוסיפו *tūsīfu*)

(17) ...לֹ֣א אֹסֵ֗ף לִשְׁמֹ֙עַ֙ אֶת־קוֹל֙ יְהוָ֣ה אֱלֹהָ֔י וְאֶת־הָאֵ֨שׁ הַגְּדֹלָ֥ה הַזֹּ֛את לֹֽא־אֶרְאֶ֥ה ע֖וֹד וְלֹ֥א אָמֽוּת:

'...I will not again hear the voice of the LORD my God or see this great fire any more, lest I die.' (Deut. 18.16 || SP אוסיף *ūsəf*)

(18) ...וְרָעָ֞ב אֹסֵ֤ף עֲלֵיכֶם֙ וְשָׁבַרְתִּ֥י לָכֶ֖ם מַטֵּה־לָֽחֶם:

'...and famine I will add upon you and will break your supply of bread.' (Ezek. 5.16)

(19) ...לֹ֥א אוֹסֵ֖ף אַהֲבָתָ֑ם כָּל־שָׂרֵיהֶ֖ם סֹרְרִֽים:

'...I will no longer love them.' (Hos. 9.15)

(20) ...עַם רַב וְעָצוּם כָּמֹהוּ לֹא נִהְיָה מִן־הָעוֹלָם וְאַחֲרָיו לֹא יוֹסֵף עַד־שְׁנֵי דּוֹר וָדוֹר׃

'...a great and powerful people; their like has never been before, nor will be again after them through the years of all generations.' (Joel 2.2)[13]

While a certain degree of overlap between jussive and indicative patterns is known to characterise the use of *yiqṭol* forms in BH (see, e.g., GKC §109d, k; JM §114l), the frequency of the phenomenon in the case of הוֹסִיף–יָסַף arguably calls for closer inspection—lest a factor specific to this verb be (partially) responsible for the unexpectedly high degree of apparent mismatch between morphology and modality.

Of general relevance is an observation made by Blau (2010, 21–23). It is widely held that BH *qal yiqṭol* represents three Proto-Semitic vocalic patterns, namely *yafʿul*, *yafʿil*, and *yifʿal*, the former two considered active and the latter stative. Dominant Hebrew *yiqṭol* is the reflex of original *yafʿul* and, due to various phonological and analogical processes, many original *yafʿil* and *yifʿal* verbs also developed *yiqṭol* forms. Only a minority of verbs preserve reflexes of their original *yafʿil* or *yifʿal* patterns, especially those with weak or guttural radicals and/or those included in the

---

[13] The form יֹסֵף in יְהוָה אֱלֹהֵי אֲבוֹתֵכֶם יֹסֵף עֲלֵיכֶם כָּכֶם אֶלֶף פְּעָמִים וִיבָרֵךְ אֶתְכֶם כַּאֲשֶׁר דִּבֶּר לָכֶם׃ (Deut. 1.11) is semantically ambiguous in terms of both vocalisation and context. It is analysable as a *qal* indicative *yiqṭol* or active participle 'the LORD will add' or as a *qal* or *hifʿil* jussive 'may the LORD add', but cf. the ensuing undoubtedly volitional וִיבָרֵךְ 'and may he bless'. MT Deuteronomy exhibits use of both unequivocal *qal* and *hifʿil* forms. For purposes of the present study, the form in Deut. 1.11 is classified as a jussive of ambiguous stem.

category of 'stative' verbs. Original *yafʿil* seems to have been particularly vulnerable to analogical levelling, with genuine reflexes preserved in *qal* I-y forms, e.g., יֵרֵד (< *yarid), and in the prefix conjugation of נָתַן, e.g., יִתֵּן (< *yantin). Blau (2010, 222) accounts for the rare preservation of *yafʿil* thus:

> Two factors cooperated in ousting *yafʿil*: Philippi's Law, shifting stressed *i* in closed syllables to *a* and transferring it into the pattern having *a* as the characteristic vowel; and, even more, *yafʿil* was reinterpreted as *hifʿil* (which before the lengthening of the characteristic *i* also had the form of *yafʿil*).

As examples, consider the BH *qal* forms in *weqaṭal* וְגַנּוֹתִי 'and I will defend' (2 Kgs 19.34; see also 20.6) and infinitive absolute גָּנוֹן 'defending' (Isa. 31.5), along with the corresponding *yiqṭol* יָגֵן '(he) will defend' (Isa. 38.6; see also Zech. 9.15; 12.8). Though the *yiqṭol* forms have the appearance of short *hifʿil* jussives, a more fitting contextual analysis is that they are old indicative *qal* *yiqṭol* (specifically, *yafʿil*) forms. In RH, however, one finds unequivocal *hifʿil* forms, e.g., imperatival הגן 'defend!' ('Aravit, Fourth Blessing).[14] Similarly, within the Bible and beyond there is evidence of the secondary reinterpretation of *qal* בָּן-בָּן-יָבִין 'understand' as *hifʿil* הֵבִין-מֵבִין-יָבִין, of *qal* שָׂם-שָׂם-יָשִׂים 'put' as *hifʿil* הֵשִׂים-מֵשִׂים-יָשִׂים, and—most relevantly—of *qal* יָרָה-יָרָה-יוֹרֶה as *hifʿil*

---

[14] The same may hold true of QH. The expression מגני עוז 'strong defenders' (4Q403 f1i.25; 4Q405 f3ii.17) is interpretable as an instance of the *hifʿil* participle (see the analysis of the Academy of the Hebrew Language's Historical Dictionary Project online *Maʿagarim*), but Abegg (1999–2009) and Wise, Abegg, and Cook (2005) construe מגני here as a noun, i.e., 'shields of'. In Second Temple Aramaic, the verb is C-stem.

הוֹרָה-מוֹרֶה-יוֹרֶה. In all cases, an ambiguous *qal yiqṭol* form seems to have been interpreted as *hifʿil*, leading to the secondary creation of unequivocal *hifʿil* suffix conjugation, participial, and other forms. Such shifts coincided with a long-term, broader move away from the *qal* pattern in favour of stems perceived as having greater semantic iconicity.[15]

2.2. Reconsidering the Evidence

Having illustrated likely cases of *qal* > *hifʿil* reinterpretation, including in the specific case of original *yafʿil* forms, we are well positioned to consider the specific case of forms of *qal* יָסַף versus those of *hifʿil* הוֹסִיף. As it turns out, one need not assume with Ginsberg that a prefix conjugation vocalisation such as יֹסֵף in וְאֵדְעָה מַה־יֹּסֵף יְהוָה דַּבֵּר...'...that I may know what more the LORD will say' (Num. 22.19) is necessarily a secondary, anachronistic, and artificial misapplication of Second Temple jussive *hifʿil* phonology and morphology to an indicative form with the intended *qal* realisation יֵסֵף*. Rather, as Huehnergard (2006, 466–71; see also JM §75f) has shown, though resembling a misused *hifʿil* jussive, Tiberian *yōsēf* is in reality a passable, if exceptional, reflex of a *qal* I-*w/y* verb with an original *yafʿil* pattern.[16] This means

---

[15] On hifilisation as a feature of Second Temple Hebrew, see Hornkohl (2023, 209–51) and the references cited there.

[16] Huehnergard details three routes of phonological development for original I-*w* prefix conjugation forms: (a) *w* > *y*, e.g., יִישַׁן < *yiyšan* < *yiwšan*; (b) elision of *w*, e.g., יֵשֵׁב, whose related imperative and infinitive also lack the first radical; (c) in the case of verbs with a dental/coronal consonant in second position, assimilation of *w*, e.g., יִצֹּר < PS *yaṣṣur* < PS *yawṣur*. The preservation of *w* in *yawsip* > יוֹסֵף is, thus,

that the ostensibly ill-fitting jussive-like *hifʿil* forms in indicative contexts in examples (13)–(20) above are alternatively analysable as aptly employed indicative forms with vocalisations traceable to archaic *qal* morphology.[17] The same can be said of consonant-final *wayyiqtol* forms (i.e., forms without vowel-final suffixes), which, despite their *hifʿil*-like phonology, may also be analysed as having *qal* morphology, e.g., וַתֹּסֶף לָלֶדֶת... 'And she again gave birth...' (Gen. 4.2).

Contrasting with these, however, are forms in which the spelling and/or vocalisation allow for no interpretation other than *hifʿil*, namely, (a) all vowel-final and similar prefix conjugation (*yiqtol* and *wayyiqtol*) forms, i.e., plural forms with an open penultimate syllable, like ...לֹא תֹסִפוּן לִרְאוֹת פָּנַי '...you will no more see my face' (Gen. 44.23) and ...וַיּוֹסִפוּ עוֹד שְׂנֹא אֹתוֹ '...and they continued still to hate him' (Gen. 37.5), where the expected reflexes of archaic *qal yafʿil* are *תֹסְפוּן and *וַיֹּסְפוּ, respectively, and (b) consonant-final forms bearing a long *i* theme vowel (whether indicated by *mater yod*, *ḥireq*, or both), e.g., יֹסִיף 'he must (not) exceed' (Deut. 25.3).

---

according to Huehnergard (2006, 466, fn. 39) "an analogical countervention of the sound rule" in (c) which would otherwise have resulted in ***yissop̄*. Huehnergard (2006, 459, 467–68) opines that *yafʿil* here ultimately developed from *yafʿul*, but this does not affect the argument here.

[17] To be sure, identically vocalised short *yiqtol* (jussive or preterite) forms also occur, e.g., יֹסֵף יְהוָה לִי בֵּן אַחֵר 'May the LORD add' (or 'The LORD has added for me another son!') (Gen. 30.24); אַל־תּוֹסֶף דַּבֵּר אֵלַי עוֹד בַּדָּבָר הַזֶּה 'Do not speak any more to me about this matter' (Deut. 3.26). These are equally analysable as *qal* or *hifʿil*.

To summarise: it would seem that in the case of prefix conjugation forms, the Tiberian reading tradition mixes the conservation of authentic reflexes of *qal* morphology with secondary *hifʿil* vocalisations. *Qal* preservation was likely conditioned on resemblance to *hifʿil*, even if this involved the apparent use of jussive forms in indicative contexts. Phonetic recasting took place where the original *qal* phonology could not easily be reconciled with *hifʿil* realisation, e.g., וַיּוֹסְפוּ* > וַיֹּסִפוּ.

In addition to suppletive forms in close proximity, as in examples (9)–(12) above, the recasting of original *qal* morphology with *hifʿil* phonology sometimes occasioned genuinely awkward combinations, e.g.,

(21) לָכֵ֗ן הִנְנִ֥י יוֹסִ֛ף לְהַפְלִ֥יא אֶת־הָֽעָם־הַזֶּ֖ה...

'Therefore, behold, I am again doing wonderful things with this people...' (Isa. 29.14)

(22) ...הִנְנִ֣י יוֹסִף֮ עַל־יָמֶ֒יךָ֒ חֲמֵ֥שׁ עֶשְׂרֵ֖ה שָׁנָֽה׃

'...Behold, I am adding fifteen years to your life (Isa. 38.5)

The constructions in (21)–(22) are doubly dubious. First, expressions involving the presentative הִנֵּה with a pronominal suffix and *yiqtol* are exceedingly rare. A participle is expected. Second, 1st-person הִנְנִי does not concord with 3rd-person יוֹסִף. Rather than positing elision of the glottal stop in a *hifʿil* prefix conjugation form, *hinnī ʾōsīf > hinnī yōsīf*,[18] it may be that the intended construction in both cases was *הִנְנִי יֹסֵף, with a *qal* participle (cf. the relevant critical notes in the BHS apparatus).

---

[18] See Khan (2013, 100; 2020, 252–53) for the historical Tiberian pronunciation of הִנְנִי as *hinnī*.

3.0. Interpreting the Data

The discussion to this point has substantiated a degree of dissonance between the Tiberian written and reading traditions revolving around forms of *qal* יָסַף and *hifʿil* הוֹסִיף. It has also been noted that the dissonance is not equally characteristic of all parts of the MT. Further, in addition to the layers of evidence available in the consonantal and vocalic components of the Tiberian tradition, the related, yet semi-independent layer reflected in the use of *mater yod* for unambiguous representation of *hifʿil* may be interrogated. Though caution must be exercised with spelling practices infamous for variation (Barr 1989; cf. Andersen and Forbes 2013), the three-way relationship among the consonantal text, vocalisation, and *plene* orthography is worth exploring in connection to the hifilisation of *qal* יָסַף. Table 4 (facing page) displays the distribution of unambiguous consonantal forms of *qal* יָסַף and *hifʿil* הוֹסִיף seen above (Table 2) alongside the distribution of the relevant MT *(way)yiqtol* forms, whether *qal*, *hifʿil*, or of ambiguous stem. Table 5 (p. 76) combines the data from Table 4 on individual books, presenting them in corporate totals.

When it comes to the distribution of forms of *qal* יָסַף and *hifʿil* הוֹסִיף, the various Masoretic corpora exhibit conspicuous differences of apparent diachronic significance.

3. Qal versus hif'il Forms of יס"ף

Table 4: MT distribution of forms of qal יָסַף and hif'il הוֹסִיף (see §§4.1 and 4.3 for citations).

Book	unequivocal consonantal		prefix conjugation vocalisation			
			indicative	hif'il		ambiguous
	qal	hif'il	qal	defective	plene	jussive/wayyiqtol
Genesis	2	0	1	5	0	6
Exodus	0	0	0	4	1	3
Leviticus	7	1	3	0	0	0
Numbers	3	0	2	0	0	3
Deuteronomy	2	0	2	4	3	1
Joshua	0	0	0	0	2	0
Judges	2	0	0	6	3	2
Samuel	5	0	0	4	9	13
Kings	2	3	0	3	4	1
Isaiah	5	0	0	2	10	2
Jeremiah	2	0	0	0	1	0
Ezekiel	0	0	1	1	0	1
Hosea	0	0	1	1	1	0
Joel	0	0	1	0	0	0
Amos	0	0	0	0	4	0
Jonah	0	0	0	0	1	0
Nahum	0	0	0	0	1	0
Zechariah	0	0	0	1	0	0
Psalms	0	1	0	0	6	1
Job	0	0	0	0	6	5
Proverbs	0	0	0	3	7	3
Ruth	0	0	0	0	1	0
Lamentations	0	0	0	0	3	0
Qohelet	0	3	0	0	2	0
Esther	0	0	0	0	0	1
Daniel	0	0	0	0	0	1
Ezra	0	1	0	0	0	0
Nehemiah	0	1	0	0	0	0
Chronicles	1	1	0	0	7	2

Table 5: MT distribution of forms of *qal* יָסַף and *hif'il* הוֹסִיף according to corpus

	unequivocal consonantal		prefix conjugation vocalisation			
	qal	*hif'il*	*qal*	*hif'il* defective	*hif'il* plene	ambiguous jussive/*wayyiqtol*
Pentateuch	13	1	8	11	4	4
Prophets	15	3	3	11	36	1
(Former	9	3	0	6	18	1)
(Latter	6	0	3	5	18	0)
Writings	1	7	0	3	30	6
(non-LBH+	0	1	0	3	22	5)
(LBH+	1	6	0	0	8	1)
TOTAL	29	11	11	25	70	11

3.1. Harmony and Dissonance within the Combined Tiberian Consonantal, Orthographic, and Vocalic Tradition

3.1.1. Tiberian Late Biblical Hebrew+

Thus, in MT LBH+[19] the three types of evidence agree, in that there is virtually no dissonance among them: (a) *hif'il* morphology predominates to the near exclusion of *qal* in unequivocal consonantal forms; (b) vocalisation of *yiqtol* is exclusively *hif'il*; and (c) *hif'il* prefix conjugation vocalisation is consistently matched by exclusively *plene hif'il* orthography.[20] The morphological harmony among consonantal text, vocalisation, and *matres lectionis* in Persian Period material tallies with additional evidence

---

[19] On LBH+ as distinguished from LBH, see above, ch. 2, fn. 4.

[20] The relevant distribution in the non-LBH+ Writings seems similar, but the dearth of unequivocal consonantal forms precludes certainty.

confirming a special affinity between the Tiberian vocalisation and the period in which LBH+ texts were composed.[21]

3.1.2. The Tiberian Pentateuch

The rest of the MT is characterised by more or less conflicting totals. Consider the Pentateuch: unequivocal consonantal forms are nearly all *qal*—with the problematic לְהוֹסִיף (Lev. 19.25) the single arguable exception (see above, §2.1 and fn. 11)—but *yiqtol* vocalisation is divided—eight *qal* and fifteen *hifʿil*. Intriguingly, however, only four of the fifteen *yiqtol* forms with indisputable *hifʿil* vocalisation have equally unambiguous *plene hifʿil* spelling. This situation obviously contrasts with the one described above for LBH+ texts. Whereas there is consonantal, vocalic, and orthographic harmony in LBH+, striking dissonance obtains in the Pentateuch. Unambiguous *qal* consonantal forms and the rare incidence of *plene* orthography with *mater yod* signalling *hifʿil* morphology contrast with rather common—though by no means universal—*hifʿil* vocalisation. The complexity of the combined Tiberian written-reading tradition in the Pentateuch is further manifested in the rather frequent preservation of archaic *qal* phonology (see above, §2.1).

---

[21] Intriguingly, the lone *qal* outlier in LBH+ is יָסְפָה (2 Chron. 9.6 || הוֹסַפְתָּ 1 Kgs 10.7), which involves the late usage of a characteristically classical *qal* parallel to *hifʿil* in what is conventionally considered earlier material. The Chronicler's penchant for classical features, even where his ostensible sources have late alternatives, is conspicuous within LBH. It is evident in the case of several features; see Hornkohl (2014a, 35, fn. 97, 88–89, 108, 177, 187–88, 197, 208, 245, 320).

3.1.3. The Tiberian Prophets

The books of the Prophets appear to occupy a sort of intermediate position between the Pentateuch and LBH+. The Prophets exhibit significant discord between evidence for preservation of *qal* in unequivocal consonantal forms and evidence for *hifʿil yiqtol*, but noticeably greater affinity than in the Pentateuch between *hifʿil* vocalisation and *hifʿil plene* orthography of *yiqtol* forms. A further point of contrast with the Pentateuch is the infrequency in the Prophets of archaic *qal* vocalisations.

3.2. Diachronic Considerations

Some preliminary points are in order in reference to the historical depth of the hifilisation of *qal* יָסַף in the Tiberian reading tradition. First, though the vocalisation in the Pentateuch and the Prophets is almost certainly somewhat anachronistic—involving the *hifʿil* reinterpretation of several *qal* forms in line with Second Temple tendencies unambiguously seen in late consonantal evidence—in no part of the Hebrew Bible is the vocalisation component of the combined Tiberian biblical tradition the lone witness to the hifilisation of *qal* יָסַף. In its use of unambiguous *plene hifʿil* spellings, both the orthographic component (represented by *mater yod*) and the purely consonantal component (excluding *matres*) also evince results of hifilisation. What is more, since consonantal and orthographic evidence for the hifilisation of *qal* יָסַף substantially predates the advent of the Tiberian vocalisation signs, it would appear that the medieval Tiberian reading tradition reliably reflects a far earlier shift. To be more specific, the historical depth of the Tiberian vocalisation finds confirmation in the unequivocal *hifʿil* evidence found in MT LBH+, the biblical and non-biblical DSS, the SP, Ben Sira, and RH, which combine to show clearly that the *qal* > *hifʿil* shift reflected in the vocalisation of the Tiberian reading tradition had already by Second Temple times profoundly impacted morphology.

Second, unambiguous consonantal evidence of hifilisation in CBH—לְהוֹסִיף (Lev. 19.25); הוֹסַפְתָּ (1 Kgs 10.7); וְהֹסַפְתִּי (2 Kgs 20.6); הֵסִיף (2 Kgs 24.7); וְהוֹסַפְתִּי (Ps. 71.14)—and extrabiblical Iron Age epigraphy—הוספ[תִ (Zakkur [*KAI* 202] B.4–5)—shows that Hebrew הוֹסִיף should be considered not an exclusively late innovation, but merely one whose dominance is restricted to late compositions, in which case the degree of *hifʿil* vocalisation in the Tiberian reading tradition of CBH texts is best seen as the Second Temple extension and standardisation of a development already underway in First Temple times.

Yet, the Second Temple characterisation of the Tiberian vocalisation should also be nuanced. As has been shown, especially in the Pentateuch, the reading tradition betrays opposing tendencies: on the one hand, secondary hifilisation; on the other, phonological reflexes explicable as instances of conditioned preservation of archaic *qal* morphology. That the preservation of the latter was possibly facilitated by passable resemblance to *hifʿil* forms in no way detracts from the reliability of the testimony. Also, while the rarity of such vocalisations from Masoretic BH beyond the Pentateuch, or their complete absence therefrom, may be casual, seen together with similar cases of disparity between Pentateuchal and non-Pentateuchal CBH collected in this volume, it is also interpretable as evidence that the Tiberian reading tradition of the Torah is especially conservative.

Focusing on the relationship between the vocalisation and the orthographic tradition regarding hifilisation of *qal* יָסַף, consider Table 6, which shows the incidence of *plene*-spelled *hifʿil* *(way)yiqṭol* forms with expected long *i* theme vowel out of all such forms according to MT corpus.

Table 6: *Plene hifʿil (way)yiqṭol* forms with expected long *i* theme vowel out of all *hifʿil (way)yiqṭol* forms with expected long *i* theme vowel per MT corpus

	plene/total	percentage *plene*
Pentateuch	4/15	26.7
Prophets	36/47	76.6
(Former Prophets	18/24	75)
(Latter Prophets	18/23	78.3)
Writings	30/33	90.9
(non-LBH Writings	22/25	88.5)
(LBH +	8/8	100)

The statistics constitute arguable evidence of linguistically significant orthographic development within the MT. Concentrating on *yiqṭol* forms where a long *i*-vowel might be expected, we find that explicit *hifʿil* spellings constitute a minority of the cases in the Pentateuch, come in three-quarters of the cases in the Prophets, and are the norm in the Writings, including LBH+, where *hifʿil* orthography is employed to the total exclusion of potential *qal* spellings. Crucially, the *plene* percentages reflect various degrees of agreement between the orthographic and vocalisation components of the combined Tiberian tradition.

Whenever its constituent texts were composed, the written form of the Masoretic Pentateuch seems to reflect a stage in orthographic development during which the spelling of *(way)yiqtol* was still largely amenable to realisation according to *qal* morphology. Beyond the Pentateuch, there is a strong and increasing tendency to utilise *(way)yiqtol* spellings exclusive to *hifʿil*. It is reasonable to assume that such spellings in LBH accurately reflect the post-exilic *hifʿil* usage common to Second Temple Hebrew material noted above.

How to account for the high degree of *hifʿil yiqtol* forms in CBH outside the Pentateuch is a more complicated question. It may be, of course, that the relatively high incidence of *hifʿil* spellings in non-Pentateuchal CBH is due partially to the anachronistic application of late linguistic conventions to this material, an enterprise from which the Pentateuch was (partially) exempted, due presumably to its relatively early compilation and/or special venerated status.

A reasonable hypothesis for historical development might run as follows. An early situation of dominant *qal* morphology gradually gave way to one of increased *hifʿil* usage due in part to *hifʿil*-like *qal yiqtol* forms. This second stage was characterised by the continued use of both consonantally unambiguous and ambiguous *qal* forms as well as by an increase in the use of consonantally and orthographically unambiguous *hifʿil* forms. Depending on the realisation and spelling of ambiguous forms, various manifestations of suppletion might obtain, whether original or secondary.

Intriguingly, the sorts of suppletion encountered in the Masoretic corpora described above show a certain diachronic progression. The clearest situations are in LBH+ and the Pentateuch: whereas LBH+ texts show virtually no suppletion—*hifʿil* dominant according to all components of the tradition—much of the suppletion in the Pentateuch seems to be secondary—*qal* dominant both consonantally and orthographically, *hifʿil* restricted chiefly, though not exclusively, to vocalisation, and even then, far from consistent.

The nature of the suppletion in the Prophets is more difficult to interpret. Is it organic, secondary, or a mixture of the two? The nature of the evidence all but precludes certainty. The greater use of *mater yod* for unequivocal *hifʿil* spelling in the Prophets vis-à-vis the Pentateuch may be due to a secondary spelling revision that impacted non-Torah CBH material more than the CBH of the Torah. Limited support for such a theory emerges from the fact that, in comparison to the Pentateuch, the Prophets show increased incidence of *plene* spelling with both *yod* and *waw* in the relevant *(way)yiqtol* forms of יָסַף and הוֹסִיף. What is clear is that, whatever its origin, there is more in the way of *qal–hifʿil* suppletion to deal with in the Prophets than in either the Pentateuch or LBH+.

Yet, the possibility that the *qal–hifʿil* suppletion in the books of the Prophets may be partially organic in nature should not be dismissed out of hand. On the assumption of an originally unified *qal* paradigm of יס"ף, it is difficult to decide how to interpret *(way)yiqtol* forms like (ו)יסף in the Prophets. While the secondary hifilisation of such forms is clearly connected with the expanded use of transparently *hif'il* suffix conjugation, participial, infinitival, and imperatival forms, it is logical to assume that these latter forms arose due to prior *hif'il* reinterpretation of ambiguous *(way)yiqtol* forms. In other words, it is entirely reasonable to posit that the *hif'il* analysis of ambiguous *(way)yiqtol* spellings *preceded* and, indeed, *led to* the development of unequivocal *hif'il* consonantal *qatal*, participle, infinitival, and imperatival forms. If so, the Prophets exhibit precisely the constellation of forms expected for a corpus that reflects a chronolect where *(way)yiqtol* forms were already read as *hif'il*, but other forms were still largely *qal*. By contrast, in LBH+ nearly all forms are unambiguously *hif'il*, while the Torah, despite a few unambiguous *hif'il* consonantal and orthographic forms, along with rather common *hif'il* vocalisation of otherwise ambiguous spellings, regularly exhibits spellings entirely amenable to *qal* interpretation as well as a sizeable minority of *(way)yiqtol* vocalisations reconcilable with *qal* morphology. If so, the alleged 'imposition' of *hif'il* morphology via the secondary insertion of *mater yod* and/or unambiguous *hif'il* vocalisation may not be an artificial imposition, after all. It may rather be a case in which original *hif'il* morphology was secondarily disambiguated via the use of *mater yod* and/or dedicated *hif'il* vocalisation. If the *hif'il* orthography and vocalisation of *(way)yiqtol* forms in the Prophets is in any way representative of their earliest chronolect, then the difference between the CBH of the Torah, with multiple *qal*-amenable orthographic and vocalic forms, and the CBH of the Prophets, where such forms are comparatively rare, may be interpreted as diachronic in nature, an isogloss separating typologically distinct sub-chronolects. It also goes without saying that the few clear orthographically transparent cases of *hifʿil* in the Pentateuch may be considered authentic early precursors of eventually more extensive *hifʿil* morphology.

Rounding out the discussion, it is worth reporting results of an examination of distribution of *qal* and *hifʿil* י"ס‎ף forms according to purported Pentateuchal source (per Friedman 1989, 246–59). See Table 7.

Table 7: *qal* and *hifʿil* forms of י"ס‎ף according to purported Pentateuchal source

	Form	J	E	P	Dtr₁	Dtr₂	Other
Consonantal	*qal*	2	1	9	2	0	2
	hifʿil	0	0	1	0	0	0
Prefix	contextual/vocalic *qal*	1	1	4	0	0	2
	plene orthographic *hifʿil*	1	0	0	0	1	2
	defective vocalic *hifʿil*	5	4	0	1	0	3
	ambiguous	5	7	0	2	0	0

Since nearly all unambiguous consonantal forms are *qal*, no single source shows a concentration of typologically late *hifʿil* consonantal forms. The one source with such a form, P, also shows the highest incidence of unambiguous *qal* consonantal forms.[22] When it comes to prefix conjugation forms, P also shows the

---

[22] And it should be recalled that the lone *hifʿil* case in question constitutes an interpretive, and perhaps textual, crux (see above, §2.1 and fn. 11).

highest incidence of pseudo-jussive forms, i.e., contextually indicative forms in which archaic *qal* vocalisation has been preserved, though these are also found in J, E, and Friedman's Other source in Deuteronomy. Finally, again in relation to prefix conjugation forms, in contrast to all other sources, P shows no incidence of *plene* orthographic *hifʿil*, defective vocalic *hifʿil*, or ambiguous forms. In sum, considering only unequivocal consonantal and orthographic evidence, there is broad preference for typologically early *qal* over later *hifʿil* morphology, with no source deviating in favour of *hifʿil*. P, with 13 of 14 forms demanding or amenable to *qal* analysis, is particularly conservative.

4.0. Appendix

4.1. Table 2 Citations

Qal: יָסְפָה (Gen. 8.12 [J]); יֹסֵף (Gen. 38.26 [J]); וְיָסֵף (Lev. 22.14 [P]); וְיָסַפְתִּי (Lev. 26.18 [P]); וְיָסַפְתִּי (Lev. 26.21 [P]); וְיָסַף (Lev. 27.13 [P]); יֹסֵף (Lev. 27.15 [P]); וְיָסַף (Lev. 27.19 [P]); וְיָסַף (Lev. 27.27 [P]); יָסָפוּ (Num. 11.25 [E]); לִסְפּוֹת (Num. 32.14 [P]); וְיָסַף (Num. 32.15 [P]); יֹסֵף (Deut. 5.22 [Dtr₁]); יֹסְפִים (Deut. 5.25 [Dtr₁]); וְיָסַפְתָּ (Deut. 19.19 [Other]); וְיָסְפוּ (Deut. 20.8 [Other]); יָסְפוּ (Judg. 8.28); יֹסֵף (Judg. 13.21); יָסְפוּ (1 Sam. 7.13); יֹסַפְנוּ (1 Sam. 12.19); יֹסֵף (1 Sam. 15.35); יָסְפוּ (2 Sam. 2.28); יֹסְפוּ (2 Kgs 6.23); וְיָסְפָה (2 Kgs 19.30); יָסַפְתְּ (Isa. 26.15a); יָסַפְתָּ (Isa. 26.15b); וְיָסְפוּ (Isa. 29.19); סְפוֹת (Isa. 30.1); וְיָסְפָה (Isa. 37.31); סְפוּ (Jer. 7.21); יֹסֵף (Jer. 45.3); יָסַפְתָּ (2 Chron. 9.6 ‖ הוֹסַפְתָּ 1 Kgs 10.7); *hifʿil*: לְהוֹסִיף (Lev. 19.25 [P]); הוֹסַפְתָּ (1 Kgs 10.7 ‖ יָסַפְתָּ 2 Chron. 9.6); וְהֹסַפְתִּי (2 Kgs 20.6); הֹסִיף (2 Kgs 24.7); וְהוֹסַפְתִּי (Ps. 71.14); וְהוֹסַפְתִּי (Qoh. 1.16); וְהוֹסַפְתִּי (Qoh. 2.9); לְהוֹסִיף (Qoh. 3.14); לְהוֹסִיף (Ezra 10.10); מוֹסִיפִים (Neh. 13.18); לְהֹסִיף (2 Chron. 28.13).

4.2. Table 3 Citations

Qal. **Meshaʿ (KAI 181)**: לספת (l. 21); יספתי (l. 29); **BDSS**: יספת (1QIsaᵃ 20.27 ‖ יָסַפְתְּ MT Isa. 26.15); יספתה (1QIsaᵃ 20.28 ‖ יָסַפְתָּ MT Isa. 26.15); ספי (1QIsaᵃ 23.7 ‖ סְפִי MT Isa. 29.1); ויספו (1QIsaᵃ 23.29 ‖ וְיָסְפוּ MT Isa. 29.19); ספות (1QIsaᵃ 24.7 ‖ סְפוֹת MT Isa. 30.1); ויסף (4Q24 f9i+10–17.22 ‖ וְיָסֵף MT Lev. 22.14); יסף (4Q41 5.2 ‖ יֹסֵף MT Deut. 5.22); יספת (4Q56 f16ii+17–20+20a.11 ‖ יָסַפְתְּ MT

Isa. 26.15); ויספ]ה (4Q56 f22–23.3 || וְיָסְפָה MT Isa. 37.31); סופי (4Q64 f1–5.4 || סְפוּ MT Isa. 29.1); {ו}יסף (4Q135 f1.1 || יֹסֵף MT Deut. 5.22); ויספתי (11Q1 5.4 || וְיָסַפְתִּי MT Lev. 26.21); ויסף (11Q1 6.2 || וְיָסַף MT Lev. 27.13); ויסף (11Q1 6.4 || וְיָסַף MT Lev. 27.15); ויסף (11Q1 6.9 || וְיָסַף MT Lev. 27.19); יספים (XQ2 1.6 || יֹסְפִים MT Deut. 5.25); **SP:** ויסף wyå̄səf || MT וַיֹּסֶף (Gen. 8.10); יספה yå̄sēfa || MT יָסְפָה (Gen. 8.12); ויסף wyå̄səf || MT וַיֹּסֶף (Gen. 18.29); ויסף wyå̄səf || MT וַיֹּסֶף (Gen. 25.1); יסף yå̄səf || MT יֹסֵף (Gen. 38.26); ויסף wyå̄səf || MT וַיֹּסֶף (Exod. 9.34); יספם yūsīfəm || MT — (Exod. 20.15d || Deut. 5.25); ויסף wyå̄səf || MT וְיָסַף (Lev. 22.14); ויסף wyå̄səf || MT וְיָסַף (Lev. 27.13); ויסף wyå̄səf || MT וְיָסַף (Lev. 27.15); ויסף wyå̄səf || MT וְיָסַף (Lev. 27.19); ויסף wyå̄səf || MT וְיָסַף (Lev. 27.27); ויסף wyå̄səf || MT וַיֹּסֶף (Num. 22.15); ויסף wyå̄səf || MT וַיֹּסֶף (Num. 22.25); ויסף wyå̄səf || MT וַיּוֹסֶף (Num. 22.26); ויסף wyå̄səf || MT וְיָסַף (Num. 32.15); יסף yå̄səf (Deut. 5.19) || MT יֹסֵף (Deut. 5.22); יספם yūsīfəm (Deut. 5.22) || MT יֹסְפִים (Deut. 5.25); **NBDSS:** יספה (4Q252 1.19 || Gen. 8.22); [ה]יֹסִפ (4Q252 1.20); **Mishna:** וְיֹסְפוּ (m. Soṭa 8.5 || Deut. 20.8). **Hifʿil. Zakkur (KAI 202):** הוספ[ת (B.4–5) **BDSS:** אם מו[סיפים (4Q37 3.7 || MT אִם־יֹסְפִים Deut. 5.25); והוספתי (4Q83 f9ii.13 || MT וְהוֹסַפְתִּי Ps. 71.14); [וסיפים (4Q129 f1R.13 || MT כִּי מ]אם מו[סיפים Deut. 5.25); אם מו[סיפים (4Q135 f1.4 || MT אִם־יֹסְפִים Deut. 5.25); אם מ/יספים (4Q137 f1.31) (?) || MT אִם־יֹסְפִים Deut. 5.25); **NBDSS:** והוסיפו (1QS 2.11); להוסיף (1QS 6.14); לוסיף (1QpHab 8.12); להוסיף (1QpHab 11.15); הוסיפו (1QHa 9.37); לוסף (1Q14 f8–10.7); לה[ו]סי[ף (4Q265 f4ii.3); [ו]הוסיפו (4Q286 f7i.8); הוסיפו (4Q298 f3–4ii.6); הוסיפו (4Q298 f3–4ii.7); הוסף (4Q299 f30.5); להוסיף (4Q416 f2iv.7); הוסף (4Q418 f81 + 81a.17); כהוסיפ]כם (4Q502 f3.1); להוסיף (4Q503 f15–16.10); להוסיף (4Q525 f1.3); **Ben Sira:** מוסיף (SirA 1r.16 = Sirach 3.27); להוסיף (SirA 1v.25 = Sirach 5.5); להוסיף (SirC 2r.7 = Sirach 5.5); **Mishna:** הוֹסִיף (Kil 1.3); הוֹסִיף (Kil. 5.6); הוֹסִיף (Kil. 7.8); מוֹסִפִין (Shev. 3.2a); מוֹסִיפִין (Shev. 3.2b); מוֹסִיף (Shev. 3.3); וְהוֹסִיף (Ter. 4.3); הוֹסִיף (Ter. 4.4a); לְהוֹסִיף (Ter. 4.4a); לְהוֹסִיף (Maas. 1.1); מוֹסִיף (Maaser2 4.3a); מוֹסִיף (Maaser2 4.3b); מוֹסִיף (Maaser2 4.3c); מוֹסִיף (Maaser2 5.5); הוֹסִיף (Orla 1.5); מוֹסִיף (Eruv. 7.7a); מוֹסִיף (Eruv. 7.7b); [שֶׁ]מּוֹסִיפִין (Pesah. 1.6a); הוֹסִיף (Pesah. 1.6b); [שֶׁ]מּוֹסִיפִין (Pesah. 1.6c); לְהוֹסִיף (Yoma 3.7a); מוֹסִיף (Yoma 3.7b); מוֹסִיף (Yoma 4.4); מוֹסִיף (Yoma 7.5); מוֹסִיפִים (Sukk. 3.15); מוֹסִיפִים (Sukk. 5.5a); מוֹסִיפִים (Sukk. 5.5b); מוֹסִיפִים (Sukk. 5.5c); וּמוֹסִיף (Taan. 2.2); מוֹסִיפִים (Meg. 4.1); מוֹסִיפִים (Meg. 4.2a); מוֹסִיפִים (Meg. 4.2b); מוֹסִיף (Ketub. 3.4); לְהוֹסִיף (Ketub. 5.1); מוֹסִיפִין (Ketub. 5.7); וּמוֹסִיפִין (Ketub. 5.9); מוֹסִיף (Ned. 3.1); מוֹסִיפִים (Sota 9.1); מוֹסִיפִין (Qidd. 4.4); מוֹסִיף (ʿArayot 11); מוֹסִיפִים (BabaM. 4.8a); מוֹסִיף (BabaM. 4.8b); מוֹסִיף (BabaM. 4.8c); מוֹסִיף (BabaM. 4.8d); מוֹסִיף (BabaM. 4.8e); הוֹסִיף (BabaM. 6.5); מוֹסִיפִין (Sanh. 1.5); מוֹסִיפִין (Sanh. 1.6); מוֹסִיפִין (Sanh. 5.5); לְהוֹסִיף (Sanh. 11.3); הוֹסִיף (Mak 3.14); מוֹסִיפִין (Shevu. 2.2); מוֹסִיפִין (Ed. 2.1); הוֹסִיף (Ed. 2.1); שְׁמוֹלוֹסִיף (Ed. 2.1); הוֹסִיף (Ed. 8.1); הוֹסִיף (Zevah. 1.3); מוֹסִף (Menah. 13.6); הוֹסִיף (Bek. 6.8); מוֹסִיפִין (Arak. 2.3a); מוֹסִיפִין (Arak. 2.3b); מוֹסִיפִין (Arak. 2.3c); וּמוֹסִיפִין (Arak. 2.5a); וּמוֹסִיפִין (Arak. 2.5b); וּמוֹסִיפִין (Arak. 2.5c); וּמוֹסִיפִין (Arak. 2.6); מוֹסִיף (Arak. 6.2); מוֹסִיפִין (Arak. 8.2); מוֹסִיפִין (Arak. 8.3); הוֹסִיפוּ (Mid. 3.1);

מוֹסִיפִין (Tamid 5.1); הוֹסִיפוּ (Maksh. 2.4); מוֹסִיפִין (Yad. 1.1); מוֹסִיפִין (Yad. 1.1); הוֹסִיף (Yad. 4.2).

4.3. Table 4 Citations

For unambiguous consonantal forms, see above, §4.1. **Prefix conjugation—qal**: לֹא־תֹסֵף (Gen. 4.12 [J]); יֹסֵף (Lev. 5.16 [P], 24 [P]; 27.31 [P]; Num. 5.7 [P]); מַה־יֹּסֵף (Num. 22.19 [E]); לֹא־תֹסֵף (Deut. 13.1 [Other]); לֹא אֹסֵף (Deut. 18.16 [Other]); אֹסֵף (Ezek. 5.16); לֹא אוֹסִף (Hos. 9.15); לֹא יוֹסֵף (Joel 2.2); **defective (way)yiqtol pointed as hif'il**: אֹסֵף (Gen. 8.21a [J]); אֹסִף (Gen. 8.21b [J]); וַיֹּסֶף (Gen. 37.5 [J]); וַיֹּסִפוּ (Gen. 37.8 [J]); תֹּסִפוּן (Gen. 44.23 [J]); תֹּאסִפוּן (Exod. 5.7 [E]); תֹּסִפוּן (Exod. 9.28 [E]); אֹסֵף (Exod. 10.29 [E]); תֹסֵף (Exod. 11.6 [E]); תֹסִפוּ (Deut. 4.2 [Dtr₁]); יֹסֵף (Deut. 13.12 [Other]); תֹּסִפוּן (Deut. 17.16 [Other]); יֹסִפוּ (Deut. 19.20 [Other]); וַיֹּסִפוּ (Judg. 3.12); וַיֹּסִפוּ (Judg. 4.1); וַיֹּסִפוּ (Judg. 10.6); וַיֹּסִפוּ (Judg. 13.1); וַיֹּסִפוּ (Judg. 20.22); הָאוֹסִף (Judg. 20.28); יֹסֵף (1 Sam. 14.44); וַיֹּסִפוּ (2 Sam. 3.34); וַיֹּסִפוּ (2 Sam. 5.22); וְאֹסְפָה (2 Sam. 12.8); יוֹסִפוּן (1 Kgs 19.2); יוֹסִפוּ (1 Kgs 20.10); יֹסֵף (2 Kgs 6.31); יֹסֵף (Isa. 29.14); יוֹסֵף (Isa. 38.5); תוֹסֵף (Ezek. 36.12); יֹסִפוּ (Hos. 13.2); תֹּסְפִי (Zeph. 3.11); יֹסֵף (Prov. 10.22); תוֹסֵף (Prov. 19.19); תֹסֵף (Prov. 23.28); **plene (way)yiqtol pointed as hif'il**: תֹסִיפוּ (Exod. 14.13 [J]); יֹסִיף (Deut. 25.3a [Other]); יֹסִיף (Deut. 25.3b [Other]); תֹסִיף (Deut. 28.68 [Dtr₂]); אוֹסִיף (Josh. 7.12); יוֹסִיף (Josh. 23.13); אוֹסִיף (Judg. 2.21); אוֹסִיף (Judg. 10.13); הָאוֹסִיף (Judg. 20.23); יוֹסִיף (1 Sam. 3.17); יֹסִיף (1 Sam. 20.13); יֹסִיף (1 Sam. 25.22); יֹסִיף (2 Sam. 3.9); יֹסִיף (2 Sam. 3.35); יֹסִיפוּ (2 Sam. 7.10); יֹסִיף (2 Sam. 7.20); יֹסִיף (2 Sam. 14.10); יוֹסִיף (2 Sam. 19.14); יוֹסִיף (1 Kgs 2.23); אוֹסִיף (1 Kgs 12.11); אֹסִיף (1 Kgs 12.14); אֹסִיף (2 Kgs 21.8); תוֹסִיפוּ (Isa. 1.5); תוֹסִיפוּ (Isa. 1.13); יוֹסִיף (Isa. 10.20); יוֹסִיף (Isa. 11.11); תוֹסִיפִי (Isa. 23.12); תֹסִיף (Isa. 24.20); תוֹסִיפִי (Isa. 47.1); תוֹסִיפִי (Isa. 47.5); תוֹסִיפִי (Isa. 51.22); יוֹסִיף (Isa. 52.1); יוֹסִפוּ (Jer. 31.12); אוֹסִיף (Hos. 1.6); תוֹסִיף (Amos 5.2); אוֹסִיף (Amos 7.8); תוֹסִיף (Amos 7.13); אוֹסִיף (Amos 8.2); אוֹסִיף (Jon. 2.5); יוֹסִיף (Nah. 2.1); יוֹסִיף (Ps. 10.18); יוֹסִיף (Ps. 41.9); תוֹסִיף (Ps. 61.7); יֹסִיף (Ps. 77.8); וַיֹּסִיפוּ (Ps. 78.17); יֹסִיף (Ps. 120.3); יֹסִיף (Job 17.9); תוֹסִיף (Job 20.9); אֹסִיף (Job 34.32); יֹסִיף (Job 34.37); תֹסִיף (Job 38.11); אוֹסִיף (Job 40.5); יוֹסִפוּ (Prov. 3.2); וְיוֹסִפוּ (Prov. 9.11); תוֹסִיף (Prov. 10.27); יֹסִיף (Prov. 16.21); יֹסִיף (Prov. 16.23); יֹסִיף (Prov. 19.4); אוֹסִיף (Prov. 23.35); יֹסִיף (Ruth 1.17); יוֹסִיפוּ (Lam. 4.15); יוֹסִיף (Lam. 4.16); יוֹסִיף (Lam. 4.22); וְיוֹסִיף (Qoh. 1.18a); יוֹסִיף (Qoh. 1.18b); וַיֹּסִיפוּ (1 Chron. 14.13); יוֹסִיפוּ (1 Chron. 17.9); יוֹסִיף (1 Chron. 17.18); תוֹסִיף (1 Chron. 22.14); אֹסִיף (2 Chron. 10.11); אֹסִיף (2 Chron. 10.14); אוֹסִיף (2 Chron. 33.8); **jussive/wayyiqtol forms of ambiguous stem**: וַתֹּסֶף (Gen. 4.2 [J]); וַיֹּסֶף (Gen. 8.10 [J]); וַיֹּסֶף (Gen. 18.29 [J]); וַיֹּסֶף (Gen. 25.1 [E]); יֹסֵף (Gen. 30.24 [J]); וַתֹּסֶף (Gen. 38.5 [J]); אַל־יֹסֵף (Exod. 8.25 [E]); וַיֹּסֶף (Exod. 9.34 [E]); אַל־תֹּסֶף (Exod. 10.28 [E]); וַיֹּסֶף (Num. 22.15 [E]); וַיֹּסֶף (Num. 22.25 [E]); וַיֹּסֶף (Num. 22.26 [E]); יֹסֵף (Deut. 1.11 [Dtr₁]); אַל־תּוֹסֶף (Deut. 3.26 [Dtr₁]); וַיֹּסֶף (Judg. 9.37); וַיֹּסֶף (Judg. 11.14); וַיֹּסֶף (1 Sam. 3.6); וַיֹּסֶף (1 Sam. 3.8); וַיֹּסֶף (1 Sam. 3.21); וַיֹּסֶף (1 Sam. 9.8); וַיֹּאסֶף (1 Sam.

18.29); וַתֹּסֶף (1 Sam. 19.8); וַיֹּסֶף (1 Sam. 19.21); וַיֹּסֶף (1 Sam. 20.17); וַיֹּסֶף (1 Sam. 23.4); וַיֹּסֶף (2 Sam. 2.22); וַיֹּסֶף (2 Sam. 18.22); וְיֹסֵף (2 Sam. 24.1); וְיֹסֵף (2 Sam. 24.3); וַיֹּוסֶף (1 Kgs 16.33); וַיּוֹסֶף (Isa. 7.10); וַיֹּסֶף (Isa. 8.5); וַתֹּסֶף (Ezek. 23.14); יֹסֵף (Ps. 115.14); וַיֹּסֶף (Job 27.1); וַיֹּסֶף (Job 29.1); וַיֹּסֶף (Job 36.1); וַיֹּסֶף (Job 42.10); אַל־תּוֹסֵף (Job 40.32); וְיוֹסֶף (Prov. 1.5); וְיוֹסֶף (Prov. 9.9); אַל־תּוֹסְףְּ (Prov. 30.6); וַתּוֹסֶף (Est. 8.3); וַיֹּסֶף (Dan. 10.18); יֹסֵף (1 Chron. 21.3); וַיּוֹסֶף (2 Chr 28.22).

4. CONSTRUCT מְאַת VERSUS ABSOLUTE מֵאָה

1.0. The Numeral 'Hundred' in Ancient Hebrew

Ancient Hebrew exhibits two forms of the numeral hundred when followed by a noun: construct מְאַת and absolute מֵאָה. Their distribution in biblical and extrabiblical material is not random.[1]

1.1. Iron Age Epigraphic Hebrew

Iron Age Hebrew epigraphy has just one relevant instance. Here the grammatical state of the numeral is construct: ומ[א]ת אמה 'and a hu[nd]red cubits' (Siloam ll. 5–6).

1.2. The Masoretic Tradition

In the MT, the ratio of construct to absolute forms is 30:53, but the respective totals show uneven distribution. In the Pentateuch, construct forms outnumber absolute by a margin of 27:5. The rest of the MT exhibits the reversed trend of 3:48—0:34 in the Prophets, 3:14 in LBH. Recalculated according to recognised chronolects, in CBH the ratio is 27:39, in LBH 3:14.

Some HUNDRED + NOUN collocations utilise only construct מְאַת or absolute מֵאָה. Since a given expression may only ever have occurred with one of the two forms, it is instructive to consider expressions co-occurring with both forms. See Table 1 (overleaf).

---

[1] See Moshavi and Rothstein (2018), on indefinite numerals in construct generally, and (117–18) on constructions with מאת specifically. Their discussion is largely synchronic.

Table 1: Nouns that occur in collocations after construct and absolute forms of 'hundred'

Noun	Construct		Absolute	
	Count	References	Count	References
אֲדָנִים 'bases'	1	Exod. 38.27 (P)	0	
אִישׁ 'people'	0		4	Judg. 7.19; 20.35; 1 Kgs 18.13; 2 Kgs 4.43
אֶלֶף 'thousand'	4	Num. 2.9 (P), 16 (P), 24 (P), 31 (P)	8	1 Kgs 20.29; 2 Kgs 3.4, 4; 1 Chron. 5.21; 21.5; 22.14; 29.7; 2 Chron. 25.6
אַמָּה/אַמּוֹת 'cubits'	0		11	1 Kgs 7.2; Ezek. 40.19, 23, 27, 47, 47; 41.13, 13, 14, 15; 42.8
יוֹם 'days'	3	Gen 7.24 (P); 8.3 (P); Est. 1.4	0	
כִּכָּר 'talents'	4	Exod. 38.25 (P), 27 (P), 27 (P); 2 Chron. 25.9	5	2 Kgs 23.33; Ezra 8.26; 2 Chron. 25.6; 27.5; 36.3
כֶּסֶף 'silver'	1	Neh. 5.11	4	Deut. 22.19 (Other) (|| SP); Judg. 16.5; 17.2, 3
מְדִינָה 'countries'	0		3	Est. 1.1; 8.9; 9.30
נְבִאִים 'prophets'	0		1	1 Kgs 18.4
עָרְלוֹת פְּלִשְׁתִּים 'Philistine foreskins'	0		2	1 Sam. 18.25; 2 Sam. 3.14
פְּעָמִים 'times'	0		2	2 Sam. 24.3 || 1 Chron. 21.3
צֹאן 'sheep and goats'	0		1	1 Kgs 5.3
צִמֻּ(וּ)קִים 'raisin clusters/cakes'	0		2	1 Sam. 25.18; 2 Sam. 16.1
קַיִץ 'summer fruit (figs)'	0		1	2 Sam. 16.1
קְשִׂיטָה 'monetary units'	0		2	Gen. 33.19 (E) (|| SP); Josh. 24.32
רֶכֶב 'chariots'	0		2	2 Sam. 8.4 || 1 Chron. 18.4
שָׁנָה 'years'	17	Gen. 5.3 (R), 6 (R), 18 (R), 25 (R), 28 (R); 11.10 (R), 25 (R); 21.5 (P); 25.7 (P), 17 (P); 35.28 (P); 47.9 (E), 28 (P); Exod. 6.16 (P), 18 (P), 20 (P); Num. 33.39 (R)	4	Gen. 17.17 (P); 23.1 (P); Isa. 65.20, 20
שְׂעָרִים 'measures'	0		1	Gen. 26.12 (|| SP)
TOTALS	30		53	

In BH, just four collocations occur with both forms of 'hundred': אֶלֶף 'thousand', כִּכָּר 'talent', כֶּסֶף 'silver', and שָׁנָה 'year'. Broadening the perspective, this is also true of אמות/אמה 'cubit(s)', preceded by construct מאת in Iron Age epigraphy (above, §1.1), but by absolute מאה in BH (including the SP, below, §1.5) and elsewhere. Taking into account only these expressions, the ratio of construct to absolute is 26:21 overall, 24:3 in the Torah, and 2:18 elsewhere. Consider examples (1)–(8).

(1) כָּל־הַפְּקֻדִים לְמַחֲנֵה אֶפְרַיִם מְאַת אֶלֶף וּשְׁמֹנַת־אֲלָפִים וּמֵאָה לְצִבְאֹתָם...
'All those numbered of the camp of Ephraim, according to their divisions, are 108,100 [= one hundred thousand...].' (MT Num. 2.24)

(2) ...וַיַּכּוּ בְנֵי־יִשְׂרָאֵל אֶת־אֲרָם מֵאָה־אֶלֶף רַגְלִי בְּיוֹם אֶחָד:
'And the people of Israel struck down of the Syrians 100,000 [= one hundred thousand] foot soldiers in one day.' (MT 1 Kgs 20.29)

(3) וַיְהִי מְאַת כִּכַּר הַכֶּסֶף לָצֶקֶת אֵת אַדְנֵי הַקֹּדֶשׁ
'The hundred talents of silver were for casting the bases of the sanctuary...' (MT Exod. 38.27)

(4) ...וַיִּתֶּן־עֹנֶשׁ עַל־הָאָרֶץ מֵאָה כִכַּר־כֶּסֶף וְכִכַּר זָהָב:
'...and he laid on the land a tribute of a hundred talents of silver and a talent of gold.' (2 Kgs 23.33)

(5) הָשִׁיבוּ נָא לָהֶם כְּהַיּוֹם שְׂדֹתֵיהֶם כַּרְמֵיהֶם זֵיתֵיהֶם וּבָתֵּיהֶם וּמְאַת הַכֶּסֶף
'Return to them this very day their fields, their vineyards, their olive orchards, and their houses, and the hundred pieces of silver' (Neh. 5.11)[2]

---

[2] The phrase וּמְאַת הַכֶּסֶף here is enigmatic. ESV takes it as 'percentage'. Others view it as a corruption of מַשַּׁאת 'loan of', here in the sense of 'interest of, collateral of' (see the critical apparatus in *BHS*).

(6) וַיָּ֫שֶׁב אֶת־אֶ֫לֶף־וּמֵאָ֤ה הַכֶּ֫סֶף לְאִמּֽוֹ
'And he restored the 1,100 [= one thousand, one hundred...] pieces of silver to his mother.' (Judg. 17.3)

(7) וְאַבְרָהָ֖ם בֶּן־מְאַ֣ת שָׁנָ֑ה
'And Abraham was a hundred years old' (MT Gen. 21.5).

(8) ...כִּ֣י הַנַּ֗עַר בֶּן־מֵאָ֤ה שָׁנָה֙ יָמ֔וּת וְהַ֣חוֹטֶ֔א בֶּן־מֵאָ֥ה שָׁנָ֖ה יְקֻלָּֽל׃
'...for the young man shall die a hundred years old, and the sinner a hundred years old shall be accursed.' (MT Isa. 65.20)

Most collocations are indefinite, but instances including the definite article are found with both structures, e.g., examples (3) and (6).

Turning to the matter of Source Criticism, consider Table 2.

Table 2: Incidence of construct מְאַת and absolute מֵאָה according to purported Pentateuchal sources (per Friedman 1989, 246–59)

	Construct	Absolute
E	1	1
P	17	2
R	8	0
Other	0	1

As the construct form dominates in the Pentateuch, it is unsurprising that no source should exhibit marked preference for the absolute form. Still, it is worth noting that routinely late-dated P, though showing minority use of the absolute form (with the word שָׁנָה 'year'), exhibits decisive affinity for the construct form (including with the word שָׁנָה 'year'), accounting for a large share of the construct forms. R also uses the construct form exclusively, whereas E shows mixed usage between two occurrences, while Freidman's Other source in Deuteronomy shows a single instance of absolute morphology. The most conspicuous tendencies are those of P and R, which differ markedly from the dominance of the absolute form in non-Pentateuchal CBH and LBH.

1.3. The Non-biblical Dead Sea Scrolls

In the NBDSS, there are four cases of construct מאת, but only one—4Q159 f1ii.8—is independent of BH influence, the remaining cases being based on BH—4Q252 1.7 || Gen. 7.24; 4Q252 1.9 || Gen. 8.3; 4Q364 f8i.2 || Gen. 35.28. Absolute cases number five; of these, four are independent—מאה מגן 'a hundred shields' (1QM 9.13); מאה יום 'a hundred days' (4Q266 f10ii.1); מאה צוא[ן] 'a hundred sheep and goats' and ומאה נשכה 'and a hundred chambers' (11Q19 44.6)—and one is a biblical quotation—מאה כסף 'a hundred (pieces of) silver' (11Q19 65.14 || מֵאָה כֶסֶף Deut. 22.19). These figures relevant to independent usages—four absolute, one construct—indicate that the absolute form is more characteristic than the construct form of the linguistic milieu in which the NBDSS were composed.

1.4. The Biblical Dead Sea Scrolls

The BDSS exhibit one instance of construct מאת: מאת ש[נה] 'a hundred years' (4Q1 f5.9 || Gen. 35.28) and five instances of absolute מאה: מאה ק[שיטה] 'a hundred monetary units' (MurX f1.3 || Gen. 33.19; מאה שנה 'a hundred years' (1QIsaᵃ 55.3 [2x] || 1Q8 28.4 || Isa. 65.20 [2x]). In all cases, the BDSS form corresponds to that of the MT. Little of diachronic import can be said on the basis of these facts, as the material is fragmentary and there is full agreement between the BDSS and the MT.

1.5. The Samaritan Pentateuch

Due to textual differences of a non-linguistic nature, the SP has more cases of HUNDRED + NOUN constructions than the MT. Overall, its ratio of construct to absolute is 36:3 (compare 27:5, in the case of the MT Torah, above, §1.2). In most cases, the SP matches the MT in terms of the grammatical state of the numeral 'hundred'. Thus, all cases of MT construct מְאַת with a corresponding form of 'hundred' in the SP are paralleled by construct מאת *mā̊t*. The SP lacks a corresponding form three times in Gen. 5 (vv. 18, 25, 28), while there are ten cases of SP construct מאת *mā̊t* in Gen. 11 not paralleled by MT 'hundred' (vv. 12, 14, 16, 18, 19, 20, 21, 22 have no parallel numeral; vv. 23 and 32 have מָאתַיִם 'two hundred'). Additionally, in two cases SP construct מאת *mā̊t* parallels MT absolute מֵאָה (Gen. 17.17; 23.1). Significantly, these two involve the specific expression 'a hundred years', which in the Masoretic Pentateuch shows a construct form 17 times, and an absolute form just twice. It seems that, in line with its penchant for linguistic harmonisation, the Samaritan tradition levelled the two exceptional cases in line with the majority. This means that the SP preserves absolute מאה *mā̊:* 'hundred' only in the case of expressions with no documented construct alternative in the Pentateuch (Gen. 26.12; 33.19; Deut. 22.19).

1.6. Rabbinic Hebrew

RH shows strong predilection for the absolute form. Focusing on the Mishna, construct מאת is unattested, while examples of absolute מאה are plentiful (40 ×).³ These latter include cases of collocations that in earlier sources utilise the construct alternative, specifically, מאה אמה 'a hundred cubits' (m. ʿEruvin 3.3, 3; 8.10; m. Middot 4.7; 5.1, 2; m. ʾOholot 14.3; 17.1; cf. Iron Age epigraphic Hebrew, §1.1, above) and מאה יום 'a hundred days' (m. Nazir 2.10; 3.4; cf. Tiberian and Samaritan BH, §§1.2 and 1.5, respectively). In RH beyond the Mishna, construct מאת is extremely rare, and seems to obtain only in direct allusion to BH. Compare the following examples from the Babylonian Talmud:

(9) בתי הניפי לי(ה) במניפיך ואני אתן ליכי מאה כבריך דנרד

'My daughter, fan me with a fan, and as a gift I will give you a hundred packages of spikenard' (b. Bava Meṣiaʿ 86a)

(10) בנתינת הכסף אתה מוצא מאת ככר. דכת' "ויהי מאת ככר הכסף לצקת" וג'.

'But with regard to the giving of the silver to the Tabernacle you find only one hundred talents, as it is written: "And the hundred talents of silver were for casting" (Exod. 38.27).' (b. Bekhorot 5a)

When the RH usage is independent of BH, the absolute form obtains (9). Only under the influence of a BH allusion is the construct alternative preserved (10). But even under BH influence, construct מְאַת does not necessarily persist in RH. Consider example (11).

---

³ M. Demai 7.7, 7, 7, 7, 7, 7, 7; m. Terumot 4.7, 10; 5.1, 2, 3, 4; 9.5; m. Shabbat 16.3; m. ʿEruvin 3.3, 3; 8.10; m. Ketubbot 4.3; 5.1, 5; 13.7; m. Nazir 2.10; 3.4; m. Bava Qamma 4.5; m. Bava Meṣiaʿ 3.8; m. Bava Batra 9.5; m. Sanhedrin 4.5; m. Ḥullin 6.4, 4; m. ʿArakhin 3.5; 6.2; m. Keritot 5.3, 3; m. Middot 4.7; 5.1, 2; m. ʾOholot 14.3; 17.1; m. Negaʿim 8.4.

(11) אבינו אברהם בשעה שנימול היה בן תשעים ותשע שנה "בהמולו בשר ערלתו". ומת בן חמש ושבעים ומאת שנה. "ויהיו חיי שרה מאה שנה ועשרים שנה ושבע שנים שני חיי שרה". יצחק אבינו מת בן מאה ושמונים שנה. "ויהיו ימי יעקב שני חייו שבע שנים וארבעים ומאת שנה".

'Our father Abraham at the time that he was circumcised was ninety-nine years old "In his circumcising of his foreskin" (Gen. 17.24)'. And he died at the age of a hundred and seventy-five years [≈ Gen. 25.7]. "And Sarah's life was a hundred and twenty-seven years—the years of Sarah's life" (Gen. 23.1). Isaac our father died at the age of a hundred and eighty years [≈ Gen. 35.28]. "And the days of Jacob's life were a hundred and forty-seven years" (Gen. 47.28).' (Seder 'Olam Rabba 2)

Instructive in example (11) is the varied treatment of forms of 'hundred' in the RH retelling of BH source material. Twice the composer of Seder 'Olam Rabba preserves BH construct מְאַת (in the non-literal allusion to Gen. 25.7 and the quotation of Gen. 47.28). In another instance, BH absolute מֵאָה is retained (in the quotation of Gen. 23.1). In the remaining case, the BH construct is brought into line with the standard RH absolute (in the allusion to Gen. 35.28). This is typical of RH citation of BH: a combination of verbatim quotation, reformulation retaining linguistic archaisms, and rephrasing with contemporary forms.

1.7. Cognate Sources

Both Old and Second Temple Aramaic have regular recourse to the absolute form of 'hundred'. OA usage is seen in the four relevant cases in the Tell Fekheriye bilingual inscription (*KAI* 309): ומאה סאון 'and a hundred ewes' (l. 20), ומאה סור 'and a hundred cows' (l. 20), ומאה נשון 'and a hundred women' (ll. 21, 22). The Second Temple Aramaic convention is demonstrated by the Targums and the Peshiṭta, which consistently resort to the absolute form of 'hundred', even when rendering a construct form in the MT.

2.0. Interpreting the Data

2.1. Diachrony

Based on the biblical and extrabiblical distribution of the construct and absolute forms of 'hundred', מאת and מאה, respectively, certain diachronic conclusions can be drawn. The most obvious would seem to be that CBH allowed for the use of both the construct and the absolute forms, generally and in the case of specific collocations. Thus, Tiberian CBH shows a construct to absolute ratio of 27:39, whereas the same ratio in LBH is 3:14. Crucially, the late abandonment of the construct form in writing independent of BH influence is confirmed by Second Temple extrabiblical corpora, especially the NBDSS and RH. A single case of the construct form in Iron Age Hebrew epigraphy, OA's use of the absolute form, and mixed usage in the BDSS and the SP support the reliability of the general impression of distribution reflected in Tiberian CBH.

2.2. The Linguistic Exceptionality of the Torah

A second phenomenon of apparent diachronic import is the conspicuous distinction between the Hebrew of the Torah and the Hebrew of the rest of the Bible. In other words, without denying the validity of the difference observed in the previous section

(§2.1) between CBH, on the one hand, and LBH and other Second Temple forms of Hebrew, on the other, there is also a clear-cut division between the Hebrew of the Torah (Tiberian and Samaritan, alike), joined by Iron Age epigraphy, and the Hebrew of all other ancient sources, including, critically, all non-Pentateuchal CBH. The relevant ratios of construct to absolute are MT Torah 27:5, SP 36:3, rest of MT 3:48 (Prophets 0:34, Writings 3:14).

This state of affairs demands an explanation that takes into account not just the distribution of the specific linguistic feature under examination, but additional traits discussed in this volume, by dint of which the linguistic profile of the Torah is exceptional.

2.2.3. Explanation 1: Differing Approaches to Preservation

According to what is perhaps the least contentious hypothesis, ancient scribes accorded the Torah special reverence not accorded to other biblical material, on account of which they took special care to preserve its linguistic profile, including archaic features, which in non-Pentateuchal material they were somewhat less careful to preserve, allowing the infiltration of later alternatives. If so, then one might reasonably suppose that the CBH of the Prophets may once have presented more cases of construct מְאַת than the extant Masoretic tradition does, but that these were replaced with absolute מֵאָה as Second Temple scribes allowed non-Pentateuchal CBH to shift in the direction of the Hebrew of their own milieu. There seems to be nothing in the distribution of the two forms of 'hundred' to contradict the reality of such a scenario.

2.2.2. Explanation 2: Diachronic Diversity within Classical Biblical Hebrew

The suitability of such an explanation in this specific case does not, however, prove its correctness here or in general. Indeed, parsimony dictates preference for the theory that accounts for the broadest swathe of data. While an approach that assumes secondary contemporisation of non-Pentateuchal CBH in the direction of Second Temple Hebrew plausibly accounts for many differences between Pentateuchal CBH and non-Pentateuchal CBH, it cannot account for all of them. Chs 1–2 in the present volume deal with features the specific distributions of which are difficult to explain as the result of such a process. It has been argued that these must rather be considered characteristic of typologically distinct CBH sub-chronolects, tentatively labelled CBH_1 and CBH_2. Crucially, a theory hypothesising phases within CBH can account for all differences between Pentateuchal and non-Pentateuchal CBH. The reality of artificial linguistic development in the course of transmission must be taken seriously, but it was evidently not so pervasive as to reshape the general profile of a given biblical chronolect. In general, the ostensible CBH_2 remains distinct from TBH and LBH. Thus, even if this subphase of CBH is deemed (partially) a result of secondary processes, a distinction between it, i.e., retouched early material and TBH and LBH, i.e., authentically later material, is perceptible.

3.0. Excursus: The Grammatical State of the Numerals 1–10 in Ancient Hebrew in Historical Perspective[4]

It might be wondered whether the developments seen in the case of forms of the numeral 'hundred' were part of a broader process of development involving the grammatical state of cardinal numerals modifying nouns in indefinite constructions. In this connection, not all forms are relevant or show a distinction. No construct form of אֶחָד or אַחַת 'one' is available in indefinite expressions, because the numeral 'one' typically follows the noun it modifies. In the case of אַרְבַּע 'four (F)', שֵׁשׁ 'six (F)', שְׁמֹנֶה 'eight (F)', and עֶשֶׂר 'ten (F)', there is no possibility of marking a distinction in state, as the respective construct and absolute forms are identical. Though such a distinction theoretically exists in the case of absolute חָמֵשׁ 'five (F)', versus construct חֲמֵשׁ 'five (F)', absolute שֶׁבַע 'seven (F)', versus construct שְׁבַע*, and absolute תֵּשַׁע 'nine (F)', versus construct תְּשַׁע*, the construct forms obtain only in fixed expressions involving more complex numerals, e.g., חֲמֵשׁ מֵאוֹת 'five hundred' and שְׁבַע עֶשְׂרֵה 'seventeen', but generally not with following nouns (the sole possible exception being ketiv חמש־אמות קנים 'five cubit reeds', qere חֲמֵשׁ־מֵאוֹת קָנִים 'five hundred reeds' [Ezek. 42.16], but the realisation of the ketiv cannot be known). Table 3 (facing page) gives the MT distribution of forms where a distinction in grammatical state obtains.

---

[4] See Moshavi and Rothstein (2018) for a synchronic discussion of the grammar of indefinite numerical construct phrases in BH.

4. Construct מְאַת versus Absolute מֵאָה

Table 3: Incidence of construct and absolute forms of numerals in the MT (for citations, see below, §4.0)

Two	שְׁנֵי	%	שְׁנַיִם	%
Pent	56	97	2	3
Proph	27	59	19	41
Writ	3	43	4	57
LBH	1	20	4	80

	שְׁתֵי	%	שְׁתַּיִם	%
Pent	33	97	1	3
Proph	16	59	11	41
Writ	3	75	1	25
LBH	2	67	1	33

Three	שְׁלֹשֶׁת	%	שְׁלֹשָׁה	%
Pent	18	42	25	58
Proph	13	33	26	67
Writ	4	36	7	64
LBH	4	40	6	60

	שְׁלֹשׁ	%	שָׁלֹשׁ	%
Pent	2	9.5	19	90.5
Proph	1	4	27	96
Writ	0	0	7	100
LBH	0	0	5	100

Four	אַרְבַּעַת	%	אַרְבָּעָה	%
Pent	0	0	10	100
Proph	1	6	16	94
Writ	0	0	1	100
LBH	0	—	0	—

Five	חֲמֵשֶׁת	%	חֲמִשָּׁה	%
Pent	2	15	11	85
Proph	0	0	12	100
Writ	0	—	0	—
LBH	0	—	0	—

Six	שֵׁשֶׁת	%	שִׁשָּׁה	%
Pent	13	72	5	28
Proph	4	40	6	60
Writ	0	0	5	100
LBH	0	0	5	100

Seven	שִׁבְעַת	%	שִׁבְעָה	%
Pent	56	80	14	20
Proph	15	44	19	56
Writ	13	68	6	32
LBH	11	85	2	15

Eight	שְׁמֹנַת	%	שְׁמֹנָה	%
Pent	2	50	2	50
Proph	0	0	3	100
Writ	0	0	2	100
LBH	0	0	2	100

Nine	תִּשְׁעַת	%	תִּשְׁעָה	%
Pent	0	—	0	—
Proph	0	0	1	100
Writ	0	—	0	—
LBH	0	—	0	—

Ten	עֲשֶׂרֶת	%	עֲשָׂרָה	%
Pent	3	14	18	86
Proph	3	14	18	86
Writ	2	0	2	50
LBH	2	67	1	33

It is difficult to discern an overall trend. In the case of the numerals 'two',[5] 'six', and 'seven', a trend of diminishing use of the construct seems clear. In the case of 'four', 'five', and 'ten', the construct form is consistently rare. In the case of 'three', both construct and absolute forms occur and are stable. Cases of 'eight' and 'nine' are too rare to sustain much in the way of argumentation.

These trends find a degree of confirmation in non-Tiberian biblical material and extrabiblical sources, but there are also inconsistencies. See Table 4 (facing page). Instability in the grammatical state of 'two' in the MT Prophets, MT LBH, the NBDSS, and the BDSS—with preference for the construct, but also some documentation of the absolute—contrasts sharply with overwhelming use of the relevant construct forms in the MT Pentateuch and the Mishna (with absolute forms in the latter only in citations of the Torah). The growing use of absolute forms of 'six (M)' and 'seven (M)' is confirmed by similar distributions in non-Tiberian and extrabiblical material, but LBH is an outlier when it comes to 'seven (M)'. The same is true of absolute 'eight', the infrequency of which in BH makes it difficult to discern any trend there. 'Nine' is virtually undocumented in BH, but is strongly construct in RH. The numeral 'ten' shows preference for the absolute state throughout all sources. The SP is in general agreement with the MT, sometimes harmonising minority forms.

---

[5] Excluded from counts of the numeral 'two' are cases involving the decades, e.g., 'twenty-two', as these almost uniformly (15 of 16 times) involve absolute forms of the numeral 'two', e.g., וּשְׁלֹשִׁים וּשְׁנַיִם מֶלֶךְ 'and thirty-two kings' (1 Kgs 20.1). The sole exception is אַרְבָּעִים וּשְׁנֵי יְלָדִים 'forty-two children' (2 Kgs 2.24).

4. Construct מְאַת versus Absolute מֵאָה

Table 4: Incidence of construct and absolute forms of numerals in the MT, non-Tiberian BH, and late extrabiblical sources (for citations, see below, §4.0)

	שתי/שני	שתי/שני	שלשת	שלשה	ארבעת	ארבעה	חמשת	חמשה	ששת	ששה	שבעת	שבעה	שמנת	שמנה	תשעת	תשעה	עשרת	עשרה
Pent.	89	3	18	25	0	11	2	11	13	5	56	14	2	2	0	0	3	18
Proph.	41	30	13	26	1	16	0	12	4	6	15	19	0	3	0	1	3	18
LBH	3	5	4	7	0	0	0	0	0	5	11	2	0	2	0	0	2	1
NBDSS	15	4	8	15	0	5	0	0	0	5	21	37	0	2	0	0	7	10
BDSS	9	2	4[6]	7	0	1[7]	0	1	15[8]	0	15[9]	8	0	0	0	0	1	2
SP	91	0[10]	18	25	0	10	2	10	14	5	53	14	2	2	0	0	3	17
Ben Sira	2	0	0	0	0	0	0	0	0	0	1	0	0	0	0	0	0	0
RH	669	9[11]	45	211	13	76	5	45	0	32	8	20	1	10	13	2	6	88

Since no general trend is discernible, it is difficult to contextualise the treatment of 'hundred'. The only thing that can be

---

[6] Excluding 4Q51 9e–i.2, where the text is unclear.

[7] ארבעה כנפים 'and four wings' (4Q73 f2.6) || וְאַרְבַּע כְּנָפַיִם (MT Ezek. 10.21).

[8] ששת ימים 'six days' (4Q132 f3–4.1; 4Q136 f1.13; 4Q140 f1.14; 4Q145 f1R.7) || שִׁבְעַת יָמִים 'seven days' (MT Exod. 13.6).

[9] שׁ[בעת ימים 's[even days' (4Q30 f32i + 33.4) || שֵׁשֶׁת יָמִים 'six days' (MT Deut. 16.8); לשבעת נחלים 'into seven channels' (1QIsaᵃ 11.5) || לְשִׁבְעָה נְחָלִים (MT Isa. 11.15).

[10] שני כרובים *šēni kērūbəm* 'two cherubim' (SP Exod. 25.18) || שְׁנַיִם כְּרֻבִים (MT Exod. 25.18); שני עדים *šēni idəm* 'two witnesses' (SP Deut. 17.6) || שְׁנַיִם עֵדִים (MT Deut. 17.6); שתי מערכות *šitti mārrēkot* 'two arrays' (SP Lev. 24.6) || שְׁתַּיִם מַעֲרָכוֹת (MT Lev. 24.6).

[11] All cases of שְׁנַיִם come in citations of עַל־פִּי | שְׁנַיִם עֵדִים (Deut. 17.6; Sota 6.3 [3×]; Mak. 1.7, 9 [2×]). All cases of שְׁתַּיִם come in a citation of Ezek. 41.23–24 (Mid. 4.1 [2×]).

said is that, similar to the case of 'hundred', the Torah shows high proportions of construct 'two', 'six', and 'seven', which elsewhere in BH (but not necessarily in other late sources) show majority absolute usage. In a limited sense, then, preference for the construct forms of these numerals may be considered distinctive of the CBH of the Pentateuch.

4.0. Citations

שני—Gen. 10.25; 24.22; 25.23, 23; 27.9; 32.8, 11; 41.50; Exod. 2.13; 26.19, 19, 21, 21, 23, 25, 25; 34.1, 4, 4; 36.24, 24, 26, 26, 28, 30, 30; 37.7; Lev. 5.7, 11; 12.8; 14.10, 22; 15.14, 29; 16.5; 23.13, 17, 19, 20; 24.5; Num. 6.10; 11.26; 15.6; 28.9, 9, 12, 20, 28; 29.3, 9, 14; Deut. 4.13; 5.22; 10.1, 3; 19.15; Judg. 3.16; 11.38; 1 Sam. 10.2; 28.8; 30.12; 2 Sam. 4.2; 8.2; 12.1; 14.6; 1 Kgs 2.32, 39; 6.23, 34, 34; 7.18, 24, 42; 12.28; 20.27; 2 Kgs 5.22, 23; 7.14; 10.8; 17.16 (qere); Jer. 24.1; Ezek. 37.22; Zech. 11.7; Song 4.5; 7.4; 1 Chron. 1.19; שנים—Exod. 25.18; Deut. 17.6; Josh. 2.1; Judg. 11.37, 39; 15.13; 1 Sam. 25.18; 1 Kgs 5.28; 10.19; 17.12; 18.23; 21.10; 2 Kgs 2.12; 17.16 (ketiv); Ezek. 21.24; 40.39, 39, 40, 40; 41.18; Zech. 4.3; Neh. 6.15; 2 Chron. 4.3, 13; 9.18; שתי—Gen. 4.19; 19.8; 29.16; Exod. 25.12, 12; 26.17; 28.7, 9, 14, 23, 26, 27; 30.4; 36.22; 37.3, 3, 27; 39.16, 16, 19, 20; Lev. 5.7, 11; 12.8; 14.4, 22, 49; 15.14, 29; Num. 6.10; 10.2; Deut. 14.6; 21.15; 1 Sam. 1.2; 2.21; 6.7, 10; 10.4; 13.1; 2 Sam. 13.6; 1 Kgs 6.32, 34; 7.16; 2 Kgs 5.22, 23; Isa. 7.21; Ezek. 37.22; 41.24; Amos 3.12; Prov. 30.15; Neh. 12.31; 1 Chron. 4.5; שתים—Lev. 24.6; 2 Sam. 2.10; 1 Kgs 3.16; 2 Kgs 2.24; (8.17, 26; 15.2, 27; 21.19;) Jer. 2.13; Ezek. 23.2; 40.9; 41.3, 22, 23, 24; 43.14; Zech. 5.9; 2 Chron. 33.21

שלשת—Gen. 30.36; 40.12, 13, 18, 19; 42.17; Exod. 3.18; 5.3; 8.23; 10.22, 23; 15.22; 19.15; Lev. 12.4; 27.6; Num. 10.33, 33; 33.8; Josh. 1.11; 2.16, 22; 3.2; 9.16; Judg. 14.14; 19.4; 1 Sam. 10.3; 2 Sam. 20.4; 24.13; 1 Kgs 10.17; Amos 4.4; Jon. 3.3; Est. 4.16; Dan. 10.3; 1 Chron. 21.12; 2 Chron. 10.5; שלשה—Gen. 6.10; 18.2; 29.2, 34; 40.10, 16; Exod. 2.2; 25.32, 32, 33, 33; 37.18, 18, 19, 19; Lev. 14.10; Num. 15.9; 28.12, 20, 28; 29.3, 9, 14; Deut. 17.6; 19.15; Josh. 18.4; Judg. 7.16; 9.43; 1 Sam. 2.21; 10.3, 3; 11.11; 13.17; 30.12, 12; 2 Sam. 6.11; 14.27; 18.14; 24.13; 1 Kgs 6.36; 7.4, 12; 12.5; 2 Kgs 2.17; 9.32; 23.31; 24.8; Isa. 17.6; Amos 4.7; Jon. 2.1, 1; Job 1.17; Dan. 10.2; 11.2; 1 Chron. 13.14; 21.12; 2 Chron. 36.2, 9; שֵׁלֶשׁ—Gen. 18.6; 38.24; 1 Sam. 13.21 (?); שָׁלֹשׁ—Gen. 11.13, 15; Exod. 23.14, 17; 27.1; 34.23, 24; 38.1; Lev. 19.23; Num. 22.28, 32, 33; 24.10; Deut. 4.41; 14.28; 16.16; 19.2, 7, 9; Judg. 9.22; 16.15; 1 Sam. 20.41; 2 Sam. 13.38; 21.1; 1 Kgs 2.39; 7.4, 5; 9.25; 10.22; 15.2; 17.21; 22.1; 2 Kgs 13.18, 19, 25; 17.5; 18.10; 24.1; 25.17; Isa. 16.14; 20.3; Jer. 36.23; Ezek. 40.48,

4. *Construct* מְאַת *versus Absolute* מֵאָה

48; 41.22; Amos 4.8; Job 1.2; 42.13; 1 Chron. 21.12; 2 Chron. 8.13; 9.21; 13.2; 31.16

ארבעת—Judg. 11.40; ארבעה—Gen. 2.10; 14.9; Exod. 25.34; 26.32, 32; 28.17; 36.36, 36; 37.20; 39.10; Judg. 9.34; 19.2; 20.47; 1 Sam. 27.7; 1 Kgs 7.2, 30; 18.34; 2 Kgs 7.3; Ezek. 1.6; 10.9, 14, 21; 40.41, 41, 42; Zech. 2.3; Job 42.16

חמשת—Num. 3.47; 18.16; חמשה—Gen. 47.2; Exod. 21.37; 26.27, 27, 37, 37; 36.32, 32, 38; Lev. 27.6; Num. 11.19; Josh. 10.26; Judg. 18.2; 1 Sam. 6.4, 4; 17.40; 21.4; 22.18; 2 Kgs 6.25; 25.19; Ezek. 8.16; 11.1; 45.12; חֲמֵשׁ—Ezek. 42.16; חָמֵשׁ—Gen. 5.6, 11, 15; 11.32; 12.4; 25.7; 43.34; 45.6, 11, 22; Exod. 26.3; 27.1, 1, 18; 36.10; 38.1, 1, 18; Lev. 27.5, 6; Josh. 14.10; 1 Sam. 25.18, 18; 2 Sam. 4.4; 1 Kgs 6.10, 24, 24; 7.16, 16; Isa. 19.18; Jer. 52.22; Ezek. 40.7, 30, 48, 48; 41.2, 2, 9, 11, 12; 2 Chron. 6.13, 13

ששת—Exod. 16.26; 20.9, 11; 23.12; 24.16; 31.15, 17; 34.21; 35.2; Lev. 12.5; 23.3; Deut. 5.13; 16.8; Josh. 6.3, 14; 1 Kgs 11.16; Ezek. 46.6; ששה—Gen. 30.20; Exod. 25.32; 26.22; 36.27; 37.18; 2 Sam. 2.11; 5.5; 6.13; 2 Kgs 15.8; Ezek. 9.2; 46.4; Est. 2.12, 12; 1 Chron. 3.4; 8.38; 9.44

שבעת—Gen. 8.10, 12; 31.23; 50.10; Exod. 7.25; 12.15, 19; 13.6; 22.29; 23.15; 29.30, 35, 37; 34.18; Lev. 8.33, 33, 35; 12.2; 13.4, 5, 21, 26, 31, 33, 50, 54; 14.8, 38; 15.13, 19, 24, 28; 22.27; 23.6, 8, 18, 34, 36, 39, 40, 41, 42; Num. 12.14, 14, 15; 19.11, 14, 16; 28.17, 24; 29.12; 31.19; Deut. 16.3, 4, 13, 15; 1 Sam. 10.8; 11.3; 31.13; 1 Kgs 8.65, 65; 16.15; 20.29; 2 Kgs 3.9; Ezek. 3.15, 16; 43.25, 26; 44.26; 45.23, 23; Job 2.13, 13; Est. 1.5; Ezra 6.22; Neh. 8.18; 1 Chron. 10.12; 2 Chron. 7.8, 9, 9; 30.21, 23, 23; 35.17

שבעה—Num. 23.1, 1, 1, 14, 29, 29, 29; 28.19, 27; Deut. 7.1; 16.9, 9; 28.7, 25; Josh. 6.4, 6, 6; 18.2, 5, 6, 9; Judg. 8.14; 16.7, 8; 1 Sam. 6.1; 2 Sam. 21.6; Isa. 11.15; Jer. 32.9; 52.25; Ezek. 39.12, 14; Zech. 3.9; 4.2; Job 1.2; 42.8, 8; Ruth 4.15; 1 Chron. 15.26, 26

שמנת—Gen. 17.12; 21.4; שמנה—Exod. 26.25; 36.30; 1 Sam. 17.12; Jer. 41.15; Ezek. 40.41

תשעה—2 Sam. 24.8

עשרת—Gen. 31.7, 41; Lev. 27.5; Judg. 17.10; Isa. 5.10; Jer. 42.7; Neh. 5.18; 2 Chron. 36.9; עשרה—Gen. 24.10, 22; 45.23; Lev. 27.7; Num. 7.14, 20, 26, 32, 38, 44, 50, 56, 62, 68, 74, 80; 11.19, 32; Josh. 22.14; Judg. 6.27; 20.10; 1 Sam. 1.8; 17.17; 25.5; 2 Sam. 18.11, 15; 1 Kgs 5.3; 7.38; 11.31; 14.3; 2 Kgs 13.7; 25.25; Jer. 41.1, 8; Amos 6.9; Zech. 8.23; Ruth 4.2; Ezra 1.10

5. *QAL* INTERNAL PASSIVE VERSUS *NIF'AL* MORPHOLOGY

Over the course of its history, ancient Hebrew underwent many morphological developments. One such development was a long, gradual, and increasingly pervasive process of reorganisation of derivational verbal morphology involving stem (*binyan*) movement, whereby many formerly G-stem (*qal*) verbs were transferred by language users to alternative stems, primarily N-stem (*nifʿal*), D-stem (*piʿʿel*), and C-stem (*hifʿil*), with no accompanying semantic change.[1] Among the affected early stem patterns was the apophonic passive of the G-stem, commonly known as the *qal* internal passive.

The fate of the *qal* internal passive in BH is an oft-recounted tale.[2] Beyond acknowledging its existence in BH, scholars have noted several important features relevant to the diachronic evolution of Hebrew. As early as the Iron Age, the form seems to have been in the process of being replaced by alternative forms.

---

[1] For extensive discussion of such shifts, along with additional bibliography, see Hornkohl (2023, 183–318). On nifalisation specifically, see Hornkohl (2021b; 2023, 183–208).

[2] Important scholarly discussions include Böttcher (1866–1868, I:98–105); Barth (1890); Lambert (1900); Blake (1901, 53–54); GKC (§52e); Ginsburg (1929; 1934; 1936); Williams (1977); WO (373–76); Hughes (1994, 71–76); JM (§58); Sivan (2009, 50–51); Blau (2010, 217–18); Reymond (2016); cf. Garbini (1960, 130 fn. 5). See Chomsky (1959, xvii–xix, 103 fn. 146) for opinions on the *qal* internal passive among medieval Jewish grammarians.

This process later accelerated and expanded, resulting in many cases of suppletion due to secondary replacement, reinterpretation of original morphology, and the eventual disuse of the form in favour of alternative morphology. After summarising these developments, the present chapter will consider an additional topic: whether distinct, diachronically meaningful patterns of *qal* internal passive use and non-use can be discerned within CBH.

1.0. The *qal* Internal Passive in the Tiberian Masoretic Tradition

1.1. Secondary Developments and Suppletion

Investigation of the *qal* internal passive is complicated by the fact that, in many cases, the original *qal* passive pronunciation of forms has been eclipsed by secondary realisations. In some instances, the new pronunciation differed only slightly from the expected *qal* passive realisation.

For example, in the suffix conjugation of the strong verb, where expected *quṭal* > *quṭṭal*, the gemination was probably due to a spontaneous phonological process that allowed for preservation of the *u*-vowel iconically associated with passive voice (Suchard 2019, 110, fn. 31). Because in this case the *u*-vowel was short, without gemination, it would likely otherwise have shortened to *shewa*; but the gemination also resulted in a form identical to that of the D-stem passive *puʿʿal*.

In other cases, like that of the prefix conjugation of the strong verb, where expected *yuqtal* > *yiqqā̊ṭēl*, consonantal forms amenable to reinterpretation were simply read with alternative passive morphology, i.e., as the more dominant *nifʿal*.

In both of the above situations, it is important to note that the secondary developments brought the morphology into line with Second Temple linguistic conventions.

In still other cases, e.g., the prefix conjugation of I-*n* forms, the expected *yuṭṭal* form underwent no change, but, due to similarity to the C-stem internal passive form, was readily analysable as *hofʿal* (*hufʿal*).

Finally, there are cases, such as that of the participle of strong verbs and I-*y* verbs—expected, respectively, to yield *qal* passive *quṭāl* and *yūṭāl*, but resulting in *quṭṭāl* and *yuṭṭāl*—where the gemination created resemblance to D-stem passive *puʿʿal*, with the lack of the characteristic D-stem prefix -מ betraying the original *qal* passive morphology. The treatment of several of the most common verb classes is summarised in the following table.

Table 1: Expected *qal* passive and received suppletive passive paradigms of common verb classes

Verb class	Form	Expected paradigm	Received paradigm	Description
Strong	SC	*quṭal*	*quṭṭal*	> *puʿʿal*
	PART	*quṭāl*	*quṭṭāl*	> *puʿʿal* (w/o -מ)
	PC	*yuqṭal*	*yiqqāṭēl*	> *nifʿal*
I-*y*	SC	*yūṭal*	*yuṭṭal*	> *puʿʿal*
	PART	*yūṭāl*	*yuṭṭāl*	> *puʿʿal* (w/o -מ)
	PC	*yūṭal*	*yiwwāṭēl*	> *nifʿal*
I-*n*	SC	*nuṭal*	*niṭṭal*	> *nifʿal*
	PART	*nuṭāl*	*niṭṭāl*	> *nifʿal*
	PC	*yuṭṭal*	*yuṭṭal*	*qal* passive (= *hufʿal*) vocalism

The specific constellation of forms, characterised by suppletion involving predictable revocalisation, reinterpretation, and irregularity is readily explained as a result of secondary processes.

Another indication of the secondary character of the suppletion is the occurrence of morphologically distinct cases of passives in proximity. Consider the instances of passives of נָתַן 'give'—first *qal* internal passive, then *nifʿal*—in the following:

(1) לָרַב תַּרְבֶּה נַחֲלָתוֹ וְלַמְעַט תַּמְעִיט נַחֲלָתוֹ אִישׁ לְפִי פְקֻדָיו יֻתַּן נַחֲלָתוֹ... וַיִּהְיוּ פְקֻדֵיהֶם שְׁלֹשָׁה וְעֶשְׂרִים אֶלֶף כָּל־זָכָר מִבֶּן־חֹדֶשׁ וָמָעְלָה כִּי | לֹא הָתְפָּקְדוּ בְּתוֹךְ בְּנֵי יִשְׂרָאֵל כִּי לֹא־נִתַּן לָהֶם נַחֲלָה בְּתוֹךְ בְּנֵי יִשְׂרָאֵל:

'To a large tribe you shall give a large inheritance, and to a small tribe you shall give a small inheritance; to every tribe shall its inheritance be given (*qal* internal passive) in proportion to its list.... And those listed were 23,000, every male from a month old and upward. For they were not listed among the people of Israel, because no inheritance was given (*nifʿal*) to them among the people of Israel.' (Num. 26.54, 62)

1.2. Late Disappearance of the *qal* Internal Passive

Related to the secondary replacement or reinterpretation of original *qal* internal passive forms is the conspicuous infrequency of the *qal* internal passive in Second Temple Hebrew sources, including LBH, SH, Ben Sira, QH, and the Tiberian reading tradition of CBH texts (Hughes 1994, 76, fn. 20; Reymond 2016, 1138–40; Qimron 2018, 221–22; Hornkohl 2023, 185–87, 194, 196–97, 199, 202, 203–7). Indeed, the *qal* internal passive is completely unproductive in RH (Sharvit 2004, 45; Reymond 2016, 1141, fn. 37; Hornkohl 2023, 198).

1.3. Late Expansion of Morphological Alternatives for the *qal* Internal Passive

A further confirmation of the secondary and late character of the morphological shifts under discussion is the disproportionately late incidence of purely consonantal *nifʿal* evidence for certain common verbs with both *qal* internal and *nifʿal* passive morphology. Thus, in the case of נת"ן, 15 of the 31 cases of unambiguous consonantal *nifʿal* forms come in the very restricted range of LBH, while for יל"ד the proportion is 11 of 17 (13 of 19, if the two cases of *nufʿal* are included). In the same LBH material, there is no instance of the *qal* internal passive of נת"ן and just one of the *qal* internal passive יל"ד.[3] Note the replacement of *qal* passive forms in Samuel (even-numbered examples) with *nifʿal* forms in Chronicles (odd-numbered examples) in the following pairs of contrasting examples:

(2) אֵלֶּה יֻלְּדוּ לְדָוִד בְּחֶבְרוֹן
'These were born (*qal passive*) to David in Hebron.' (2 Sam. 3.5)

(3) שִׁשָּׁה נוֹלַד־לוֹ בְחֶבְרוֹן
'six were born (*nifʿal*) to him in Hebron' (1 Chron. 3.4)

(4) וְגַם־הוּא יֻלַּד לְהָרָפָה
'He too was born (*qal passive*) to the Raphaites' (2 Sam. 21.20)

(5) וְגַם־הוּא נוֹלַד לְהָרָפָא
'He too was born (*nifʿal*) to the Raphaites' (1 Chron. 20.6)

Significantly, the late reinterpretation of *qal* passive forms as D- and C-stem passive forms is also in line with Second Temple linguistic trends, as the broader processes of both pielisation and

---

[3] נת"ן: *nifʿal*—Est. 2.13; 3.14; 5.3, 6; 7.2, 3; 8.13; 9.12, 13, 14; Dan. 8.12; 11.6; 1 Chron. 5.20; 2 Chron. 2.13; 18.14; יל"ד: *qal* passive—1 Chron. 1.19; *nifʿal*—Qoh. 4.14; 7.1; Ezra 10.3; 1 Chron 2.3, 9; 3.1, 4, 5 (*nufʿal*); 7.21; 20.6, 8 (*nufʿal*); 22.9; 26.6.

hifilisation are acknowledged phenomena associated with later forms of ancient Hebrew (Hornkohl 2023, 209–88).

1.4. The Antiquity of *Nifʿal* Morphology

Given the tenor of the discussion above, focusing on examples of late and secondary movement from *qal* passive to *nifʿal* morphology,[4] one might be tempted to conclude that *nifʿal* forms are universally late. Such would be a misreading of the evidence. The use of *nifʿal* and, therefore, the potential for nifalisation were not restricted to post-exilic times. Though there is a meaningful association between nifalisation and the Second Temple period, the relationship is not exclusive.

Especially important in this connection is early unambiguous *nifʿal* evidence from sources unaffected by the vagaries of scribal transmission or secondary development of the reading tradition, such as *nifʿal* forms in Iron Age Hebrew inscriptions, e.g., the imperative השמר 'take care!' (Lachish 3.21), the infinitive להנ[קב 'to be he[wn]' (Siloam 1.2), and the prefix conjugation form ילקח 'be taken' (Arad 111.4).[5]

Turning to the Hebrew Bible, many intransitive verbs are commonly represented by unequivocal *nifʿal* consonantal forms in CBH texts, with little to no evidence of *qal* synonymy. Thus, נִפְרַד 'separate (intr.)' has consistent *nifʿal* spelling and vocalisation

---

[4] Additional cases of secondary nifalisation involve *qal* verbs with stative, medio-passive, intransitive, and weakly transitive semantics that shift to *nifʿal* (see Hornkohl 2023, 183–208).

[5] N-stem נאנח 'groan' occurs in the 8th-century Deir ʿAlla inscription (*KAI* 312 B.12).

throughout BH. Likewise, though a vestige of *qal* שָׁאַר 'remain' is attested once in CBH (1 Sam. 16.11), the synonymous *nifʿal* נִשְׁאַר is unambiguously represented in all biblical chronolects.[6]

Since *nifʿal* morphology was available at an early date, it is only logical that classical texts might show evidence of *qal–nifʿal* synonymy as a result of early nifalisation. And, indeed, this is precisely what one finds. Consider the combination of apparently synonymous *qal* passive and *nifʿal* patterns used in close in proximity in:

(6) וְכִי־יַכֶּה֩ אִ֨ישׁ אֶת־עַבְדּ֜וֹ אֽוֹ אֶת־אֲמָת֗וֹ בַּשֵּׁ֙בֶט֙ וּמֵ֣ת תַּ֣חַת יָד֑וֹ נָקֹ֖ם יִנָּקֵֽם׃ אַ֥ךְ אִם־י֛וֹם א֥וֹ יוֹמַ֖יִם יַעֲמֹ֑ד לֹ֣א יֻקַּ֔ם כִּ֥י כַסְפּ֖וֹ הֽוּא׃

'When a man strikes his slave, male or female, with a rod and the slave dies under his hand, he shall surely be avenged (*qal, nifʿal*). But if the slave survives a day or two, he may not be avenged (*qal* internal passive), for the slave is his money.' (Exod. 21.20–21)

(7) וַיְהִ֣י כְעָבְרָ֗ם וְאֵ֨לִיָּ֜הוּ אָמַ֣ר אֶל־אֱלִישָׁ֗ע שְׁאַל֙ מָ֣ה אֶֽעֱשֶׂה־לָּ֔ךְ בְּטֶ֖רֶם אֶלָּקַ֣ח מֵעִמָּ֑ךְ וַיֹּ֣אמֶר אֱלִישָׁ֔ע וִֽיהִי־נָ֛א פִּֽי־שְׁנַ֥יִם בְּרוּחֲךָ֖ אֵלָֽי׃ וַיֹּ֙אמֶר֙ הִקְשִׁ֣יתָ לִשְׁא֑וֹל אִם־תִּרְאֶ֨ה אֹתִ֜י לֻקָּ֤ח מֵֽאִתָּךְ֙ יְהִֽי־לְךָ֣ כֵ֔ן וְאִם־אַ֖יִן לֹ֥א יִהְיֶֽה׃

'When they had crossed, Elijah said to Elisha, "Ask what I shall do for you, before I am taken (*nifʿal*) from you." And Elisha said, "Please let there be a double portion of your spirit on me." And he said, "You have asked a hard thing; yet, if you see me being taken (*qal* internal passive) from you, it shall be so for you, but if you do not see me, it shall not be so."' (2 Kgs 2.9–10)

---

[6] See Hornkohl (2023, 203, fn. 16) for further unambiguous consonantal evidence of *nifʿal* morphology in CBH.

Also relevant in this connection is the instance of *qere–ketiv* in the following example:

(8) יֻתַּן [K] ינתן־לָ֜נוּ שִׁבְעָ֤ה אֲנָשִׁים֙ מִבָּנָ֔יו וְהוֹקַֽעֲנוּם֙ לַֽיהוָ֔ה בְּגִבְעַ֖ת שָׁא֣וּל בְּחִ֣יר יְהוָ֑ה ס וַיֹּ֥אמֶר הַמֶּ֖לֶךְ אֲנִ֥י אֶתֵּֽן׃

'Let seven of his sons be given (*ketiv nifʿal, qere qal* internal passive) to us, so that we may hang them before the LORD at Gibeah of Saul, the chosen of the LORD.' (2 Sam. 21.6)

Given the historical depth of passive encoding via *nifʿal* morphology in BH, there seems no reason to doubt the antiquity of either component of the tradition here. If so, this is simply "a genuine instance of early textual fluctuation" (Hornkohl 2023, 206; cf. Hughes 1994, 76).

2.0. Usage Patterns in Classical Biblical Hebrew

Based on the foregoing description, it is apparent that any diachronic account of the development of the *qal* internal passive in ancient Hebrew must take into account the intricacies of a complicated combination of facts, including, among other things, (a) early development of *nifʿal* forms with little to no evidence of *qal* competition, as seen in unambiguous biblical and extrabiblical consonantal evidence; (b) early synonymy of *qal* and *nifʿal* forms, as seen in unambiguous biblical and extrabiblical consonantal evidence; (c) late standardisation of *nifʿal* morphology at the expense of formerly dominant *qal* passive morphology, as seen in unambiguous biblical and extrabiblical consonantal evidence; (d) secondary subversion of early *qal* passive morphological dominance via the opportune reinterpretation of consonantal forms amenable to secondary *nifʿal* realisation, as seen in BH reading traditions associated with the Second Temple period—i.e., the specific period associated with (c)—e.g., the Tiberian and Samaritan pronunciation traditions.

2.1. Classical Biblical Hebrew versus Late Biblical Hebrew

There is a marked distinction between CBH and LBH when it comes to usage of the *qal* internal passive. Despite the reality of authentic *nifʿal* forms and of blurring due to secondary nifalisation in CBH texts, the *qal* internal passive remains well represented in the relevant material. It was evidently still a productive element within CBH grammar, at least in the case of specific verbs, notwithstanding already pervasive *nifʿal* encroachment. By the time of LBH, by contrast, the *qal* internal passive had largely fallen into disuse, a situation confirmed by late extrabiblical sources and, to some extent, by non-Tiberian biblical material with late affinities.

2.2. Variations in Usage involving Classical Biblical Hebrew

Despite displaying a great deal of linguistic diversity, CBH is generally considered sufficiently homogenous to be regarded as a single chronolect. Based on affinities with Iron Age epigraphic Hebrew, CBH seems broadly to reflect the literary language practices of Iron Age II, approximately 1000–600 BCE, or, in terms of biblical historiography, the monarchic period. Yet, a large section of the CBH corpus deals with pre-monarchic times and, as such, may incorporate earlier traditions, including linguistic material.

While there is little reason to challenge the general correctness of the CBH label or its literary and historical associations, it is legitimate to wonder whether language change is discernible within CBH.

When it comes to the matter of the *qal* internal passive, several significant distributional patterns emerge.[7] These include comprehensive *nifʿal* dominance, i.e., the general absence of *qal* passive morphology from all strata of BH; CBH preference for *qal* passive versus LBH preference for *nifʿal* morphology; and inner-CBH differences in *qal* passive and *nifʿal* distributional patterns. In order properly to contextualise the discussions that follow, it is important to note that none of the relevant roots are represented by *qal* passive or *nifʿal* forms in Iron Age Hebrew epigraphic sources, that the relevant *qal* passive forms occur outside Tiberian BH only in non-Tiberian biblical traditions (BDSS, SP) or in extrabiblical allusions to Tiberian BH (e.g., m. Makhshirin 1.1–6, in reference to Lev. 11.38), and that the relevant *nifʿal* forms are frequent in post-biblical Hebrew, including material independent of BH (NBDSS, Ben Sira, RH).

2.2.1. Comprehensive *nifʿal* Dominance

Consider the respective *qal* internal passive and *nifʿal* data for the roots כר"ת 'be cut, cut off' and רא"י 'be seen, appear' in Tables 2 and 3 (facing page).

---

[7] In the following sections, the discussion is limited to verbs with both *qal* internal passive and *nifʿal* representation. It is further restricted to verbs with more than just a handful of occurrences, as the rest are too rare to have statistical significant distributions. Possible semantic distinctions are dealt with on a case-by-case basis, as necessary.

5. Qal Internal Passive versus nifʿal Morphology

Table 2: כר"ת—*Qal* internal passive versus *nifʿal*

	consonantal *qal* passive	*nifʿal* consonantal	*nifʿal* vocalisation (consonantally ambiguous)
Torah	0	23	5
Fmr Prophets	1	3	6
Lat. Prophets	1	9	13
Non-LBH Writings	0	3	8
LBH	0	0	3

qal **passive—consonantal**: Judg. 6.28; Ezek. 16.4; *nifʿal*—**consonantal**: Gen. 17.14 (P); Exod. 12.15 (P), 19 (P), 30.33 (P), 38 (P); 31.14 (P); Lev. 7.20 (P), 21 (P), 25 (P), 27 (P); 17.4 (P), 9 (P); 18.29 (P); 19.8 (P); 20.17 (P), 18 (P); 22.3 (P); 23.29 (P); Num. 9.13 (P); 15.30 (R), 31 (R); 19.13 (P), 20 (P); Josh. 3.16; 4.7, 7; Isa. 22.25; 29.20; Jer. 7.28; Joel 1.5, 16; Obad. 1.10; Nah. 2.1; Zeph. 1.11; Zech. 9.10; Ps. 37.28, 34, 38; **vocalisation (consonantally ambiguous)**: Gen. 9.11 (P); 41.36 (E); Lev. 17.14 (P); Num. 11.33 (E); 15.31 (R); Josh. 3.13; 9.23; 2 Sam. 3.29; 1 Kgs 2.4; 8.25; 9.5; Isa. 11.13; 48.19; 55.13; 56.5; Jer. 33.17, 18; 35.19; Hos. 8.4; Obad. 1.9; Mic. 5.8; Zeph. 3.7; Zech. 13.8; 14.2; Ps. 37.9, 22; Job 14.7; Prov. 2.22; 10.31; 23.18; 24.14; Ruth 4.10; Dan. 9.26; 2 Chron. 6.16; 7.18

Table 3: רא"י—*Qal* internal passive versus *nifʿal*

	consonantal *qal* passive	*nifʿal* consonantal	*nifʿal* vocalisation (consonantally ambiguous)
Torah	0	17	31
Fmr Prophets	0	14	9
Lat. Prophets	0	6	6
Non-LBH Writings	1	3	4
LBH	0	6	4

qal **passive—consonantal**: Job 33.21; *nifʿal*—**consonantal**: Gen. 8.5 (P); 9.14 (P); 12.7 (J); 35.1 (E); 48.3 (P); Exod. 3.16 (E); 4.1 (E), 5 (E); 16.10 (P); Lev. 9.4 (P); 13.7 (P), 7 (P), 14 (P), 19 (P); 14.35 (P); Num. 14.10 (P), 14 (J); Judg. 13.10, 21; 19.30; 1 Sam. 1.22; 3.21; 2 Sam 17.17; 1 Kgs 3.5; 6.18; 9.2; 10.12; 11.9; 18.1, 2; 2 Kgs 23.24; Isa. 16.12; Jer. 13.26; 31.3; Ezek. 10.1; 21.29; Mal. 3.2; Ps. 102.17; Prov. 27.25; Song 2.12; Dan. 1.15; 8.1, 1; 2 Chron. 1.7; 3.1;

9.11;[8] **vocalisation (consonantally ambiguous)**: Gen. 1.9 (P); 12.7 (J); 17.1 (P); 18.1 (J); 22.14 (R); 26.2 (J), 24 (J); 35.9 (P); 46.29 (J); Exod. 3.2 (J); 6.3 (P); 13.7 (E), 7 (E); 23.15 (E), 17 (E); 33.23 (E); 34.3 (J), 12 (E), 20 (J), 23 (J); Lev. 9.6 (P), 23 (P); 13.57 (P); 16.2 (P); Num. 16.19 (P); 17.7 (P); 20.6 (P); Deut. 16.4 (Other), 16 (Other), 16 (Other); 31.15 (E); Judg. 5.8; 6.12; 13.3; 2 Sam. 22.11, 16; 1 Kgs 8.8, 8; 9.2; 18.15; Isa. 1.12; 47.3; 60.2; Ezek. 10.8; 19.11; Zech. 9.14; Ps. 18.16; 42.3; 84.8; 90.16; Dan. 1.13; 2 Chron. 5.9, 9; 7.12[9]

In both cases, unambiguous consonantal evidence for *nifʿal* morphology substantially outweighs that for *qal* internal passive.[10] This, in turn, makes it probable that some portion of the ambiguous consonantal forms are also authentically *nifʿal*—in agreement with their vocalisation. If these verbs ever had productive *qal* internal passive forms, the figures indicate that by the CBH period, they had been effectively eclipsed by *nifʿal*, which forms continued to serve in later Hebrew.[11]

---

[8] Excluded from the count of consonantal *nifʿal* forms of רא״י is the form לֵרָאוֹת in phrases of the type אֶת־פְּנֵי יְהוָה אֱלֹהֶיךָ לֵרָאוֹת (Exod. 34.24; see also Deut. 31.11; Isa. 1.12). Though the pointing reflects *nifʿal* realisation, the consonantal form consistently reflects original *qal* morphology; see Hornkohl (2023, 55–66, esp. 56–57).

[9] Included in the list of ambiguous consonantal forms of רא״י with *nifʿal* vocalisation are the three cases of לֵרָאוֹת cited in the previous footnote.

[10] In terms of semantics: in the case of כר״ת, the *qal* passive form is used only with inanimate subjects; the *nifʿal* most commonly occurs with human subjects, but is also used for the cutting (off) of non-human subjects (e.g., Num. 11.33; Josh. 3.13; Job 14.7). For רא״י, the lone *qal* passive has an inanimate subject and the sense of 'be seen, visible', which features are also possible for the *nifʿal* (e.g., 1 Kgs 6.18). It would thus seem in all cases that, at the very least, the *nifʿal* could have been used wherever the *qal* passive was (though perhaps not vice-versa).

[11] *Nifʿal* כר״ת and רא״י are reflected in unequivocal consonantal evidence in QH, RH, and Ben Sira.

2.2.2. Classical Biblical Hebrew against Late Biblical Hebrew

In line with what was said above (§§1.2; 2.1), the distributional pattern of one root with common *qal* passive and *nifʿal* alternatives—namely, יל"ד 'be born'—shows consistent *qal* passive dominance in CBH consonantal evidence against *nifʿal* dominance in LBH, along with suspiciously common *nifʿal* vocalisation of morphologically ambiguous written forms in CBH texts. See Table 4.

Table 4: יל"ד—*Qal* internal passive versus *nifʿal*

	qal passive consonantal	*nifʿal* consonantal	*nifʿal* vocalisation (consonantally ambiguous)
Torah	11	3	8
Fmr Prophets	6	1	3
Lat. Prophets	4	1	1
Non-LBH Writings	6	1	7
LBH	1	11	0

***qal* passive—consonantal**: Gen. 4.26 (J); 6.1 (J); 10.21 (J), 25 (J); 24.15 (J); 35.26 (P); 36.5 (P); 41.50 (E); 46.22 (P), 27 (P); 50.23 (E); Judg. 13.8; 18.29; 2 Sam. 3.2 [*ketiv*], 5; 21.20, 22; Isa. 9.5; Jer. 20.14, 15; 22.26; Ps. 87.4, 5, 6; 90.2; Job 5.7; Ruth 4.17; 1 Chron. 1.19; ***nifʿal*—consonantal**: Gen. 21.3 (P), 5 (P); 48.5 (P); 1 Kgs 13.2; Hos. 2.5; Ps. 22.32; Qoh. 4.14; 7.1; Ezra 10.3; 1 Chron. 2.3, 9; 3.1, 4, 5 (*nufʿal*); 7.21; 20.6, 8 (*nufʿal*); 22.9; 26.6;[12] **vocalisation (consonantally ambiguous)**: Gen. 4.18 (J); 10.1 (P); 17.17 (P); 46.20 (P); Lev. 22.27 (P); Num. 26.60 (P); Deut. 15.19 (Other); 23.9 (Other); 2 Sam. 3.2 [*qere*]; 5.13; 14.27; Isa. 66.8; Ps 78.6; Job 1.2; 3.3; 11.12; 15.7; 38.21; Prov. 17.17

Throughout CBH, the *qal* internal passive dominates over the *nifʿal* in unambiguous consonantal forms (by a margin of 27:6). In LBH, the trend is reversed (1:11). The forms tallied in the

---

[12] This count excludes the two cases of *nufʿal* נוּלְדוּ (1 Chron 3.5; 20.8).

'ambiguous' column are all prefix conjugation forms vocalised as *nifʿal*. One might expect the proportions of *qal* passive and *nifʿal* morphology among the consonantally ambiguous forms to resemble those of the consonantally unambiguous forms in each respective portion of the Hebrew Bible, but this cannot be confirmed.

2.2.3. Distinctive *qal* Internal Passive and *nifʿal* Distributional Patterns within Classical Biblical Hebrew

Several verbs exhibiting both *qal* internal passive and *nifʿal* forms show interesting distributions within the Hebrew Bible, in general, and within CBH, more specifically. All very clearly exhibit the aforementioned dichotomy between CBH and LBH (and other late forms of ancient Hebrew), with late disuse of the *qal* passive in favour of *nifʿal*. Crucially, though, the significant shift—be it reduction in *qal* internal passive usage or increase in *nifʿal* usage—coincides not with the onset of LBH, but within CBH, distinguishing the CBH of the Torah from the CBH of the relevant works in the Prophets and Writings. See Tables 5–7.

Table 5: לק״ח—*Qal* internal passive versus *nifʿal*

	consonantal *qal* passive	*nifʿal* consonantal	*nifʿal* vocalisation (consonantally ambiguous)
Torah	5	0	0
Fmr Prophets	2	7	0
Lat. Prophets	7	1	0
Non-LBH Writings	1	0	0
LBH	0	2	0

qal passive—consonantal: Gen. 2.23 (J); 3.19 (J), 23 (J); 12.15 (J); 18.4 (J); Jdg. 17.2; 2 Kgs 2.10; Isa. 49.24, 25; 52.5; 53.8; Jer. 29.22; 48.46; Ezek. 15.3; Job 28.2; *nifʿal*—consonantal: 1 Sam. 4.11, 17, 19, 21, 22; 21.7; 2 Kgs 2.9; Ezek. 33.6; Esth. 2.8, 16

Passive semantics in the case of לק"ח are expressed exclusively via the *qal* internal passive in the CBH of the Torah. While use of the *qal* passive is also characteristic of CBH beyond the Torah—especially so in the high rhetoric and poetry of the Latter Prophets—clear-cut *nifʿal* usage is found only outside the Torah—especially in the prose of the Former Prophets.

Table 6: נת"ן—*Qal* internal passive versus *nifʿal*

	consonantal *qal* passive	*nifʿal* consonantal	*nifʿal* vocalisation (consonantally ambiguous)
Torah	3	2	7
Fmr Prophets	4	3	5
Lat. Prophets	0	11	24
Non-LBH Writings	1	0	2
LBH	0	15	13

qal passive—consonantal: Lev. 11.38 (P); Num. 26.54 (P); 32.5 (P); 2 Sam. 21.6 [*qere*]; 1 Kgs 2.21; 2 Kgs 5.17; Job 28.15; *nifʿal*—consonantal: Exod. 5.18 (E); Lev. 24.20 (P); 2 Sam 21.6 [*ketiv*]; 2 Kgs 18.30; 19.10; Isa. 36.15; 37.10; 51.12; Jer. 21.10; 32.4, 4; 34.3; 37.17; 38.3, 3; 39.17; Est. 2.13; 3.14; 5.3, 6; 7.2, 3; 8.13; 9.12, 13, 14; Dan. 8.12; 11.6; 1 Chron. 5.20; 2 Chron. 2.13; 18.14; **vocalisation (consonantally ambiguous):** Gen. 9.2 (P); 38.14 (J); Exod. 5.16 (E); Lev. 10.14 (P); 19.20 (P); 26.25 (P); Num. 26.62 (P); Josh. 24.33; 1 Sam. 18.19; 25.27; 2 Kgs 22.7; 25.30; Isa. 9.5; 29.12; 33.16; 35.2; Jer. 13.20; 32.24, 25, 36, 43; 38.18; 46.24; 51.55; 52.34; Ezek. 11.15; 15.4; 16.34; 31.14; 32.20, 23, 25, 29; 33.24; 35.12; 47.11; Job 9.24; 15.19; Qoh. 10.6; 12.11; Est. 3.15; 4.8; 6.8; 8.14; Dan. 11.11; Ezra 9.7; Neh. 10.30; 13.10; 1 Chron. 5.1; 2 Chron. 28.5; 34.16.

When it comes to passive semantics of נת"ן, the Torah shows mixed, nearly balanced usage. The CBH Prophets and LBH, by contrast, show pronounced preference for *nifʿal*. This is especially true of the Latter Prophets and LBH, which corpora exhibit *nifʿal* to the total exclusion of *qal* passive. This picture is based on unequivocal consonantal evidence. The *nifʿal* vocalisations of ambiguous consonantal forms may be assumed to be variously authentic or secondary in line with the relevant consonantal evidence of the respective corpus, though each assumption is unverifiable conjecture which can be neither confirmed nor disconfirmed.

Table 7: נק״ם—*Qal* internal passive versus *nifʿal*

	consonantal *qal* passive	*nifʿal* consonantal	*nifʿal* vocalisation (consonantally ambiguous)
Torah	3	1	0
Fmr Prophets	0	2	2
Lat. Prophets	0	5	1
Non-LBH Writings	0	0	0
LBH	0	1	0

qal passive—consonantal: Gen. 4.15 (E), 24 (J); Exod. 21.21 (E); *nifʿal*—consonantal: Exod. 21.20 (E); Judg. 16.28; 1 Sam. 18.25; Isa. 1.24; Jer. 15.15; 46.10; Jer. 50.15; Ezek. 25.15; Est. 8.13; vocalisation (consonantally ambiguous): Judg. 15.7; 1 Sam. 14.24; Ezek. 25.12

Involving admittedly few tokens, majority use of *qal* internal passive in the Pentateuch gives way to exclusive use of *nifʿal* in the rest of the Hebrew Bible (with a few instances of *nifʿal* vocalisations of ambiguous consonantal forms). Thus, the shift from *qal* passive to *nifʿal* appears to be an inner-CBH development.

3.0. Interpreting the Data

According to the foregoing investigation of passive morphological options, an unmistakable diachronic pattern of usage emerges. Generally speaking, the early typological situation was one of mixed *qal* passive and *nifʿal* usage. From this there eventually evolved a situation of *nifʿal* dominance. Some verbs show this very distribution of *qal* passive and *nifʿal* forms (§§2.1; 2.2.2). In the case of other verbs, however, in agreement with broad evidence for early nifalisation, the ostensible substitution of *qal* passive with *nifʿal* was largely complete by the age of the most ancient CBH texts, such that there is little to no evidence of *qal* passive usage (§2.2.2). Finally—and most intriguingly for the argument sustained in this volume—the passive morphology of some verbs exhibits an evident diachronic development that, rather than distinguishing CBH from LBH, distinguishes the CBH of the Torah from both the rest of CBH (Prophets and Writings) and LBH.

As in other such cases discussed in this monograph, two non-mutually exclusive explanations suggest themselves. According to one hypothesis, the CBH of all biblical corpora once showed rather more homogenous usage patterns of *qal* passive and *nifʿal* morphology, but in the process of redaction, compilation, and transmission, scribes allowed greater influence of late linguistic conventions—in this case, *nifʿal* encroachment—in the CBH of the Prophets and Writings than they did in the case of the Torah's CBH—this owing to the Pentateuch's relatively early crystallisation and to the high status it held among readers.

There is some evidence supporting this view, but it is far from unequivocal. Where possible, apparently original *qal* passive forms were reinterpreted as *nifʿal* or analysed as *hufʿal* (*hofʿal*) forms in the Tiberian reading tradition. Also, certain non-Tiberian biblical sources and traditions known for their Second Temple linguistic affinities, such as the contemporised BH of 1QIsaiah[a] and the SP, especially the latter's pronunciation tradition, tend to replace the *qal* internal passive with alternatives, be they passive, impersonal, or active (Kutscher 1974, 362; Ben-Ḥayyim 2000, 177; Reymond 2016, 1138–41; Hornkohl 2021b, 8–9; 2023, 194). By contrast, many *qal* passive forms in Tiberian BH are paralleled by forms amenable to *qal* passive analysis in the BDSS. Moreover, as noted above, the biblical *qal* passive morphological tradition seems quite stable in extrabiblical material that cites BH. Crucially lacking is any smoking-gun evidence of textual material representing the CBH Prophets and Writings exhibiting their presumed greater early use of *qal* passive morphology.

The alternative hypothesis is that the various Masoretic corpora by and large faithfully preserve typologically distinct usage patterns of passive morphology, especially in unambiguous consonantal forms. The Torah's typologically early affinity for *qal* passive forms in the case of several verbs contrasts with the typologically later preference for the *nifʿal* forms of such verbs in the CBH Prophets and Writings. This state of affairs does not necessarily imply the early composition of the Tiberian Torah in its extant form—though this well may be the case—but it does seem to indicate the preservation of a typologically early linguistic tradition, which tallies with the notion that the content of the

Pentateuch, whenever it achieved its ultimate form, incorporates genuinely ancient, i.e., pre-monarchic, material in a form that preserves pre-monarchic linguistic features.

At this juncture, it is opportune to consider the distribution of the relevant passive morphological alternatives in the sources that purportedly comprise the Pentateuch. Table 8 displays the figures for the verb forms above according to purported source (per Friedman 1989, 246–59).

Table 8: Statistics of *qal* internal passive and *nifʿal* forms of specific verbs per purported Pentateuchal source

כר״ת	J	E	P	R	Other	נת״ן	J	E	P	R	Other
qal pass.	0	0	0	0	0	*qal* pass.	0	0	3	0	0
nif.	0	0	21	2	0	*nif.*	0	1	1	0	0
ambig.	0	2	2	1	0	ambig.	1	1	5	0	0
רא״י						נק״ם					
qal pass.	0	0	0	0	0	*qal* pass.	1	2	0	0	0
nif.	2	4	11	0	0	*nif.*	0	1	0	0	0
ambig.	9	7	11	1	3	ambig.	0	0	0	0	0
יל״ד						TOTALS					
qal pass.	5	2	4	0	0	*qal* pass.	11	4	7	0	0
nif.	0	0	3	0	0	*nif.*	2	6	36	2	0
ambig.	1	0	5	0	2	ambig.	11	10	23	2	5
לק״ח						Totals w/o כר״ת and רא״י					
qal pass.	5	0	0	0	0	*qal* pass.	11	4	7	0	0
nif.	0	0	0	0	0	*nif.*	0	2	4	0	0
ambig.	0	0	0	0	0	ambig.	2	1	10	0	2

Focusing on the totals, the high number of unambiguous consonantal *nifʿal* forms (36) is conspicuous. This is misleading, though, as a large proportion of this figure (32) consists of forms of כר״ת and רא״י, neither of which show any cases of *qal* internal passive morphology. Narrowing the focus to roots represented by both *qal* passive and *nifʿal* morphology, several important usage patterns emerge. J shows strong preference for *qal* internal passive morphology, while E and J are similar in terms of the relative frequencies of *qal* passive and *nifʿal* morphology. Significant here is the persistence of *qal* passive morphology in all relevant sources, with preference for *qal* passive forms in verbs showing a *nifʿal* alternative. This is in line with the general trend characteristic of the Torah observed above, i.e., its typological con-servatism in its rather common maintenance of *qal* passive morphology relative to synonymous *nifʿal* morphology. Notably, this distinguishes all putative Torah sources from the CBH of the Prophets and the Writings (see Tables 5–7, above, with the relevant discussions). It also reveals the affinity of P, which many regard as an exilic or post-exilic composition, to J and, especially, E regarding passive morphology, as well as its clear distinction from LBH, late non-Tiberian biblical sources, and late extrabiblical material.

6. זע"ק VERSUS צע"ק

The distribution of the synonymous roots צע"ק and זע"ק in ancient Hebrew sources is not haphazard.[1] Rather, a diachronic trend is perceptible (Hornkohl 2014a, 78–82). Both roots are well represented throughout the Masoretic biblical tradition as well as in non-Masoretic biblical and late extrabiblical material; neither is attested in Iron Age Hebrew epigraphy.[2] On the basis of the evidence, an early minority form, זע"ק, appears to have supplanted its majority counterpart, צע"ק, in late sources. But the sources also seem to reveal a gradual process, with an intermediate period of mixed usage, albeit with certain interesting exceptions. Within this broad picture there is clear evidence of a distinction between CBH and LBH, but also, intriguingly, possible signs of diachronic development within CBH.

---

[1] The synonymy of lexemes with the roots צע"ק and זע"ק is seen in nouns and verbs, e.g., the nouns צְעָקָה (20×) and זְעָקָה (18×) '(out)cry', the *qal* verbs צָעַק (48×) and זָעַק (61×) 'cry out', *nifʿal* נִצְעַק (6×) and נִזְעַק (6×) 'be mustered', *hifʿil* הִצְעִיק (1×) and הִזְעִיק (7×) 'muster'. It is also seen in the use of alternant forms in proximity, e.g., the nouns in Gen. 18.20–21; Jer. 48.3–5, 34; Neh. 5.1, 6; the *qal* forms in Judg. 10.10, 12, 14; Ps. 107.6, 13, 19, 28; Neh. 9.4, 27–28; noun and *qal* verb combinations in 1 Sam. 4.13–14; Isa. 65. 14, 19; Jer. 25.34, 36; 48.3–5, 20, 31, 34; Neh. 9.4, 9, 27–28.

Etymologically, the situation is unclear. For example, BDB (277a, 858a) paradoxically considers זע"ק a biform of צע"ק, but simultaneously cites distinct Arabic cognates in زعق and صعق.

[2] The reconstructed OA form שׁ[קה 'outcry' in Sefire Treaty Text 1 (a.30; ca. 750 BCE) is, unfortunately, broken; see *CAL s.v.* צעקה.

1.0. The Hebrew of the Second Temple Period

In the standard Tiberian biblical tradition, both roots are common, with a צע"ק to זע"ק ratio of 76:91. See Table 1 for the frequency statistics of the relevant verbal and nominal forms.

Table 1: Tiberian biblical distribution of verbal and nominal forms with the roots צע"ק and זע"ק by book

	צָעַק	צָעֵק	נִצְעַק	הִצְעִיק	צְעָקָה	צע"ק	זָעַק	נִזְעַק	הִזְעִיק	זְעָקָה	זע"ק
Genesis	3	0	0	0	3	6	0	0	0	1	1
Exodus	10	0	0	0	5	15	1	0	0	0	1
Numbers	3	0	0	0	0	3	0	0	0	0	0
Deuteronomy	3	0	0	0	0	3	0	0	0	0	0
Joshua	1	0	0	0	0	1	0	1	0	0	1
Judges	2	0	4	0	0	6	7	4	2	0	13
Samuel	0	0	1	1	2	4	12	1	2	0	15
Kings	7	1	1	0	0	9	1	0	0	0	1
Isaiah	5	0	0	0	1	6	6	0	0	3	9
Jeremiah	3	0	0	0	4	7	8	0	0	6	14
Ezekiel	0	0	0	0	0	0	4	0	0	1	5
Hosea	0	0	0	0	0	0	2	0	0	0	2
Joel	0	0	0	0	0	0	1	0	0	0	1
Jonah	0	0	0	0	0	0	1	0	1	0	2
Micah	0	0	0	0	0	0	1	0	0	0	1
Habakkuk	0	0	0	0	0	0	2	0	0	0	2
Zephaniah	0	0	0	0	1	1	0	0	0	0	0
Zechariah	0	0	0	0	0	0	0	0	1	0	1
Psalms	5	0	0	0	1	6	5	0	0	0	5
Proverbs	0	0	0	0	0	0	0	0	0	1	1
Job	2	0	0	0	3	5	1	0	1	1	3
Lamentations	1	0	0	0	0	1	1	0	0	0	1
Qohelet	0	0	0	0	0	0	0	0	0	1	1
Esther	0	0	0	0	0	0	1	0	0	2	3
Ezra	0	0	0	0	0	0	0	0	0	0	0
Nehemiah	1	0	0	0	1	2	2	0	0	2	4
Chronicles	1	0	0	0	0	1	4	0	0	0	4
Total	47	1	6	1	21	76	60	6	7	18	91

The most conspicuous tendency of obvious diachronic import is that of Second Temple material. Tiberian LBH shows a pronounced preference for זע"ק. Thus, the ratio of צע"ק to זע"ק in the LBH corpus consisting of Qohelet, Esther, Nehemiah, and Chronicles is 3:12.

Significantly, LBH is joined by several late extrabiblical and non-Masoretic biblical corpora in its preference for זע"ק over צע"ק. The root צע"ק is entirely absent from the non-biblical DSS, against 16 instances of זע"ק, in four of which זע"ק parallels Masoretic צע"ק:[3]

(1) וַיֹּאמֶר יְהוָה אֶל־מֹשֶׁה מַה־תִּצְעַק אֵלָי
ויואמר יה[ו]ה [א]ל מושה מה תזעק אלי
'The LORD said to Moses, "Why do you cry out to me?"' (MT Exod. 14.15 || 4Q365 f5ai.4)

(2) וַיִּלֹּנוּ הָעָם עַל־מֹשֶׁה לֵּאמֹר מַה־נִּשְׁתֶּה: וַיִּצְעַק אֶל־יְהוָה
וילון העם ע[ל מ]ושה ל[אמור מה נשתה ויזעק מושה אל [יהוה]
'So the people murmured against Moses, saying, "What can we drink?" And he/Moses cried out to the LORD' (MT Exod. 15.24–25 || 4Q365 f6aii+6c.10)

---

[3] In light of the 'biblical' character of these quotations/allusions, the suitability of the label 'non-biblical' for the texts in which they are embedded is debateable. Though arguably anachronistic, it is employed here for the sake of simplicity, reflecting the eventual distinction between what was canonised and what was not. It makes no claim as to how contemporary authors and scribes thought of the texts.

(3) עַל־דְּבַר֙ אֲשֶׁ֣ר לֹא־צָעֲקָ֣ה בָעִ֔יר
עֹל דבר לוא זעק[ה] בעיר

'because she did not cry out in the city' (MT Deut. 22.24 || 11Q19 66.2–3)

(4) כִּ֣י בַשָּׂדֶ֞ה מְצָאָ֗הּ צָעֲקָ֨ה הַֽנַּעֲרָ֤ה [*ketiv* הנער] הַמְאֹ֣רָשָׂ֔ה וְאֵ֥ין מוֹשִׁ֖יעַ לָֽהּ
כי בשדה מצאה זעקה הנערה המאורשה ואין מושיע לה

'for he met her in the field: the engaged woman cried out, but there was no one to rescue her.' (MT Deut. 22.27 || 11Q19 66.7–8)

Cases of זע"ק outnumber those of צע"ק in the BDSS as well; in this material the ratio of צע"ק to זע"ק is 11:27, with five cases in which biblical צע"ק is paralleled by BDSS זע"ק, e.g.,[4]

(5) לֹ֥א יִצְעַ֖ק וְלֹ֣א יִשָּׂ֑א וְלֹֽא־יַשְׁמִ֥יעַ בַּח֖וּץ קוֹלֽוֹ
לוא יזעק ולוא ישא ולוא ישמיע בחוץ קולו

'He will not cry out or shout; he will not publicise himself in the streets.' (MT Isa. 42.2 || 1QIsaᵃ 35.11)

(6) וַיִּצְעֲק֣וּ אֶל־יְ֭הוָה בַּצַּ֣ר לָהֶ֑ם וּֽ֝מִמְּצֽוּקֹתֵיהֶ֗ם יוֹצִיאֵֽם
ויזעקו אל יהוה ב[צר] להם ממציקותיהם וישיעם

'They cried out to the LORD in their distress; he delivered them from their troubles.' (MT Ps. 107.28 || 4Q88 3.19–21)

Likewise, in Aramaic sources the preference for זע"ק is very strong. The 5th-century BCE Egyptian Aramaic documents from Elephatine contain derivations of both roots, but nearly all later material, including BA, QA, and Syriac in general, employs זע"ק

---

[4] The other three instances of interchange are MT Isa. 33.7 || 1QIsaᵃ 27.7; MT Isa. 46.7 || 1QIsaᵃ 39.12; and MT Isa. 65.14 || 1QIsaᵃ 52.21. The opposite interchange takes place in MT 2 Sam. 2.23 || 4Q11 f3–4.4.

to the exclusion of צע"ק. Decisively, TA favours זע"ק even where the MT has צע"ק. Contact with Aramaic was likely a factor in the post-exilic Hebrew drift toward preference for זע"ק over צע"ק.

Rounding out the picture, the use of צע"ק persists in other late biblical and extrabiblical material—Ben Sira, SH, and RH—in the face of the encroachment of זע"ק. This is to be expected for Ben Sira, known for his archaising penchant, as well as for the SP, which in this instance outstrips even the Tiberian Torah in antiquarian fervour—apparently levelling the minority זע"ק cases safeguarded in the Masoretic Pentateuch to harmonise with majority צע"ק. For its part, RH is an unexpected outlier among Second Temple Hebrew traditions, anomalously preferring צע"ק over זע"ק (see Hornkohl 2014a, 81, fn. 28). For considerations on the potential methodological difficulty occasioned by RH's preservation of צע"ק against the late encroachment of זע"ק, see below, §2.0.

2.0. Classical Biblical Hebrew

CBH differs from LBH and other late material in terms of the relative distributions of צע"ק and זע"ק. Contrasting appreciably with LBH's strong predilection for זע"ק over צע"ק (12:3), the Tiberian Torah displays a more decisive reverse preference for צע"ק over זע"ק (27:2). Based on this information alone, it is reasonable to argue for a diachronic difference. One might also posit a post-exilic shift. However, the story is more complicated than this. See Table 2 (overleaf).

Table 2: Tiberian biblical distribution of verbal and nominal forms with the roots צע"ק and זע"ק by section

	צָעַק	צֶעֱק	נִצְעַק	הִצְעִיק	הַצְעָקָה	צע"ק	זָעַק	נִזְעַק	הִזְעִיק	זְעָקָה	זע"ק
Pentateuch	19	0	0	0	8	27	1	0	0	1	2
Prophets	18	1	6	1	8	34	45	6	6	10	67
Former	10	1	6	1	2	20	20	6	4	0	30
Latter	8	0	0	0	6	14	25	0	2	10	37
the Twelve	0	0	0	0	1	1	7	0	2	0	9
Writings	10	0	0	0	5	15	14	0	1	7	22
non-LBH	8	0	0	0	4	12	7	0	1	2	10
LBH	2	0	0	0	1	3	7	0	0	5	12

While exhibiting persistence of צע"ק, the CBH Prophets and non-LBH Writings are also characterised by significant זע"ק usage. According to these statistics, then, the precise nature of the late development at issue lies not in the increased usage of זע"ק *per se*, since its derivatives are common in many CBH texts, but in the non-use of צע"ק, non-use that is characteristic exclusively of LBH and other late sources.

Having precisely defined the nature of the diachronic development in question, we are equipped to return briefly to the aforementioned 'problem' of late material, such as RH, that does not partake therein. Methodologically, a late source's preservation—even consistent preservation—of a single characteristically classical feature in no way contradicts its overall late linguistic periodisation. This is because early features remained available to late writers. The regnant diachronic approach permits the persistence of early features; it excludes the possibility of consistently thorough classical style on the part of late writers. More problematic in the present context would be the regular occurrence of a late feature in early material, but since no CBH text with more than a single potential case is entirely free of instances of צע"ק, there are no grounds for methodological concern.

The figures in Table 2, above, highlight the contrast between the clearcut dominance of זע"ק in LBH and the still-significant incidence of צע"ק in CBH, but this broad characterisation obscures a degree of distributional variation at a more granular level. As such, it is worth making a few observations on specific books and larger corpora in the Tiberian tradition.

First, though the corpus-centric statistics in Table 2 are generally representative of the figures associated with their constituent works, as depicted in Table 1, above, the book of Kings is an exception. With a 9:1 ratio of צע"ק to זע"ק, Kings is a definite outlier among the books of the Prophets and in this regard is more reminiscent of the books of the Torah.

Second, given the probable pre-exilic origin of several of the constituent works in the Twelve (Minor Prophets), their 1:9 ratio of צע"ק to זע"ק is somewhat unexpected. One wonders whether the current preference for זע"ק might be partially artificial, a result of secondary levelling in favour of the more prevalent Second Temple form.[5] This is mere conjecture, though, as there is no tangible textual evidence to support the theory.

Third, on the basis of the difference between the CBH Prophets, with pronounced dominance of זע"ק, and the non-LBH Writings, with nearly balanced use of צע"ק and זע"ק, it would be

---

[5] See Hornkohl (2014a, 88) for a similar explanation of corpus-wide harmonisation behind the otherwise anomalous dominance in the Twelve of names ending in the short theophoric suffix יָה- rather than long יָהוּ-.

reasonable to speculate as to the possible influence of genre—perhaps the archaic or archaising style of poetry prolonged the use of the perceived old צע"ק, when contemporary prose style would more regularly opt for זע"ק.

3.0. Interpreting the Data

While the widely accepted CBH–LBH dichotomy of ancient Hebrew periodisation is consistent with a great deal of diachronic variety in BH and has largely withstood scholarly scrutiny, finer gradations—such as early poetic ABH and late pre-exilic, exilic, and early post-exilic TBH—have been suggested, with mixed reviews. None of the diachronic paradigms reflected by these chronolects seems a good fit for the biblical distribution of צע"ק and זע"ק.

Recapping the pertinent statistics from above, the צע"ק to זע"ק ratio in the principal biblical sections according to the Tiberian tradition are reproduced in Table 3.

Table 3: Tiberian distribution of צע"ק and זע"ק in the principal biblical sections

	צע"ק	זע"ק
Pentateuch	27	2
Prophets	34	67
Non-LBH Writings	12	10
LBH	3	12

As observed above, while LBH, with rare usage of צע"ק, differs from CBH, where צע"ק is common, this is not the only shift perceptible in the data. The LBH reduction in צע"ק is obviously related to increased use in זע"ק. Crucially, however, this latter development evidently took place before LBH's heyday. While rare in the Tiberian Torah, זע"ק is common elsewhere in CBH, and dominant in the CBH Prophets. The main question, then, is how to interpret the obvious numerical disparity between the CBH of the Tiberian Torah and the CBH of the relevant books in the Prophets and Writings when it comes to the use of זע"ק.

It is first of all worth asking whether the distribution of forms in the Tiberian Torah is genuine. Despite some evidence of textual variation involving צע"ק and זע"ק in the text of the Pentateuch, it does not materially alter the picture that emerges from the MT. As mentioned above, the SP, which shows greater incidence of צע"ק than the MT Torah—to the total exclusion of זע"ק—decisively supports the authenticity of Tiberian Pentateuchal partiality for צע"ק. For their part, the shifts from צע"ק to זע"ק in DSS material in examples (1)–(4) above are evidence of textual instability. Yet, as the DSS renditions are in line with Second Temple linguistic conventions, they should arguably be considered conditioned secondary developments, rather than evidence of random textual fluidity.

If the Tiberian linguistic tradition is to be regarded as historically reliable in this detail, then perhaps the most straightforward explanation for the conspicuous difference in the use of זע"ק between the CBH Prophets and Writings, on the one hand, and the Torah, on the other, should be seen as a function of inner-CBH diachronic development. According to a reading of the evidence that assumes some temporal correlation between content and linguistic tradition, it is reasonable to hold that צע"ק and זע"ק coexisted as far back as BH reaches, with צע"ק the dominant option. Subsequently, *but prior to the post-Restoration period of LBH*,

ק"יז saw increased usage at the expense of צ"עק, though, crucially, use of the latter persisted in a substantial minority of cases. Finally, only some post-Restoration corpora exhibit the exclusive employment of ק"יז to the total exclusion of צ"עק (though other late sources continue to utilise צ"עק). If the scenario outlined here is correct, then the process according to which ק"יז gained total ascendency (in some late material) was long and gradual, beginning with relatively early proliferation of ק"יז forms, i.e., in CBH, and culminating with virtual abandonment of צ"עק in LBH and similar material.

According to the approach advanced here, the frequency of ק"יז constitutes an isogloss distinguishing the CBH of the Torah from the CBH of the relevant Prophets and Writings. In theory, this difference might be organic, accurately reflecting genuine linguistic patterns characteristic of the period in which the material in question was composed. This presupposes a fairly stable linguistic tradition in the face of the vicissitudes of compositional development and textual transmission. It also can be interpreted to mean that the Tiberian Torah, whenever it achieved its extant form, reliably preserves details of a recognisably early form of CBH. Given the differences in content between the relevant sections of the Bible, this linguistic difference may be understood as one of several manifestations of real-world diachronic diversity between CBH sub-chronolects, i.e., a pre-monarchic Pentateuchal linguistic tradition, CBH_1, and a monarchic linguistic tradition in the Prophets and Writings, CBH_2.

According to an alternative approach, the extant linguistic picture is to be seen at least partially as a product of secondary processes. Notwithstanding a dearth of textual evidence to support the notion, it may be that all CBH texts—in the Pentateuch, Prophets, and Writings—once showed similar distributions of צע"ק and זע"ק, the former dominating the latter, as in the Torah. While Second Temple scribes managed meticulously to preserve the linguistic situation in the Pentateuch, they were less conscientious when it came to material outside the Torah, allowing contemporisation of the language under the influence of late Hebrew and Aramaic linguistic tendencies. While in line with the discussions on certain features treated in this volume, a dearth of concrete evidence for textual variation in this specific case leaves the suggestion in the realm of conjecture and arguably makes it less convincing than the argument for organic typological difference outlined above.

Even less compelling is the argument that the dominance of צע"ק in the Tiberian Torah is artificial. The dissonance in successive verses between זְעֲקַת 'outcry' (Gen. 18.20) and הַכְּצַעֲקָתָהּ 'if according to its outcry' (Gen. 18.21) would have been a prime target for linguistic levelling, if such a procedure had been implemented to achieve consistency. Rather, this linguistic irregularity in the Tiberian Torah, albeit slight, can be taken as an indication of the authenticity of its linguistic tradition. As observed above, one need look no further than the SP for the implementation of artificial homogenisation in the case of this feature.

It is worth noting in this connection that the distribution of the two roots does not seem to be a function of putative source. Basing source identification on Friedman (1989, 246–55), the two occurrences of זע"ק in the Tiberian Torah come in the

Yahwist's Gen. 18.20 and the Priestly Exod. 2.23b. Both sources also more frequently utilise צע״ק—J: Gen. 4.10; 18.21; 19.13; 27.34, 34, etc.; P: Exod. 3.15; 14.10, 15.

This leaves us with one of two historical reconstructions, each of which presupposes not only a difference between CBH and LBH, but different sub-forms of CBH. Whether the distributional pattern seen in the Torah was also once more characteristic of the CBH Prophets and Writings or not, as things currently stand, the CBH of the Torah and LBH look like early and late diachronic extremes, respectively, with the CBH Prophets and Writings somehow transitional between the two. Crucially, however, the 'transitional' CBH of the Prophets and Writings is typologically distant from LBH and also distinct from the TBH that some scholars associate with the late pre-exilic, exilic, and early post-exilic periods.

7. 1CPL נַחְנוּ VERSUS אֲנַחְנוּ

There are three variants of the 1CPL independent subject pronoun in BH. The standard form, with some 120 occurrences, is אֲנַחְנוּ (pausal אֲנָחְנוּ). The RH-like form אנו comes as the *ketiv* form (read according to the *qere* as standard אֲנַחְנוּ) in Jer. 42.6 (see Hornkohl 2014a, 125–28, for recent discussion and references). The form נַחְנוּ (pausal נָחְנוּ) comes just five times in BH (Gen. 42.11; Exod. 16.7, 8; Num. 32.32; Lam. 3.42[1]).

1.0. Distribution Outside Tiberian Biblical Hebrew

Standard BH אֲנַחְנוּ is also typical of the BDSS, the NBDSS, and SH; it is a minority form in RH, where it is used in the more formal registers of prayers and blessings, as well as in quotations or imitation of the Bible. The form אָנוּ dominates in RH and is also known from QH (approximately 20 ×). The form נחנו is found in Iron Age inscriptional Hebrew (Lachish 4.10–11) and possibly once in a highly fragmentary NBDSS text (2Q29 f1.2).

Beyond Hebrew, forms like אֲנַחְנוּ are found in Aramaic, Phoenician, and Neo-Assyrian and Neo-Babylonian; forms like נַחְנוּ are found in Arabic, Ethiopic, and Early and Middle Akkadian (Elitzur 2018a, 94).

---

[1] The apparent case in 2 Sam. 17.12 is wrongly included in some reference works, e.g., the Groves-Wheeler (1991–2016) electronic database. In view of the syntax, BDB (59b) correctly identifies the relevant form in the expression וְנַחְנוּ עָלָיו as a *weqaṭal* in the sense 'we will descend upon him' (see also Elitzur 2018a, 94, fn. 27).

2.0. Typology

The RH form אָנוּ is generally held to be a secondary, inner-Hebrew, development, based either on 1CS אֲנִי (e.g., Sáenz-Badillos 1993, 184; Fernández 1997, 18; Blau 2010, §4.2.2.6.1; see Hornkohl 2014a, 125. fns 58, 60 for further references) or the 1CPL object/possessive suffix (GKC §32d). There is debate among scholars as to the typological priority of אֲנַחְנוּ versus נַחְנוּ. According to one approach, נַחְנוּ is the primitive form, the initial *'alef* having been added on the basis of analogy to the 1CS pronouns אֲנִי and אָנֹכִי (e.g., JM §39a Blau 2010, §4.2.2.6.1; see Hornkohl 2014a, 125. fn. 53, and Elitzur 2918a, 94, for further references). This is in agreement with Hetzron's (1976) principle of archaic heterogeneity. Others (e.g., Harris 1939, 78–79; Kutscher 1982, §42) think the form beginning with *'alef* the earlier of the two, the loss of the initial glottal stop attributable to that consonant's weakness.

3.0. Interpreting the Data

The distributional evidence and typological considerations arguably point to נַחְנוּ as an archaic form. Table 1 (facing page) presents the distribution of נַחְנוּ and אֲנַחְנוּ within the principal sections in Tiberian BH. As evidence of the antiquity of the form without *'alef*, JM (§39a) notes that נַחְנוּ appears four times in the Pentateuch. Its documentation in Iron Age Hebrew epigraphy is also significant. Conversely, its appearance in TBH Lamentations should not be considered diachronically diagnostic, because the form without *'alef* was needed there for purposes of the acrostic.

Table 1: Incidence of נַחְנוּ and אֲנַחְנוּ within the principal sections in Tiberian BH

	אֲנַחְנוּ	נַחְנוּ
Torah	28	4
Former Prophets	32	0
Latter Prophets	19	0
Non-LBH Writings	11	1
LBH	31	0

Regarding the situation in the Pentateuch—standard אֲנַחְנוּ dominates. Elitzur (2018a, 94) observes that נַחְנוּ is restricted in the Torah to quoted speech within narrative, though it is important to note that even in such quotations, standard אֲנַחְנוּ is more common. Even if נַחְנוּ is typologically more ancient that אֲנַחְנוּ, in terms of ancient Hebrew diachrony, both forms appear to have been available for usage in CBH. Further, linguistic development was such that, according to the historical snapshot offered by CBH texts, it is clear that ostensibly secondary אֲנַחְנוּ had become established as the standard form. The form נַחְנוּ can in no way be classified as characteristic of any form of CBH, whether of the Torah or of the relevant Prophets and Writings. The most that can be said is that the CBH of the Tiberian Torah uniquely preserves the typologically archaic form נַחְנוּ, with no trace of it in the rest of CBH or, for that matter, in the combined written-reading Samaritan tradition of the BH of the Torah, where all forms of the 1CPL independent subject pronoun are standard אנחנו ā̊nā̊nnu.

As in the case of additional features discussed in this volume, one must question the historical depth of the distinction between the Tiberian Torah and the rest of Tiberian CBH. Is the restriction of the employment of typologically archaic נַחְנוּ in the Torah against its absence in the rest of CBH authentic, or might נַחְנוּ have once occurred elsewhere in CBH, but have been levelled in compositional and/or transmissional processes? The textual evidence is insufficient to point decisively one way or the other.[2]

The source critical situation is presented in Table 2.

Table 2: Incidence of נַחְנוּ and אֲנַחְנוּ according to purported Pentateuchal sources (per Friedman 1989, 246–55)[3]

	נַחְנוּ	אֲנַחְנוּ
J	1	17
E	0	3
P	3	3
Dtr¹	0	4
Other	0	1

Assuming the correctness of the theory that נַחְנוּ is typologically and diachronically prior to אֲנַחְנוּ, it is interesting that all purported Pentateuchal sources exhibit usage of standard אֲנַחְנוּ, that use of נַחְנוּ is shared by both J and P, and that P, of all sources, exhibits the usage profile most consistent with preservation of archaic usage.

---

[2] Elitzur (2018a, 93–94) discusses two further distinctive Pentateuchal forms: הָאֵל for הָאֵלֶּה 'these' and כֶּשֶׂב for כֶּבֶשׂ 'sheep'. As these have no clear typological priority vis-à-vis their standard alternants, however, they are merely noted here.

[3] נַחְנוּ—Gen. 42.11 (J); Exod. 16.7 (P), 8 (P); Num. 32.32 (P); אֲנַחְנוּ—Gen. 13.8 (J); 19.13 (J); 29.4 (J); 37.7 (J); 42.11 (J), 13 (J), 21 (E), 31, (J), 32 (J); 43.8 (J), 18 (E); 44.9 (J), 16 (J); 46.34 (J); 47.3 (J), 19 (J), 19 (J); Exod. 10.26 (E); Num. 9.7 (P); 10.29 (J); 20.4 (P), 16 (J); 32.17 (P); Deut. 1.28 (Dtr¹), 41 (Dtr¹); 5.3 (Dtr¹), 25 (Dtr¹); 12.8 (Other).

PART II:
VARIATION LIMITED TO THE WRITTEN COMPONENT OF THE TIBERIAN BIBLICAL TRADITION

8. FS הוא VERSUS היא

The dominant written form of the FS independent subject pronoun across ancient Hebrew sources and traditions is היא(ה). Its pronunciation in Tiberian is *hī*, in Samaritan *ī*. These data are in line with broader Semitic evidence. From this perspective, the written component of the Tiberian tradition of the Pentateuch represents a conspicuous outlier. Whereas the combined Tiberian written-reading tradition in the MT Prophets and Writings routinely exhibits the unified orthographic-vocalic form הִיא (in 282 of 291 cases), in the Torah such unity is rare (just 18 of 212 cases). Instead of הִיא, standard outside the Pentateuch and in ancient Hebrew more generally, the 3FS independent pronoun in the Tiberian Torah is most of the time written הוא, but consistently pointed and read as a *qere perpetuum* as הִיא.[1]

Two questions call for answers. First, how to explain the anomalous spelling הוא for 3FS referents in the written component of the Tiberian Torah? Second, how to account for the fact

---

[1] The figures above include four occasions in the Hebrew Bible where readers are explicitly instructed via the *ketiv-qere* mechanism to read FS הִיא where MS הוא is written (Deut. 13.6; 1 Kgs 17.15; Isa. 30.33; Job 31.11) and five further cases in which the *ketiv-qere* gives the opposite instruction, namely, to read MS הוּא for written FS היא (1 Kgs 17.15; Ps. 73.16; Job 31.11; Qoh. 5.8; 1 Chron. 29.16). Thus, 1 Kgs 17.15 and Job 31.11 each involve both changes. The figures should be taken as representative, but scholars differ on their counts. Throughout the MT, written-reading agreement on הִיא comes in approximately 300 of 500 instances.

that the distribution of the anomaly is limited to the written component of the Tiberian Torah?

1.0. Explanations for the Spelling הוא with 3FS Referents

Broadly speaking, explanations for the routine written-reading mismatch in the Tiberian Pentateuch come in two types: graphic and linguistic.

1.1. Graphic Explanations

According to a well-rehearsed argument in favour of a graphic origin for the phenomenon, the written component of the Tiberian Torah is said to go back to a manuscript characterised by defective spelling, where the 3MS and 3FS independent subject pronouns shared the written form הא.[2] Subsequently, either *mater waw* was mechanically inserted, even where הא represented the 3FS independent pronoun, or formerly distinctive *waw*s and *yod*s became too similar to distinguish (as seen in some DSS manuscripts) and were uniformly copied as *waw*s. No attempt was made to correct the anomalous forms out of respect for the sanctity of the Pentateuch (for various renditions of the proposed course of events, see GKC §32l; Cross 1998, 222–23; JM §39c).

Of course, these explanations leave several nagging questions unanswered, especially the matter of why only in the word היא 'she', and in no other word, the *yod* was consistently mistaken

---

[2] Defective spellings of the 3MS form are found in Iron Age epigraphy, e.g., Arad 18.10, 12; Kuntillet ʿAjrud 9.1; Lachish 21.5; Meshaʿ (*KAI* 181) 6, 21; Deir ʿAlla (*KAI* 312) 1.

for a *waw*. Fassberg (2012, 171–72) also observes that such a mechanical graphic account fails to explain the Masoretic Pentateuch's 18 exceptions in which the written and reading traditions agree on FS הִיא.

1.2. Linguistic Explanations

Linguistic explanations also come in different flavours.

1.2.1. An Epicene 3CS Independent Subject Pronoun

One linguistic proposal is that the written component of the Tiberian Torah preserves an otherwise undocumented epicene 3CS pronoun ה(ו)א *hū*, which the corresponding reading tradition brought into line with the more standard convention of distinct 3MS and 3FS forms, as elsewhere in the Tiberian tradition and in ancient Hebrew more generally (Green 1872, 96; Lambert 1931, 35, fn. 3; Rendsburg 1982; Tropper 2001; Morgenstern 2007, 49–50; Elitzur 2018a, 84–88). Difficulties with this approach include (a) absence of the alleged feature outside the written component of the Tiberian Pentateuch; (b) a distinction between 3MS and 3FS morphology throughout BH grammar, including that reflected in the written component of the Tiberian Pentateuch; and (c) a distinction between 3MS and 3FS morphology in the Semitic languages more broadly.[3]

---

[3] Distinctions in masculine and feminine inflectional morphology are not necessarily matched by gender distinction in pronouns. My friend and colleague Geoffrey Khan notes (personal communication) that in many NENA dialects the gender distinction has been lost in pronouns, but not in inflection.

1.2.2. Variant 3FS Morphology

If, as argued above, arguments focusing on graphic confusion and epicene morphology are to be rejected, then a different sort of linguistic explanation must be sought. One such approach has been explored by Cohen (2007, 113–15), with further support supplied by Fassberg (2012). According to this view, the הוא spelling common to the 3MS and 3FS independent subject pronouns in the written component of the Tiberian Torah reflects distinct morphological forms, respectively, 3MS *huʾa > *huwa or *hūw and 3FS *hiʾa > *hiwa or *hīw, which in the corresponding Pentateuchal reading tradition, and the Masoretic biblical reading tradition more generally, shortened to hū and hī, respectively. While limitations inherent in the extant data make it impossible to prove such a proposal, the approach is consistent with several facts. First and foremost, it makes sense of the otherwise anomalous 3FS spelling הוא in the written component of the Tiberian Torah. Moreover, it is not incompatible with the minority DSS spelling היאה, which can be viewed as the explicit *plene* spelling of a comparatively archaic form (Qimron 1986, 57–58; 2018, 261–62; cf. Kutscher 1974, 433–34). In positing the contemporaneous use of two allomorphs of the 3FS independent subject pronoun, it also comprehends diversity seen more generally in BH pronominal morphology. Finally, if the Pentateuchal written tradition's occasional use of standard FS היא in face of dominant FS הוא is in any way indicative of the degree of its use, its agreement with the dominant hī realisation of the Tiberian reading component of the Torah is reminiscent of the relationship between other dissonant written and reading features, involving the levelling of disparate features in favour of early alternants, sometimes even via the extension of minority options, in agreement with Second Temple conventions.

Before proceeding, however, it is worth pausing to consider potential complications in the suggested approach. According to the development of the 3FS independent subject pronoun hypothesised by Cohen (2007, 114–15), at some point *hiʾa* developed to *hiwa*. Yet, as Fassberg (2012, 175, fn. 13) notes, this is hardly the expected phonological development, a *y* glide being expected contiguous to an *i*-vowel, as in Arabic هِيَ. If a realisation such as *hiwa* or *hiw* (Fassberg 2012, 177) stands behind the spelling of FS הוא in the Tiberian Torah, then perhaps the unexpected shift of *hiʾa* to *hiw(a)* came about due to analogical pressure from the corresponding—and more common—3MS form, where the development *huʾa* to *huwa* is expected. Here it is worth noting the tendency in the Semitic languages to simplify contrastive morphology between opposing masculine and feminine forms via analogy, such that forms formerly distinguished by multiple features are ultimately distinguished by fewer or just one, e.g., Proto-Semitic 2MPL *-tum(u)* and 2FPL *-tin(n)(a)* developing in Hebrew to *-tɛm* and *-tɛn*, respectively (with a similar reduction in distinguishing features in other Semitic languages, too).

As to development of the putative realisation *hiw(a)*—according to Fassberg (2012, 177), FS הוא in the written component of the Tiberian Pentateuch may conceivably reflect the realisation *hū*—due not to original epicene morphology, but to phonetic neutralisation along the lines of *hiwʾa* > *hiwa* > *hiw* > *hū*. Alternatively, *hiwʾa* may have eventually developed the standard 3FS realisation *hī*.⁴ For while the diphthong *iw* most commonly resolves to *ū* in ancient Hebrew, the alternative development to *ī* is not unknown (Blau 2010, 97, §3.4.3.3).

2.0. Interpreting the Data

Whatever the correct explanation for FS הוא in the Tiberian Pentateuch—whether due to graphic or linguistic factors—the phenomenon raises a series of additional questions. Why the distinction between the Tiberian Torah's written component and the testimony of all other ancient Hebrew witnesses? Why the distinction between the written component of the Tiberian Torah and the combined written-reading tradition of the rest of the Tiberian Bible? Why the apparent distinction between the written component of the Tiberian Torah and the Tiberian Torah's corresponding vocalisation component? What, if any, diachronic ramifications are there?

If the phenomenon in question is purely graphic, there are several potential diachronic implications. It has been demonstrated that the books of the Tiberian Torah share a particularly defective orthography vis-à-vis the rest of the Tiberian Bible (Andersen and Forbes 1986, 285, 313–14; below, ch. 12). While the spelling הא is no longer characteristic of Tiberian manuscripts, the assumption that it might once have been is not inconsistent with the relatively defective orthography of extant Tiberian exemplars. Whether such הא spellings were once more common in

---

⁴ The extant Tiberian realisation הִוא *hī* differs from **hiw*, the latter presupposing the Tiberian pointing הִוְא; cf. שָׁוְא 'vanity, falseness, emptiness'.

the Prophets and Writings cannot be determined. One might contend that the apparent conflation of הוא and היא in the Pentateuch—in contrast with their rather consistent distinction in the rest of the Bible—is evidence that the *mater* was added to originally defective spelling in the Pentateuch, but was organic in the Prophets and Writings. But this is simplistic. It is just as possible that defective הא was formerly common throughout the biblical text, that an indistinct *mater* was secondarily added throughout, but that only in the Pentateuch was anomalous FS הוא preserved due to the Torah's early crystallisation and perceived sanctity. In the rest of the Bible, conversely, scribes may have felt freer to correct the text in line with standard usage. Nothing can be said with any certainty.

The possible diachronic import of the linguistic alternatives is also extremely speculative and complicated. The proposal of an epicene 3CS independent subject pronoun הוא has been rejected above. But entertaining its acceptance for the sake of argument, the distinction between the written component of the Torah, on the one hand, and the reading component of the Torah together with the combined written and reading tradition of the rest of the Bible, on the other, would presumably be explained according to one of two scenarios. The Torah's written component uniquely preserves unconventional morphology either because its traditions alone actually date to a time when that morphology was in use or because a once more common morphology has been specially preserved in the written component of the Torah, while it was superseded by later, more conventional morphology in the Torah's reading tradition and in the combined written-reading tradition of the Prophets and Writings.

On the Masoretic Pentateuch's 18 exceptions in which its written and reading traditions agree on FS הִיא—while any mechanical graphic explanation cannot account for these, the linguistic alternatives are only marginally more successful. The random distribution of the lot, found scattered among purported sources in Genesis–Numbers (see below, end of this section), belies any simplistic source-critical explanation.[5] The most compelling suggestion would be that these exceptions reflect early penetrations, whether primary or secondary, of standard 3FS pronominal into the Torah's anomalous majority 3FS pronominal morphology. In the case of many other features discussed in this volume, the CBH_1 of the Torah is distinct from non-Pentateuchal CBH_2, but includes a minority of features standard in CBH_2.

The preferred explanation here, that MS and FS הוא in the written component of the Tiberian Torah reflect the distinct pronunciations *hu(wa)* and *hiw(a)*, respectively, raises some of the same, and more complicated, diachronic possibilities. On the basis of Fassberg's (2012, 175–77) critique of Cohen's (2007, 113–15) theory, Hornkohl (2023, 168) has sketched the schematisation of various paths of development for the 3FS independent subject pronoun in ancient Hebrew, as seen in Figure 1 (facing page).

---

[5] Gen. 14.2; 19.20; 20.5; 26.7; 38.25; 40.10; Exod. 1.16; Lev. 5.11; 11.39; 13.6, 10, 21; 16.31; 20.17, 18; 21.9; Num. 5.13, 14.

Figure 1: Reconstructed developmental paths for the 3FS independent subject pronoun in ancient Hebrew

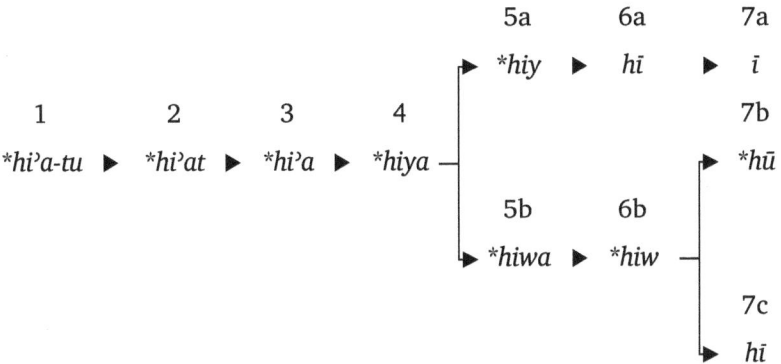

From a typological perspective, perhaps the most significant point to observe is that the realisations proposed as underlying the written and reading components of the Tiberian Torah, namely, *hiwa and *hiy, each represent developments from the single conjectural form *hiya. If diachrony comes into the picture, it would involve the possible secondary levelling of a once more diverse situation in accordance with a later situation of uniformity. Perhaps the 3FS realisation *hiw(a) and the corresponding spelling הוא were once found more commonly in the pre-Tiberian Bible, i.e., beyond the Pentateuch, but were brought into conformity with Second Temple linguistic conventions in the CBH Prophets and Writings, and preserved only in the Pentateuch, thanks to its early consolidation and revered status.

While all the explanations entertained above are possible, none can be considered more than conjecture. Given the dearth and nature of the evidence, such conjecture is useful—even necessary—for attempting to construct narratives that explain the relevant facts. From this perspective, the explanation proposing synchronic allomorphs is arguably more plausible than the respective alternative explanations assuming graphic confusion or an epicene pronoun. Whatever the case may be, all theories are compatible with arguments that account for the difference between the written and reading components of the Tiberian Torah and for the affinity between the reading component of the Tiberian Torah and the combined written-reading tradition of Tiberian CBH Prophets and Writings.

Finally, it is worth noting that the distribution in the Pentateuch of majority FS הוא and minority FS היא is not a function of putative source, as the incidence of both forms cuts across the sources.

9. FPL ן- VERSUS -נָה

Across ancient Hebrew sources and traditions, the dominant form of the FPL verbal suffix is vowel-final -נָה.[1] In terms of biblical material, this is true of the written and reading components of both the Tiberian biblical tradition and the SP, as well as of BDSS manuscripts. Beyond biblical sources, it is also true of QH and the Mishna (see Hornkohl 2023, 171–81 for further references and discussion). A minority alternative is orthographically consonant-final ן-. At issue in the present chapter is the character and biblical distribution of this minority form within the Masoretic tradition, which is often arguably levelled in the Tiberian pronunciation tradition via the apparently secondary addition of a final vowel, resulting in the anomalously defective vowel-final graphic combination ןָ-. Both forms plausibly derive from PS -*na* (cf. Arabic).

In terms of frequency, the prefix conjugation (*yiqtol*, *wayyiqtol*) is the only category for which meaningful patterns may be perceived and, as such, is the focus of the present chapter. The FPL imperative and the infinitive construct with 3FPL suffix occur too infrequently for the detection of distributions of any significance. Nor are their respective patterns of incidence sufficient materially to alter conclusions based on the distribution of the prefix conjugation.

---

[1] See Blau (2010, 203–4, §§4.3.3.1.2n–4.3.3.2.1n) on the ancient Hebrew FPL endings in the broader comparative Semitic context.

1.0. The Combined Tiberian Biblical Tradition

Hornkohl (2023, 172) presents the following tabulation of FPL prefix conjugation forms in the Tiberian biblical tradition (according to L).

Table 1: Distribution of 2/3FPL prefix conjugation forms in Tiberian BH (see Hornkohl 2023, 179, for citations)

	־נָה	־ןֶ	־ן		־נָה	־ןֶ	־ן
Genesis	15	1	12	Obadiah	1	0	0
Exodus	7	0	11	Jonah	0	0	0
Leviticus	10	0	0	Micah	4	0	0
Numbers	11	0	1	Zechariah	9	0	1
Deuteronomy	1	0	2	Malachi	1	0	0
Joshua	3	0	0	Psalms	20	0	0
Judges	5	0	0	Job	12	0	0
Samuel	15	0	3	Proverbs	10	0	0
Kings	8	0	0	Ruth	16	0	0
Isaiah	37	0	0	Song of Songs	1	0	0
Jeremiah	29	0	0	Lamentations	3	0	0
Ezekiel	58	0	7	Esther	2	0	0
Hosea	4	0	0	Daniel	4	0	0
Joel	1	0	0	Nehemiah	1	0	0
Amos	3	0	0	Chronicles	4	0	0
				TOTAL	295	0	1

Several facts emerge from the statistics. First, vowel-final orthography and pronunciation dominate, with a comparatively small minority of consonant-final spellings and a lone instance where consonant-final pronunciation coincides with consonant-final spelling in the form of ־ןֶ. Notwithstanding the extant Masoretic vocalisation, it is reasonable to speculate that consonant-final orthography implies formerly more frequent consonant-final pronunciation (more on this below).

Second, consonant-final spellings are not evenly distributed throughout the biblical text. Instances of FPL prefix conjugation forms terminating in ן- accumulate appreciably in the Pentateuch, where they account for more than a third of the cases, i.e., 27 of 71. Indeed, the Torah accounts for over 70 percent of the 38 cases of FPL prefix conjugation forms ending in ן- in the Masoretic Hebrew Bible.

Within the Pentateuch the distribution is uneven. Consonant-final forms are common in Genesis (13 of 28 cases) and dominant in Exodus (11 of 18), and, though few, also in Deuteronomy (2 of 3); in these books the ratio of נָה- to ן- is 23 to 25. By contrast, consonant-final spellings are absent from Leviticus (out of 10 cases) and nearly so in Numbers (1 of 12).

Beyond the Pentateuch, consonant-final forms are rare, accounting for just 11 of the 224 cases of FPL prefix conjugation forms. They are found in just three loci. In Samuel, one-sixth of the 18 cases show ן-, while Ezekiel, with more FPL prefix conjugation forms than any other book, has an incidence of just over 1 in 10 (7 of 65), which is similar to Zechariah's 1 in 10.

2.0. The Pentateuch

The conspicuous concentration of FPL ן- in the Pentateuch, especially Genesis, Exodus, and Deuteronomy, is remarkable. The absence of ן- forms in Leviticus might lead one to assume that the distribution of נה- versus ן- is, perhaps at least in part, a function of putative source. As Table 2 shows, the data seem to point in a different direction.

Table 2: FPL prefix conjugation forms with -נה and -ן according to reputed source (identification of sources according to Friedman 1989, 246–55; for citations, see below, §5.0, Table 4)

	-נה	-ן
J	9	10
E	13	8
P	21	6
DTR[1]	1	1
Other	0	1
	44	26

All sources with more than a single case of each alternant show some degree of mixing of vowel- and consonant-final FPL prefix conjugation morphology. In J and E the figures for both forms are significant. For its part, P shows definite preference for -נה, though consistently has -ן in Genesis–Exodus and -נה in Leviticus–Numbers. If the purported sources showing mixed usage were at one time more consistent in this regard, or if P in Leviticus and Numbers once showed greater heterogeneity, is impossible to determine, as original tendencies may well have become blurred in the processes of redaction and transmission.

In this connection, it is worth mentioning that individual sections show a mixture of forms (even if reflecting a single putative source): Gen. 19 (J): 2 -נה, 2 -ן; 41 (E): 9 -נה, 2 -ן. Consider the combination of forms in the following short spans.[2]

---

[2] Beyond the Pentateuch, note also the mixture of forms in 1 Sam. 18.7; Ezek. 16.55.

(1) וַיַּצֵּג אֶת־הַמַּקְלוֹת אֲשֶׁר פִּצֵּל בָּרְהָטִים בְּשִׁקֲתוֹת הַמָּיִם אֲשֶׁר תָּבֹאןָ הַצֹּאן
לִשְׁתּוֹת לְנֹכַח הַצֹּאן וַיֵּחַמְנָה בְּבֹאָן לִשְׁתּוֹת: וַיֶּחֱמוּ הַצֹּאן אֶל־הַמַּקְלוֹת
וַתֵּלַדְןָ הַצֹּאן עֲקֻדִּים נְקֻדִּים וּטְלֻאִים:

'He set the sticks that he had peeled in front of the flocks in the troughs, that is, the watering places, where the flocks would come to drink. And since they bred when they came to drink, the flocks bred in front of the sticks and so the flocks brought forth striped, speckled, and spotted.' (Gen. 30.38–39 [J])

(2) וְהִנֵּה אֲנַחְנוּ מְאַלְּמִים אֲלֻמִּים בְּתוֹךְ הַשָּׂדֶה וְהִנֵּה קָמָה אֲלֻמָּתִי וְגַם־נִצָּבָה
וְהִנֵּה תְסֻבֶּינָה אֲלֻמֹּתֵיכֶם וַתִּשְׁתַּחֲוֶיןָ לַאֲלֻמָּתִי:

'Behold, we were binding sheaves in the field, and behold, my sheaf arose and stood upright. And behold, your sheaves gathered around it and bowed down to my sheaf.' (Gen. 37.7 [J])

As Barr (1989, 127–30) observes, most of the verbs in question occur too infrequently in FPL forms to extrapolate much from their incidence. The exception is הָיָה 'be', with 44 cases total. In the Torah, the ratio of -נה to -ן is 11 to 9; elsewhere it is 19 to 5. This is in line with the observation made above regarding the uniqueness of the Torah in evincing forms with -ן. It is no surprise that the most commonly occurring verb is the one that most frequently preserves irregularity.[3]

Finally, no obvious phonological or prosodic factor governing the selection between alternants is apparent.

---

[3] In this connection it is worth mentioning that all cases of -ן in P, which, again, are restricted to Genesis–Exodus, involve the verb הָיָה (6 ×). By contrast, in Leviticus, P has only the -נה form of הָיָה (2 ×).

3.0. Orthographic versus Linguistic Explanations

As in other cases of apparently defective spelling of final $\bar{a}$-vowels—most notably, 2MS verbal ת- and nominal ךָ- (see Hornkohl 2023, 101–44) and נער with feminine singular referent (see below, ch. 9)[4]—though the phenomenon is explicable in purely orthographic terms, the combined Tiberian written-reading tradition furnishes evidence of pronunciation diversity supportive of a morphological, i.e., linguistic, explanation.

Standard feminine plural morphology in BH comes in both vowel- and consonant-final alternatives. Consult Table 3.

Table 3: FPL morphological variety in Tiberian Biblical Hebrew[5]

	-נה	־ן
2FPL independent pronoun	4	1
3FPL independent pronoun	48	—
2FPL nominal suffix (affixed to noun/preposition)	4	14
3FPL nominal suffix (affixed to noun/preposition)	68	180
2FPL suffix on infinitive construct	—	1
3FPL suffix on infinitive construct	4	6
3FPL suffix on verb (finite or participle)	—	9
FPL imperative	17	5

In a few categories, Masoretic BH exhibits no morphological variety, but in many there seems to have been some degree of diversity or fluctuation. Intriguingly, in all the above categories,

---

[4] Hornkohl (2023, 103, fn. 3) also lists the 3FS object/possessive suffix יָהּ-, e.g., אֵלֶיהָ 'to her', not *אֵלֶיהָה, and the *ketiv* עת with *qere* עַתָּה 'now' (Ezek. 23.43; Ps. 74.6); cf. the consistent form עת in Iron Age Hebrew epigraphy (Arad; Lachish; Murabbaʿat).

[5] Cf. also the problematic 2FPL וְהִשְׁלַכְתֶּנָה (Amos 4.3).

the written and pronunciation components of the tradition are in harmony, agreeing on vowel- or consonant-final morphology, with no indication of dissonance between spelling and vocalisation.

In this context of FPL morphology, the endings of the prefix conjugations stand out. According to the pronunciation tradition, just a single case—the poetic תִּהְיֶיןָ 'they will be' (Gen. 49.26)—is consonant-final. All other cases of consonant-final orthography are pointed ןָ-, i.e., as vowel-final, in opposition to the consonant-final realisation expected of the written form. Yet the anomalous character of this spelling for final $\bar{a}$, for which a *mater heh* is expected (and most often present), coupled with the known oscillation between vowel- and consonant-final FPL morphology more broadly, almost certainly points to a phonological distinction behind the orthographic diversity (Andersen and Forbes 1986, 180–81; Barr 1989, 130–31; Hornkohl 2023, 174). The view adopted here is that the spelling נה- reflects vowel-final realisation and that the spelling ן- originally reflected consonant-final realisation. In line with Second Temple convention, however, the realisation of ן- was almost universally levelled for purposes of linguistic harmonisation with the dominant vowel-final alternative, thereby creating the consonantal-vocalic dissonance preserved in the anomalous ןָ- of the extant combined Tiberian written-reading tradition. The consonant-final ending of poetic תִּהְיֶיןָ 'they will be' (Gen. 49.26) was presumably left as is due to its embedding in archaic poetry, where non-standard morphology was more readily tolerated.

4.0. Interpreting the Data

Vowel- and consonant-final variation in FPL morphology seems to be an ancient feature in Hebrew and the Semitic languages, more broadly (Blau 2010, 203–4, §§4.3.3.1.2n–4.3.3.2.1n). As noted above, each can be derived from PS -*nā*. As such, both the -נה and -ן FPL prefix conjugation morphological alternants may be considered early. By contrast, based on Second Temple biblical and extrabiblical evidence, there is no doubt that vowel-final prefix conjugation (and imperatival) forms eventually came to dominate as standard. With just a few exceptions, this is seen in the combined Samaritan written-reading tradition, the BDSS, Jerome's Latin transcriptions, Ben Sira, the QH of the NBDSS, and RH (Hornkohl 2023, 174–77).

It is, then, reasonable to postulate a situation of early diversity in FPL prefix conjugation morphology that gradually gave way to standardisation of vowel-final forms. The difference between the consonantal and vocalic components of the Tiberian tradition can be interpreted as a result of the manifestation of distinct phases in this process, with the orthography preserving an earlier phase of diversity and the vocalisation showing later extension of vowel-final morphology. From this perspective, it is not surprising that Tiberian LBH evinces total agreement between its constituent written and reading components, or that the consonant-final form is comparatively rare in TBH Ezekiel and Zechariah. The preservation of a mixed picture of vowel- and apparent consonant-final morphology in the Torah, with a sizeable minority of FPL ן- endings, along with the rather smaller minority in Samuel, also fits with the proposed theory.

The diachronic development as described does not, however, explain every fact. What of CBH texts that contain FPL prefix conjugation forms, but eschew completely the use of consonant-final morphology? And, especially, why such a dichotomy between the CBH of the Torah and the CBH of the relevant works in the Prophets and Writings when it comes to the preservation of consonant-final FPL morphology? While in any situation of viable alternants language users may consistently opt for one over the other—as in Leviticus and Numbers in the Torah (though in the Torah, too, there may be a degree of secondary blurring)—one wonders whether the nearly homogenous use of FPL נָה- in the CBH Prophets and Writings is authentic. It is possible—though neither provable nor disprovable—that the lop-sided preference for vowel-final נה- in CBH outside the Torah is artificial, the result of the secondary imposition of post-exilic morphological norms on an Iron Age II situation that otherwise, as in the Torah, would have shown greater morphological diversity. For its part, the Torah may have better preserved ancient heterogeneity by dint of its relatively early consolidation and perceived sanctity. While this account is by no means certain or, for that matter, even necessary, the hypothesised textual preservation of primary, diachronically authentic, data combined with secondary features variably applied within the biblical corpus, explains the diachronically complex dichotomy involving FPL prefix conjugation morphology in the CBH of the Tiberian Pentateuch and beyond.

5.0. Appendix

Table 4: FPL Prefix Conjugation Forms in the Tiberian Pentateuch According to Putative Source (per Friedman 1989, 246–55)

	-נה	-ן
Genesis	3.7 וַתִּפָּקַ֫חְנָה (J)	
		19.33 וַתַּשְׁקֶ֫יןָ (J)
		35 וַתַּשְׁקֶ֫יןָ (J)
		36 וַתַּהֲרֶ֫יןָ (J)
	24.61 וַתִּרְכַּ֫בְנָה (J)	
	61 וַתֵּלַ֫כְנָה (J)	
		26.35 וַתִּהְיֶ֫יןָ (P)
		27.1 וַתִּכְהֶ֫יןָ (J)
	30.38 וַיֵּחַ֫מְנָה (J)	30.38 תָּבֹ֫אןָ (J)
		39 וַתֵּלַ֫דְןָ (J)
	31.14 וַתֹּאמַ֫רְנָה (E)	
		33.6 וַתִּגַּ֫שְׁןָ (E)
		6 וַתִּשְׁתַּחֲוֶ֫יןָ (E)
	37.7 וַתִּשְׁתַּחֲוֶ֫יןָ (J)	37.7 תְסֻבֶּ֫יןָה (J)
	41.2 וַתִּרְעֶ֫יןָה (E)	
	3 וַתַּעֲמֹ֫דְנָה (E)	
	4 וַתֹּאכַ֫לְנָה (E)	
	7 וַתִּבְלַ֫עְןָה (E)	
	18 וַתִּרְעֶ֫יןָה (E)	
	20 וַתֹּאכַ֫לְנָה (E)	
	21 וַתָּבֹ֫אןָה (E)	
		41.24 וַתִּבְלַ֫עְןָ (E)
		36 תִּהְיֶ֫יןָ (E)
	53 וַתִּכְלֶ֫יןָה (E)	
	54 וַתְּחִלֶּ֫יןָה (E)	
		49.26 תְּהִיֶ֫יןָ (J)
Exodus	1.10 תִקְרֶ֫אןָה (E)	
		1.17 וַתִּירֶ֫אןָ (E)
		18 וַתְּחַיֶּ֫יןָ (E)
		19 וַתֹּאמַ֫רְןָ (E)
	2.16 וַתָּבֹ֫אןָה (J)	
	16 וַתִּדְלֶ֫נָה (J)	

	16 וַתְּמַלֶּאנָה (J)	
	18 וַתָּבֹאנָה (J)	
		2.19 וַתֹּאמַרְןָ (J)
	8.5 תִּשָּׁאַרְנָה (E)	
	7 תִּשָּׁאַרְנָה (E)	
		15.20 וַתֵּצֶאןָ (E)
		25.27 תְּהְיֶיןָ (P)
		26.3 תִּהְיֶיןָ (P)
		27.2 תִּהְיֶיןָ (P)
		28.21 תִּהְיֶיןָ (P)
		21 תִּהְיֶיןָ (P)
Leviticus	4.2 תֶּעָשֶׂינָה (P)	
	13 תֵּעָשֶׂינָה (P)	
	22 תֵּעָשֶׂינָה (P)	
	27 תֵּעָשֶׂינָה (P)	
	5.17 תֵּעָשֶׂינָה (P)	
	7.30 תְּבִיאֶינָה (P)	
	10.19 וַתִּקְרֶאנָה (P)	
	23.15 תִּהְיֶינָה (P)	
	17 תִּהְיֶינָה (P)	
	17 תֵּאָפֶינָה (P)	
Numbers		25.2 וַתִּקְרֶאןָ (J)
	27.1 וַתִּקְרַבְנָה (P)	
	2 וַתַּעֲמֹדְנָה (P)	
	35.11 תִּהְיֶינָה (P)	
	13 תִּהְיֶינָה (P)	
	14 תִּהְיֶינָה (P)	
	15 תִּהְיֶינָה (P)	
	36.3 תִּהְיֶינָה (P)	
	4 תִּהְיֶינָה (P)	
	6 תִּהְיֶינָה (P)	
	6 תִּהְיֶינָה (P)	
	11 וַתִּהְיֶינָה (P)	
Deuteronomy	1.44 תַּעֲשֶׂינָה (DTR[1])	
		21.15 תִּהְיֶיןָ (Other)
		31.21 תִּמְצֶאןָ (DTR[1])

10. נער VERSUS נערה WITH FEMININE SINGULAR REFERENT

In most manifestations of ancient Hebrew, nouns with the root נע"ר and the basic meaning 'young male' and 'young female' are morphologically distinguished, e.g., Tiberian נַעַר and נַעֲרָה, the feminine bearing a dedicated feminine singular suffix. In the case of biblical material, this is true of the pronunciation component of the aforementioned Tiberian Masoretic tradition, the combined Samaritan written and pronunciation tradition, and BDSS material. Beyond biblical sources, the same distinction is made in QH, Ben Sira, and RH.

1.0. Dissonance in the Tiberian Torah

Partially exceptional in this connection is the written component of the Tiberian Masoretic tradition. While throughout the Prophets and the Writings—in CBH and LBH alike—the Tiberian written and reading components agree on the morphologically distinct feminine singular form נַעֲרָה, the written component of the Masoretic Pentateuch represents an outlier. Here, in 34 of the 35 instances where the tradition's pronunciation component prescribes reading נַעֲרָה, the written component is נער.[1]

---

[1] The information pertinent to MT is based on L. Notably, however, the tradition as reflected in L is confirmed by Talmudic discussions of the lone case of *plene* נַעֲרָה in Deut. 22.19 (y. Ketubbot 3.9 || y. Sanhedrin 7.11; b. Ketubbot 40b), over which considerable exegetical energy was expended.

Cases of FS (נער(ה are limited to three loci in the Pentateuch: Gen. 24; 34; Deut. 22. In the eight relevant cases in Genesis,[2] the written form נער is simply vocalised with a final -$\bar{a}$, as נַעֲרָ֫, with no explicit *ketiv-qere* guidance. From the perspective of its defective ending, i.e., lacking a final *mater heh*, it is a case of implicit *qere perpetuum*.

In 26 of the remaining 27 cases in the Torah, all in Deut. 22,[3] readers are explicitly instructed via the *ketiv-qere* mechanism—consisting of the consonant-vowel combination נַעֲרָ֫ within the main text and an accompanying marginal note with the consonants נערה—to pronounce vowel-final נַעֲרָה instead of the pronunciation one might naturally associate with written נער, i.e., נַעַר.

In just one instance in the Torah, the orthographic and pronunciation components of the tradition agree on morphologically feminine singular הַנַּעֲרָה 'the young woman' (Deut. 22.19). The uniqueness of this form within the Pentateuch receives overt acknowledgement in the Masoretic paratext via the marginal note לית מלא בתורה = ל׳ מל׳ בתור 'no other *plene* (spelling) in the Torah'.

The distribution of the various forms is not obviously a function of putative source, as all cases in Genesis belong to J, while all those in Deuteronomy belong to the Law Code ('Other', according to Friedman 1989, 246–55).

---

[2] Gen. 24.14 (J), 16 (J), 28 (J), 55 (J), 57 (J); 34.3 (J), 3 (J), 12 (J).

[3] Deut. 22.15 (Other), 15 (Other), 16 (Other), 20 (Other), 21 (Other), 23 (Other), 24 (Other), 25 (Other), 26 (Other), 26 (Other), 27 (Other), 28 (Other), 29 (Other).

2.0. Explanations

Two issues require clarification: first, the apparent dissonance between the written and vocalic components of the Tiberian Torah manifest in mismatched consonant-final spellings and vowel-final realisations; second, the resulting disparity between the Tiberian Torah, evincing the aforementioned dissonance, and the rest of the Tiberian Bible, where the written and reading components of the tradition are in agreement, and other ancient Hebrew sources. There are two basic approaches: orthographic and linguistic.

2.1. Orthography

One possibility is that the distinctions in question are purely orthographic, not linguistic, in nature. On this argument, Tiberian BH consistently reflects morphologically distinct masculine singular and feminine singular forms, but in most cases in the Torah the feminine singular is written with defective vowel-final orthography. Feminine singular נַעֲרָ is thus, it is argued, a case of *qere perpetuum* akin to other instances of final -$\bar{\mathring{a}}$ with no accompanying *mater heh*, thus resembling the minority 2/3FPL ending ןָ- (more commonly נָה-, but see above, ch. 9) and the majority 2MS endings ךָ- and תָ- (less commonly כָה- and תָה-) (GKC §17c; cf. Hornkohl 2023, 101–44). From the narrow perspective of the Torah, the spelling נער for a feminine singular referent cannot be considered anomalous, as this is by far the dominant spelling throughout the corpus.

If the dominant feminine singular written form נער in the Masoretic Torah is to be chalked up to spelling convention, the distinction between the Torah, on the one hand, and the Prophets and Writings, on the other, is also purely orthographic. The Torah might preserve archaic orthography, whereas the Prophets and Writings show more standard vowel-final orthography. Such spelling trends might have some diachronic significance, with the defective orthography considered characteristic of early texts and the *plene* of later texts, but it is important to acknowledge the possibility of secondary processes having profoundly blurred original spelling practices. For example, while it seems likely that the *plene* spelling of cases of נערה in Esther are authentic, perhaps cases in Judges were once spelled נער and only secondarily standardised in conformity with late spelling practices. By the same token, perhaps early cases of Pentateuchal נער with feminine singular reference were preserved, while certain cases of נערה in the Torah were secondarily shortened under the influence of the majority form נער there—though the existence of a lone *plene* form נַעֲרָה in the Torah at Deut. 22.19 seems to militate against the notion of wholesale secondary harmonisation in the Tiberian written component of the Pentateuch.

Summing up the potential diachronic significance of the orthographic explanation, a plausible hypothesis is that the written component of the Masoretic Torah reflects archaic spelling conventions. While these conventions may also have been operative in extra-Pentateuchal CBH texts, they have been superseded by the more standard spelling with final *mater heh*, probably due to secondary scribal intervention. If CBH texts beyond the Torah ever knew the defective vowel-final orthography, the difference between them and the Torah, i.e., preservation of the defective vowel-final orthography in the Torah and secondary imposition of the standard *plene* vowel-final orthography elsewhere in CBH, is probably due to the relatively early literary unification of the Torah and to special reverence, whereby its orthography became fixed earlier than that of the rest of BH, including other CBH material.

Notwithstanding what has been said, a compelling argument against a fundamentally orthographic explanation for נער with a feminine singular referent in the Torah lies precisely in its oddness. From the broader perspective of the entire Masoretic Bible, as well as other biblical traditions and extrabiblical ancient Hebrew sources, the defective spelling of the -*ā̊* suffix in any feminine singular form is anomalous in the extreme. Why are there not more feminine substantives with defective -*ā̊* suffixes?

2.2. Language

A more reasonable proposal is that the distinction between the Tiberian Torah's written form נער for a feminine singular referent and נערה elsewhere in Tiberian BH, and in every other ancient Hebrew tradition and source, is linguistic in character. If so, then the written and reading components of the Tiberian biblical tradition in the Torah reflect slightly dissonant manifestations of Hebrew.

The basic idea here is that the Tiberian Torah's written component preserves a form of ancient Hebrew with an epicene lexeme נער in the gender-neutral sense of 'young person'. The usage is often compared to Greek ὁ παῖς 'the child (M)' versus ἡ παῖς 'the child (F)' (cf. English *baby*, *infant*, *child*, *adolescent*, *youth*, *teenager*). While many BH terms for pre-adults have distinct masculine and feminine forms, many (apparently) do not, employing unmarked morphology generally associated with masculine gender, e.g., זֶרַע 'seed', גָּמוּל 'weaned', יוֹנֵק 'nursing child', עוּל 'nursing child', עוֹלֵל 'child', עוֹלָל 'child', וָלָד 'child', טַף 'children'. Perhaps ancient Hebrew נער was also early on a member of this morphologically ungendered category and only later developed distinct feminine singular morphology (Gesenius 1815, 162; Elitzur 2018a, 84–86).

Against the proposal of an epicene understanding of נער, one might raise the matter of feminine morphosyntactic agreement. In nearly every case of consonantal נער where the referent is feminine, there obtains feminine agreement with a finite verbal form, participle, adjective, or pronoun. Clearly, even if נער with a feminine singular referent might lack feminine morphology, it was construed as grammatically feminine. Yet, this is not an insurmountable difficulty for the proposal, as several BH lexemes that lack feminine morphology and normally trigger masculine agreement can receive feminine morphosyntactic treatment with feminine referents, e.g., דֹּב 'bear' (2 Kgs 2.24; Isa. 11.17), גָּמָל 'camel' (Gen. 32.16), בָּקָר 'cattle' (Gen. 33.13; Job 1.14). Cf. also the use of the morphologically masculine plural אֱלֹהִים 'gods' for the feminine singular referent עַשְׁתֹּרֶת 'Ashtoret' (1 Kgs 11.5) (JM §§134c–d). Thus, morphosyntactic feminine agreement does not fatally contradict the hypothesis that נער may once have been gender neutral.

Potential counterevidence of a different sort is the existence of unequivocal feminine plural forms alongside allegedly epicene נער. While written נער seems to serve for both genders in the

Torah when the referent is singular, with just one exceptional case of written נערה, arguable support for early gender distinction may be seen in the occurrence of gender-distinct plural forms in the Torah. The apparent gender-flexible character of masculine plural נערים, with both generic (Exod. 10.9) and strictly masculine (Gen. 14.24; 22.3, 5, 19; 25.27; 48.16; Exod. 24.5; Num. 22.22) referents, is unsurprisingly. More significant is the feminine plural—does not feminine plural נְעָרוֹת presuppose the existence of a corresponding dedicated feminine singular נַעֲרָה? Conspicuously glaring in this connection is the use of feminine plural נְעָרֹת in Gen. 24.61, in a passage including five cases of consonantal נער with feminine singular reference; see also Exod. 2.5. Could semantics be a determining factor? The dedicated feminine plural form in Gen. 24.61 has the secondary meaning 'female servants', in contrast to the preceding feminine singular forms, which have the more basic sense of 'young woman'. The same sense of female servant also applies to the only other feminine plural form in the Torah, at Exod. 2.5. These few cases are intriguing, but ultimately insufficient as evidence. One can only speculate that early epicene נערים-נער secondarily developed feminine plural נערות, from which, in turn, dedicated feminine singular נערה was possibly back-formed.

3.0. Interpreting the Data

Whether נער with feminine singular referent is best interpreted as an orthographic or linguistic phenomenon, the distinction between the CBH of the Torah, with נער, and the CBH of the Prophets and Writings, with נערה, demands an explanation. Perhaps the most straightforward argument would centre on the antiquity of the Patriarchal and Mosaic traditions. Notwithstanding the composite nature of the extant Torah (as represented in various Hebrew traditions and ancient translations) and the date it reached its basic formation, the content in some fashion reflects pre-monarchic times. It is not too farfetched to hypothesise that the language, too, might preserve pre-monarchic features.

Several pertinent considerations must be mentioned. First, while such a view is not necessarily at odds with the still-influential Graf-Wellhausen and similar source-critical approaches, it obviously must engage with them, especially with claims that large sections of the Torah were written in the exilic or post-exilic period. Crucial as evidence in this regard is the linguistic contrast between acknowledged post-exilic Hebrew material and all purported Pentateuchal sources. Persian and Hellenistic Period writings consistently exhibit concentrations of diagnostically late linguistic features uncharacteristic of any part of the Pentateuch, where the language, despite a degree of diversity, is thoroughly classical.

On the other hand, the chronolect of the Pentateuch is by and large the same as that of the CBH Prophets and Writings. According to a simple view of biblical historiography, this is to be expected for the books of Joshua and Judges, which also purport to recount pre-monarchic history, and perhaps also for Samuel, which deals with the origins of the monarchy, but one might expect the obvious emergence of a later chronolect or sub-chronolect in Kings and the pre-exilic Latter Prophets, much of which material deals with the period of the divided monarchy.

While the preservation of old language as part of ancient traditions may be a decisive factor in the subdivision of CBH into earlier and later substrata, it is inadequate to explain both the extensive diachronic similarity of all CBH material and the distribution of the specific linguistic features examined in the present monograph, which sometimes extend beyond the confines of the Pentateuch (e.g., certain features of the pre-monarchic onomasticon), but often exhibit patterns that clearly distinguish the Pentateuch from the rest of CBH.

As in other cases, perhaps the best approach is to interpret the extant evidence as a combination of both primary ancient features and secondary developments. According to one version of such an approach, CBH sources in general—Torah, Prophets, and Writings—may once have been more widely characterised by cases of נער with feminine singular referent, perhaps alongside more innovative נערה, and in the course of compilation, redaction, and/or transmission during the Second Temple period or thereafter, cases of נער with feminine singular referent in the CBH Prophets and Writings were standardised in line with contemporary, i.e., post-exilic, conventions. Due to its early consolidation and revered status, the Torah, by contrast, largely escaped the secondary levelling processes applied to the rest of CBH. This does not preclude the possibility of the late addition of brief insertions to the CBH corpus. If material was added to CBH material—Torah, Prophets, or Writings—these would likely have been adapted to the prevailing norms of the section in question—נער in the Torah, נערה elsewhere. Against this, the difficulty of successful late imitation of classical style, even in short additions, should not be ignored (see above, Introduction, §5.0).

11. ABSTRACT NOUNS ENDING IN *-ŪT*

Elitzur (2018a, 88–92) presents an interesting discussion on a distinction between the Pentateuch and the rest of the Bible when it comes to abstract nouns ending in *-ūt*. Basing his analysis on König (1895–1897 2/1, 205–6), but excluding words with vowel-final base forms, e.g., בָּרוּת, כְּסוּת, פְּדוּת—in which cases the *ū* is a part of the root and the ending is actually *-t*—Elitzur (2018a, 88 and fn. 15) observes:

> Abstract nouns ending in *-ūt* are rare in the Pentateuch and are usually written defectively, without *waw*, whereas in the Prophets/Writings they are frequent and are generally spelled plene, with *waw*.... Note, however, that a final stressed *ū* vowel, which is not in the construct state or declined, is also usually written plene in the Pentateuch. Nevertheless, in the instances examined here, the spelling is defective.

He then provides a table showing that the relevant absolute forms of the lexemes גַּבְלֻת 'twistedness', כְּבֵדֻת 'heaviness', כְּרִיתֻת 'divorce', מִסְכְּנֻת 'storage', עֵדֻת 'testimony', צְמִ(י)תֻת 'perpetuity', קוֹמְמִיּוּת 'erectness', and שְׂרִ(י)רוּת 'rebelliousness' come 45 times in the Torah and are written with defective *-ūt* in 35 of those cases.[1] These and other nouns ending in *-ūt* come some 115 times outside the Torah and are written *plene* on 114 of those occasions. The obvious question is whether the regularity of defective spelling

---

[1] The ten cases of *plene -ūt* involve קוֹמְמִיּוּת (1×) and שְׂרִ(י)רוּת (9×). Elitzur (2018a, 89) notes only one case of כְּרִיתֻת in the Torah, but this should be corrected to two.

of the suffix in the Pentateuch is to be explained as due to mismatch between the written and reading components. In other words, does the rarity of *plene* -*ūt* in the Pentateuch imply that a significant portion of the words with defective -*ūt* originally ended in a different suffix, so that the realisation -*ūt* was secondarily imposed under the influence of later linguistic norms? Elitzur (2018a, 90, fn. 19) raises several possibilities as to the nature of the alternative ending, without committing himself to any of them.

1.0. Diachrony

The use of nouns ending in -*ūt* is commonly seen as especially characteristic of post-exilic forms of ancient Hebrew (see, e.g., Hornkohl 2011, 161, fn. 763, and the references there). Cohen (2012, 371–73) problematises this characterisation, noting, among other things, comparable numbers of lexemes in the Torah and LBH. Elitzur (2018a, 90, fn. 17) accepts Cohen's view, arguing that

> [t]he source of the error is the failure to distinguish between the different lexemes in counting the occurrences; the many occurrences of the lexeme מַלְכוּת in the late biblical books tipped the balance. The use of the word מַלְכוּת is one of the characteristic features of LBH, apparently under the influence of Aramaic.

Yet, Cohen's methodology is open to question. It is not clear that counting lexemes is sufficient. The example of מַלְכוּת itself (on which see Hornkohl 2014a, 318–25; Hurvitz 2014, 165–70) shows that one must also be sensitive to the frequency of tokens of given lexemes, especially as the LBH corpus is far smaller than that of either the Pentateuch or non-Pentateuchal CBH. The prevalence of nouns in -*ūt* in Aramaic and RH is also a factor to be given due weight in discussions of the diachronic character of the ending in BH. Finally, if the lexemes under discussion in this chapter are deemed to be words that end in a suffix other than -*ūt*, this would obviously reduce the number of CBH cases of words with that ending. For example, the lone ostensible form of characteristically post-exilic מַלְכוּת in the Torah is in the Oracles of Balaam in Num. 24.7, the language of which is considered by several scholars ABH (see Mandell 2013, 325). Though the lexeme's diagnostic lateness is not necessarily contradicted by sporadic early usage (Hornkohl 2014a, 6, fn. 15), it is interesting to note that the specific form מלכתו in Num. 24.7 is written defectively, opening up the possibility that it was intended to reflect מַלְכָתוֹ rather than מַלְכֻתוֹ.[2]

2.0. Interpreting the Data

There is no denying the orthographic distinctiveness of the absolute forms of the nine -*ūt*-final lexemes, both within the Torah and within the Hebrew Bible. As Elitzur (2018a, 88) observes based on Barr (1989, 113–14), stressed *u*-vowels in closed syllables in absolute and undeclined forms are normally written *plene* in the Tiberian Torah, specifically, and in Tiberian BH, more generally. Moreover, the same ending is nearly always written *plene* outside the Torah.

The question is whether this glaring distinction is merely orthographic in nature or reflects diverse morphology. If it is

---

[2] I thank my friend and colleague Ben Kantor for this observation.

even partially linguistic, then some portion of the cases would be explicable as instances of alternative endings secondarily interpreted as words ending in *-ūt* in conformity to more standard, and possibly later, Hebrew. It is, of course, also possible that defective spellings of the *-ūt* ending were also once more frequent in CBH beyond the Torah, and only secondarily became *plene* in the process of textual growth and transmission.

Some evidence for the possible orthographic character of the distinction between the Torah and the Prophets and Writings comes in the minority *plene* spelling of עֵדוּת 'testimony' (27 × defective in the Torah; 8 × *plene*) and in the *plene* spellings of קוֹמְמִיּוּת 'erectness' (1 ×) and שְׁרִ(י)רוּת 'rebelliousness' (1 ×) in the Tiberian Pentateuch. If these are early *plene* spellings, or at least *plene* spellings in line with early pronunciation, then they confirm the possibility of *-ūt* forms in the Torah. Of course, they in no way necessitate the *-ūt* interpretation of defectively spelled forms in the Torah. Also, it is not impossible that their *plene* spelling is itself secondary, early evidence of reinterpretation of the morphology in line with a different, presumably later, morphological system, which the reading tradition reflected in the vocalisation only extended.

Due to the nature of the evidence, little can be said with certainty. The Tiberian Torah certainly exhibits archaism in this regard, but it is unclear whether the archaism in question is merely orthographic or morphological.

Source-critically, most occurrences of *-ūt* lexemes in the Torah come in P (38 of 45). Of these, most spellings are defective (29 of 38). The other sources show incidence as follows: E (1 defective); R (1 defective); Dtr¹ (2 of 3 defective); Other (2 defective). The relevant citations per Friedman (1989, 246–55) are:

גְּבֻלֹת—defective: Exod. 28.22 (P); 39.15 (P); כְּבֵדָת—defective: Exod. 14.25 (E); כְּרִיתֻת—defective: Deut. 24.1 (Other), 3 (Other); מִסְכֵּנָת—defective: Deut. 8.9 (Dtr¹); עֵדָת—defective: Exod. 16.34 (P); 25.16 (P), 21 (P), 22 (P); 26.34 (P); 27.21 (P); 30.6 (P), 6 (P), 26 (P), 36 (P); 31.7 (P), 18 (P); 32.15 (E); 34.29 (P); 38.21 (P); 39.35 (P); 40.5 (P), 20 (P); Lev. 24.3 (P); Num. 1.50 (P), 53 (P); 4.5 (P); 7.89 (P); 9.15 (R); 10.11 (P); 17.22 (P); 18.2 (P); *plene*: Exod. 26.33 (P); 40.3 (P), 21 (P); Lev. 16.13 (P); Num. 1.53 (P); 17.19 (P), 23 (P), 25 (P); צְמִ(י)תֻת—defective: Lev. 25.23 (P), 30 (P); קוֹמְמִיּוּת—*plene*: Lev. 26.13 (P); שְׁרִירוּת—*plene*: Deut. 29.18 (Dtr¹)

If -*ūt* endings are especially characteristic of later forms of ancient Hebrew, their accumulation in the Torah in P may be significant. The apparent significance of this fact is tempered, though, by the frequency of עֵדָ(ו)ת, accounting for 35 of the 45 occurrences in the Torah and 35 of the 38 in P, as well as by the appearance of nouns ending in -*ūt* in other purported Pentateuchal sources.

12. ORTHOGRAPHY

In each of the eleven foregoing chapters, it has been argued that inner-CBH distinctiveness separating the CBH of the Tiberian Torah from extra-Pentateuchal CBH may be linguistic and diachronic in nature. Chs 1–7 dealt with features on which the written and reading components of the combined Tiberian tradition agree on such distinctiveness. Chs 8–11 focused on distinction only as far as the written component is concerned, the pronunciation component smoothing out distinctions in conformity to the combined Masoretic biblical written-pronunciation standard outside the Pentateuch. In other words, the features discussed in chs 8–11 involve apparent dissonance between the written and pronunciation components in the Torah, while the two components are in sync in regard to the relevant features in the rest of the Masoretic Bible.

There is, of course, an alternative view. One may view the features discussed in chs 8–11 as instances of purely orthographic, rather than linguistic, peculiarity. In that case, FS הוא, the feminine plural *yiqṭol* suffix ־ן, and נער with a feminine singular referent are to be considered linguistically identical to their respective forms as written and vocalised in the MT beyond the Torah, the difference being restricted to the level of their written representation (consisting of consonants plus *matres lectionis*). While the inaccessibility of the full phonological reality behind such written forms makes a purely orthographic explanation for such features in the Torah impossible either to prove or to disprove, the broad context of the discussions above—coming after chs 1–7, in which mere orthographic explanations are inadequate to account for the diversity—favours a linguistic rather than orthographic explanation.

This does not, however, mean that the orthography of the Masoretic Pentateuch should be considered unremarkable in the context of that of the rest of the Bible, in general, and of CBH, more specifically. Indeed, the overall defective nature of the Torah's orthography is distinctive within the MT. The significance of this fact may be questioned. For while meaningful correlations between orthography and chronology can be drawn—defective spelling customs chronologically preceding *plene* spelling customs—the reality of secondary developments in the spelling of the relevant Tiberian biblical evidence raises doubts as to its authenticity and reliability, i.e., to the depth of its historical testimony. The question boils down to whether meaningful early data can be perceived among the noise of secondary developments.

1.0. The Development of Ancient Hebrew Spelling

The spelling in the earliest uncontested Hebrew texts is most compellingly interpreted as largely defective in terms of medial vowels and *plene* in terms of final vowels (Zevit 1980 traces the development). Several apparent instances of *plene* medial vowels may be explained as diphthongs or as historical spellings thereof, e.g., בעוד 'while still' (Siloam l. 2), מוצא 'spring' (Siloam l. 5), whereas several apparent cases of word-final defective vowels are explicable as non-Tiberian consonant-final variants, עת 'now' (Arad 2.1; 3.1; 18.3; 40.4; Lachish 2.3, 3; 3.4; 4.1, 2), הית 'there was (FS)' (Siloam l. 3), והנ 'and behold' (Arad 40.9). Bona fide word-medial *plene* spellings include ארור 'cursed' (Silwan tomb l. 2), איש 'man' (Arad 40.7, 8), הברית 'the covenant' (Ketef Ḥinnom 1.4), והפקידמ 'and you will commit them into the charge (Arad 24.14–15), להעיד 'to warn' (Arad 24.18), טוב 'good' (Lachish 4.2).

No text in the Masoretic Bible is characterised by spelling conventions as regularly defective as those of the Iron Age Hebrew inscriptions. Contrast, for example, the consistent medial defectiveness of the nominal plural endings ־ם -*im* and ־ת -*ot* in the inscriptions with their regular *plene* orthography in all BH evidence. This means either that the earliest biblical texts were written later than the inscriptions or, alternatively, that their orthography, once more defective, was updated over the course of their literary and textual development and transmission.

Evidence for the latter alternative is forthcoming from several DSS versions of biblical texts. Whereas most biblical manuscripts from Qumran and other sites in the Judaean Desert are characterised by orthography as *plene* as, if not more *plene* than, that of the MT, a few manuscripts exhibit consistently more defective orthography. It is reasonable to interpret these as offering a slightly earlier snapshot of the biblical spelling tradition than that seen in the Tiberian tradition.

1.1. Pre-Tiberian Orthography

1.1.1. 4QDeuteronomy[d] (4Q31)

4QDeut[d] (4Q31) presents a version of Deut. 2.24–36 and 3.14–4.1 textually approximate to MT Deuteronomy, with plusses of את in 4QDeut[d] 1.6 || MT Deut. 2.25 and of על in 4QDeut[d] 2.17 || MT Deut. 3.27 and a minus of ו- in 4QDeut[d] 2.2 || MT Deut. 3.15.

The most conspicuous difference between the two is orthographic. While both texts utilise final and medial *matres lectionis*, and while the texts frequently exhibit defective and *plene* spellings in the same places, on the thirteen occasions where they differ, it is 4QDeut[d] that consistently presents the more defective spelling, apparently preserving a typologically earlier orthographic portrait than that exhibited in MT Deuteronomy.

4QDeut[d] (4Q31) 1.5–17 [link] || MT Deut. 2.24–36

5	את סיחן מלך חשבון האמרי ואת ארצו החל רש והתגר בו מלחמה היום הזה
25–24	...אֶת־סִיחֹן מֶלֶךְ־חֶשְׁבּוֹן הָאֱמֹרִי וְאֶת־אַרְצוֹ הָחֵל רָשׁ וְהִתְגָּר בּוֹ מִלְחָמָה: הַיּוֹם הַזֶּה
6	אחל תת פחדך ויראתך על פני העמים תחת כל השמים אשר ישמעון את שמעך
25	אָחֵל תֵּת פַּחְדְּךָ וְיִרְאָתְךָ עַל־פְּנֵי הָעַמִּים תַּחַת כָּל־הַשָּׁמָיִם אֲשֶׁר יִשְׁמְעוּן שִׁמְעֲךָ
7	ורגזו וחלו מפניך ואשלחה מלאכים ממדבר קדמת אל סיחון מלך חשבון דברי שלום
26–25	וְרָגְזוּ וְחָלוּ מִפָּנֶיךָ: וָאֶשְׁלַח מַלְאָכִים מִמִּדְבַּר קְדֵמוֹת אֶל־סִיחוֹן מֶלֶךְ חֶשְׁבּוֹן דִּבְרֵי שָׁלוֹם
8	לאמר אעברה בארצך בדרך בדרך אלך לא אסור ימין ושמאל אכל בכסף
28–26	לֵאמֹר: אֶעְבְּרָה בְאַרְצֶךָ בַּדֶּרֶךְ בַּדֶּרֶךְ אֵלֵךְ לֹא אָסוּר יָמִין וּשְׂמֹאול: אֹכֶל בַּכֶּסֶף
9	תשברני ואכלתי ומים בכסף תתן לי ושתיתי רק אעברה ברגלי כאשר עשו לי
29–28	תַּשְׁבִּרֵנִי וְאָכַלְתִּי וּמַיִם בַּכֶּסֶף תִּתֶּן־לִי וְשָׁתִיתִי רַק אֶעְבְּרָה בְרַגְלָי: כַּאֲשֶׁר עָשׂוּ־לִי
10	בני עשו הישבים בשעיר והמואבים הישבים בער עד אשר אעבר את הירדן
29	בְּנֵי עֵשָׂו הַיֹּשְׁבִים בְּשֵׂעִיר וְהַמּוֹאָבִים הַיֹּשְׁבִים בְּעָר עַד אֲשֶׁר־אֶעֱבֹר אֶת־הַיַּרְדֵּן
11	אל הארץ אשר יהוה אלהינו נתן לנו ולא אבה סיחן מלך חשבון העברנו בו כי
30–29	אֶל־הָאָרֶץ אֲשֶׁר־יְהוָה אֱלֹהֵינוּ נֹתֵן לָנוּ: וְלֹא אָבָה סִיחֹן מֶלֶךְ חֶשְׁבּוֹן הַעֲבִרֵנוּ בּוֹ כִּי־
12	הקשה יהוה אלהיך את רוחו ואמץ את לבבו למען תתו בידך כיום הזה ויאמר
31–30	הִקְשָׁה יְהוָה אֱלֹהֶיךָ אֶת־רוּחוֹ וְאִמֵּץ אֶת־לְבָבוֹ לְמַעַן תִּתּוֹ בְיָדְךָ כַּיּוֹם הַזֶּה: וַיֹּאמֶר
13	יהוה אלי ראה החלתי תת לפניך את סיחן ואת ארצו החל רש לרשת את ארצו
31	יְהוָה אֵלַי רְאֵה הַחִלֹּתִי תֵּת לְפָנֶיךָ אֶת־סִיחֹן וְאֶת־אַרְצוֹ הָחֵל רָשׁ לָרֶשֶׁת אֶת־אַרְצוֹ:
14	ויצא סיחן לקראתנו הוא וכל עמו למלחמה יהצה ויתנהו יהוה אלהינו לפנינו
33–32	וַיֵּצֵא סִיחֹן לִקְרָאתֵנוּ הוּא וְכָל־עַמּוֹ לַמִּלְחָמָה יָהְצָה: וַיִּתְּנֵהוּ יְהוָה אֱלֹהֵינוּ לְפָנֵינוּ
15	ונך אתו ואת בנו ואת כל עמו ונלכד את כל עריו בעת ההוא ונחרם את כל
34–33	וַנַּךְ אֹתוֹ וְאֶת־בָּנָיו וְאֶת־כָּל־עַמּוֹ: וַנִּלְכֹּד אֶת־כָּל־עָרָיו בָּעֵת הַהִוא וַנַּחֲרֵם אֶת־כָּל־
16	עיר מתם והנשים והטף לא השארנו שריד רק הבהמה בזנו לנו ושלל הערים
35–34	עִיר מְתִם וְהַנָּשִׁים וְהַטָּף לֹא הִשְׁאַרְנוּ שָׂרִיד: רַק הַבְּהֵמָה בָּזַזְנוּ לָנוּ וּשְׁלַל הֶעָרִים
17	אשר לכדנו מערער אשר על שפת נחל ארנן והעיר אשר בנחל ועד הגלעד לא היתה
36–35	אֲשֶׁר לָכָדְנוּ: מֵעֲרֹעֵר אֲשֶׁר עַל־שְׂפַת־נַחַל אַרְנֹן וְהָעִיר אֲשֶׁר בַּנַּחַל וְעַד־הַגִּלְעָד לֹא הָיְתָה

4QDeutᵈ (4Q31) 2.1–21 ‖ MT Deut 3.14–4.1

1 גבול הגשורי והמעכתי ויקרא אתם על שמו את הבשן חות יאיר עד היום הזה
14 גְּב֣וּל הַגְּשׁוּרִ֔י וְהַמַּֽעֲכָתִ֑י וַיִּקְרָ֨א אֹתָ֤ם עַל־שְׁמוֹ֙ אֶת־הַבָּשָׁ֔ן חַוֺּ֣ת יָאִ֔יר עַ֖ד הַיּ֥וֹם הַזֶּֽה׃

2 ולמכיר נתתי את הגלעד   ולראובני ולגדי נתתי מן הגלעד   עד נחל ארנן
15-16 וּלְמָכִ֖יר נָתַ֣תִּי אֶת־הַגִּלְעָ֑ד׃ וְלָרֻֽאוּבֵנִ֣י וְלַגָּדִ֗י נָתַ֜תִּי מִן־הַגִּלְעָ֣ד וְעַד־נַ֣חַל אַרְנֹ֗ן

3 תוך הנחל וגבל ועד יבק הנחל גבול בני עמון. והערבה והירדן וגבל
16-17 תּ֤וֹךְ הַנַּ֙חַל֙ וּגְבֻ֔ל וְעַד֙ יַבֹּ֣ק הַנַּ֔חַל גְּב֖וּל בְּנֵ֣י עַמּֽוֹן׃ וְהָ֣עֲרָבָ֔ה וְהַיַּרְדֵּ֖ן וּגְבֻ֑ל

4 מכנרת ועד ים הערבה ים המלח תחת אשדת הפסגה מזרחה   ואצו אתכם
17-18 מִכִּנֶּ֗רֶת וְעַ֨ד יָ֤ם הָֽעֲרָבָה֙ יָ֣ם הַמֶּ֔לַח תַּ֖חַת אַשְׁדֹּ֣ת הַפִּסְגָּ֑ה מִזְרָֽחָה׃ וָאֲצַ֥ו אֶתְכֶ֖ם

5 בעת ההיא לאמר יהוה אלהיכם נתן לכם את הארץ הזאת לרשתה חלצים
18 בָּעֵ֥ת הַהִ֖וא לֵאמֹ֑ר יְהוָ֣ה אֱלֹֽהֵיכֶ֗ם נָתַ֨ן לָכֶ֜ם אֶת־הָאָ֤רֶץ הַזֹּאת֙ לְרִשְׁתָּ֔הּ חֲלוּצִ֣ים

6 תעברו לפני אחיכם בני ישראל כל בני חיל   רק נשיכם   טפכם ומקנכם ידעתי
18-19 תַּֽעַבְר֞וּ לִפְנֵ֣י אֲחֵיכֶ֗ם בְּנֵֽי־יִשְׂרָאֵ֛ל כָּל־בְּנֵי־חָֽיִל׃ רַ֠ק נְשֵׁיכֶ֣ם וְטַפְּכֶם֮ וּמִקְנֵכֶם֒ יָדַ֕עְתִּי

7 כי מקנה רב לכם ישבו בעריכם אשר נתתי לכם   עד אשר יניח יהוה   לאחיכם
19-20 כִּֽי־מִקְנֶ֥ה רַ֖ב לָכֶ֑ם יֵֽשְׁבוּ֙ בְּעָ֣רֵיכֶ֔ם אֲשֶׁ֥ר נָתַ֖תִּי לָכֶֽם׃ עַ֠ד אֲשֶׁר־יָנִ֨יחַ יְהוָ֥ה ׀ לַֽאֲחֵיכֶם֮

8 ככם וירשו גם הם את הארץ אשר יהוה אלהיכם נתן להם בעבר הירדן
20 כָּכֶם֒ וְיָרְשׁ֣וּ גַם־הֵ֔ם אֶת־הָאָ֕רֶץ אֲשֶׁ֨ר יְהוָ֧ה אֱלֹֽהֵיכֶ֛ם נֹתֵ֥ן לָהֶ֖ם בְּעֵ֣בֶר הַיַּרְדֵּ֑ן

9 ושבתם איש לירשתו אשר נתתי לכם   ואת יהושע צויתי בעת ההיא
20-21 וְשַׁבְתֶּ֗ם אִ֚ישׁ לִֽירֻשָּׁת֔וֹ אֲשֶׁ֥ר נָתַ֖תִּי לָכֶֽם׃ וְאֶת־יְהוֹשׁ֣וּעַ צִוֵּ֔יתִי בָּעֵ֥ת הַהִ֖וא

10 לאמר עיניך הראת את כל אשר עשה יהוה אלהיכם לשני המלכים האלה
21 לֵאמֹ֑ר עֵינֶ֣יךָ הָרֹאֹ֗ת אֵת֩ כָּל־אֲשֶׁ֨ר עָשָׂ֜ה יְהוָ֤ה אֱלֹֽהֵיכֶם֙ לִשְׁנֵי֙ הַמְּלָכִ֣ים הָאֵ֔לֶּה

11 כן יעשה יהוה לכל הממלכת אשר אתה עבר שמה   לא תיראם כי יהוה
21-22 כֵּן־יַעֲשֶׂ֤ה יְהוָה֙ לְכָל־הַמַּמְלָכ֔וֹת אֲשֶׁ֥ר אַתָּ֛ה עֹבֵ֖ר שָֽׁמָּה׃ לֹ֖א תִּֽירָא֑וּם כִּ֚י יְהוָ֣ה

12 אלהיכם הוא הנלחם לכם   ואתחנן אל יהוה בעת ההיא לאמר   אדני
22-24 אֱלֹ֣הֵיכֶ֔ם ה֖וּא הַנִּלְחָ֥ם לָכֶֽם׃ ס וָאֶתְחַנַּ֖ן אֶל־יְהוָ֑ה בָּעֵ֥ת הַהִ֖וא לֵאמֹֽר׃ אֲדֹנָ֣י

13 יהוה אתה החלת להראת את עבדך את גדלך ואת ידך החזקה אשר
24 יְהוִ֗ה אַתָּ֤ה הַֽחִלּ֙וֹתָ֙ לְהַרְא֣וֹת אֶֽת־עַבְדְּךָ֔ אֶ֨ת־גָּדְלְךָ֔ וְאֶת־יָדְךָ֖ הַחֲזָקָ֑ה אֲשֶׁ֤ר

14 מי אל בשמים ¹בארץ אשר יעשה כמעשיך וכגבורתך   אעברה נא ואראה
24-25 מִי־אֵל֙ בַּשָּׁמַ֣יִם וּבָאָ֔רֶץ אֲשֶׁר־יַעֲשֶׂ֥ה כְמַעֲשֶׂ֖יךָ וְכִגְבוּרֹתֶֽךָ׃ אֶעְבְּרָה־נָּ֗א וְאֶרְאֶה֙

15 את הארץ הטבה אשר בעבר הירדן ההר הטוב הזה והלבנון   ויתעבד
25-26 אֶת־הָאָ֣רֶץ הַטּוֹבָ֔ה אֲשֶׁ֖ר בְּעֵ֣בֶר הַיַּרְדֵּ֑ן הָהָ֥ר הַטּ֛וֹב הַזֶּ֖ה וְהַלְּבָנֹֽן׃ וַיִּתְעַבֵּ֨ר

16 יהוה בי למענכם ולא שמע אלי ויאמר יהוה אלי רב לך אל תסף דבר
26 יְהוָ֥ה בִּי֙ לְמַ֣עַנְכֶ֔ם וְלֹ֥א שָׁמַ֖ע אֵלָ֑י וַיֹּ֨אמֶר יְהוָ֤ה אֵלַי֙ רַב־לָ֔ךְ אַל־תּ֥וֹסֶף דַּבֵּ֛ר

17 אלי עוד בדבר הזה   עלה על ראש הפסגה ושא עיניך ים   וצפנה ותימנה
26-27 אֵלַ֛י ע֖וֹד בַּדָּבָ֥ר הַזֶּֽה׃ עֲלֵ֣ה ׀ רֹ֣אשׁ הַפִּסְגָּ֗ה וְשָׂ֥א עֵינֶ֛יךָ יָ֥מָּה וְצָפֹ֖נָה וְתֵימָ֣נָה

18 ומזרחה וראה בעיניך כי לא תעבר את הירדן הזה   וצו את יהושע וחזקהו
27-28 וּמִזְרָ֖חָה וּרְאֵ֣ה בְעֵינֶ֑יךָ כִּי־לֹ֥א תַעֲבֹ֖ר אֶת־הַיַּרְדֵּ֥ן הַזֶּֽה׃ וְצַ֥ו אֶת־יְהוֹשֻׁ֖עַ וְחַזְּקֵ֥הוּ

19 וַאמצהו כי הוא יעבר לפנֹי העם הזה והוא ינחל אתם את הארץ אשר
28 וְאַמְּצֵהוּ כִּי־הוּא יַעֲבֹר לִפְנֵי הָעָם הַזֶּה וְהוּא יַנְחִיל אוֹתָם אֶת־הָאָרֶץ אֲשֶׁר

20 תראה   ונשב בגיא מול בית פעור
28-29 תִּרְאֶה: וַנֵּשֶׁב בַּגַּיְא מוּל בֵּית פְּעוֹר: פ

21 ועתה ישראל שמע אל החקים ואל המשפטים אשר אנכי מלמד אתכם לעשות.
4.1 וְעַתָּה יִשְׂרָאֵל שְׁמַע אֶל־הַחֻקִּים וְאֶל־הַמִּשְׁפָּטִים אֲשֶׁר אָנֹכִי מְלַמֵּד אֶתְכֶם לַעֲשׂוֹת

The orthographic discrepancies are collected in the Table below.

Table 1: Summary of orthographic discrepancies between 4QDeut[d] (4Q31) and MT Deuteronomy

DSS	MT	Gloss	4QDeut[d] (4Q31)	MT Deut.
קדמת	קְדֵמֹות	'Kedemoth'	1.7	2.26
סיחן	סִיחֹון	'Sihon'	1.7	2.26
ושמאל	וּשְׂמֹאול	'or left'	1.8	2.27
חלצים	חֲלוּצִים	'equipped'	2.5	3.18
יהושע	יְהֹושֻׁוּעַ	'Joshua'	2.9	3.21
הממלכת	הַמַּמְלָכֹות	'the kingdoms'	2.11	3.21
תיראם	תִּירָאוּם	'you will (not) fear them'	2.11	3.22
החלת	הַחִלֹּותָ	'you have begun'	2.13	3.24
להראת	לְהַרְאֹות	'to show'	2.13	3.24
הטבה	הַטֹּובָה	'the good'	2.15	3.25
תסף	תֹּוסֶף	'do (not) continue'	2.16	3.26
ינחל	יַנְחִיל	'he will give possession'	2.19	3.28
אתם	אֹותָם	'them'	2.19	3.28

1.1.2. 4QPalaeoJob^c (4Q101)

One of twelve DSS biblical scrolls written in palaeo-Hebrew script (see Tov 2004b, 246–48; 2012, 97, fn. 163, 123, 207), 4QPalaeo-Job^c (4Q101) is a highly fragmentary manuscript with a single textual difference vis-à-vis MT Job in ה[איחל] (f3.4) || אֲיַחֵל (MT Job 14.14). Beyond this, all differences are orthographic, with 4QPalaeoJob^c consistently exhibiting more defective spelling than L (see Seow 2011).

4QPalaeoJob^c (4Q101) f1–2.1–10 [link] || MT Job 13.18–27

אֹ֯י	1
הִנֵּה־נָ֤א עָרַ֣כְתִּי מִשְׁפָּ֑ט יָ֝דַ֗עְתִּי כִּי־אֲנִ֥י אֶצְדָּֽק׃	18
מי הוא ירב עמדי כי עתה אחריש ואגוע	2
מִֽי־ה֭וּא יָרִ֣יב עִמָּדִ֑י כִּֽי־עַתָּ֖ה אַחֲרִ֣ישׁ וְאֶגְוָֽע׃	19
אל תעש עמדי אז מפניך לא אסתר	3
אַךְ־שְׁ֭תַּיִם אַל־תַּ֣עַשׂ עִמָּדִ֑י אָ֝֗ז מִפָּנֶ֥יךָ לֹ֣א אֶסָּתֵֽר׃	20
	4
כַּ֭פְּךָ מֵעָלַ֣י הַרְחַ֑ק וְ֝אֵמָ֥תְךָ֗ אַֽל־תְּבַעֲתַֽנִּי׃	21
	5
וּ֭קְרָא וְאָנֹכִ֣י אֶעֱנֶ֑ה אֽוֹ־אֲ֝דַבֵּ֗ר וַהֲשִׁיבֵֽנִי׃	22
כמה לי עונות וחטאות פשעי וחטאתי הדעני	6
כַּמָּ֣ה לִ֭י עֲוֺנ֣וֹת וְחַטָּא֑וֹת פִּֽשְׁעִ֥י וְ֝חַטָּאתִ֗י הֹדִיעֵֽנִי׃	23
למה פניך תסתיר ותחשבני לאיב לך	7
לָֽמָּה־פָנֶ֥יךָ תַסְתִּ֑יר וְתַחְשְׁבֵ֖נִי לְאוֹיֵ֣ב לָֽךְ׃	24
העלה נדף תערוץ ואת קש יבש תרדף	8
הֶעָלֶ֣ה נִדָּ֣ף תַּעֲר֑וֹץ וְאֶת־קַ֖שׁ יָבֵ֣שׁ תִּרְדֹּֽף׃	25
כי תכתב עלי מררות ותרשני עונת נערי	9
כִּֽי־תִכְתֹּ֣ב עָלַ֣י מְרֹר֑וֹת וְ֝תוֹרִישֵׁ֗נִי עֲוֺנ֥וֹת נְעוּרָֽי׃	26
ותשם בסד רגלי ותשמור כל ארחתי	10
וְתָ֘שֵׂ֤ם בַּסַּ֨ד ׀ רַגְלַ֗י וְתִשְׁמ֥וֹר כָּל־אָרְחוֹתָ֑י עַל־שָׁרְשֵׁ֥י רַ֝גְלַ֗י תִּתְחַקֶּֽה׃	27

4QPalaeoJob^c (4Q101) f3.1–8 ‖ MT Job 14.13–18

¹ מי יתן בש̊אל תצפנני תסתירני עד שוב אפך
¹³ מִי יִתֵּן ׀ בִּשְׁאוֹל תַּצְפִּנֵנִי תַּסְתִּירֵנִי עַד־שׁוּב אַפֶּךָ

² תשית לי חק ותזכרני
תָּשִׁית לִי חֹק וְתִזְכְּרֵנִי׃

³ אם ימות גבר היחיה כל ימי צבאי
¹⁴ אִם־יָמוּת גֶּבֶר הֲיִחְיֶה כָּל־יְמֵי צְבָאִי

⁴ איחלה עד בא̇ חליפתי תקרא ואנכי אענך
¹⁵⁻¹⁴ אֲיַחֵל   עַד־בּ֗וֹא חֲלִיפָתִי׃ תִּקְרָא וְאָנֹכִי אֶעֱנֶךָּ

⁵ למ̇עשה ידיך תכסף כי
¹⁶⁻¹⁵ לְמַעֲשֵׂה יָדֶיךָ תִכְסֹף׃ כִּי־

⁶ עתה צעדי תספר לא תשמור על חטאתי
עַתָּה צְעָדַי תִּסְפּוֹר לֹא־תִשְׁמוֹר עַל־חַטָּאתִי׃

⁷ חתם̇ בצרר פשעי̇ ותספל על עוני
¹⁷ חָתֻם בִּצְרוֹר פִּשְׁעִי וַתִּטְפֹּל עַל־עֲוֺנִי׃

⁸ ואלם הר נפל יבול וצור יעתק ממקמו
¹⁸ וְאוּלָם הַר־נוֹפֵל יִבּוֹל וְצוּר יֶעְתַּק מִמְּקֹמוֹ׃

The orthographic discrepancies are collected in the Table below.

Table 2: Summary of orthographic discrepancies between 4QPaleoJob^c (4Q101) and MT Job

DSS	MT	Gloss	4QPaleoJob^c (4Q101)	MT Job
לאיב	לְאוֹיֵב	'as an enemy'	f1–2.7	13.24
עונת	עֲוֺנוֹת	'iniquities'	f1–2.9	13.26
נערי	נְעוּרָי	'my youth'	f1–2.9	13.26
ארחתי	אָרְחוֹתָי	'my paths'	f1–2.10	13.27
בא	בּוֹא	'coming of'	f3.4	14.14[1]
תספר	תִּסְפּוֹר	'(you) count'	f3.6	14.16
בצרר	בִּצְרוֹר	'in a bundle'	f3.7	14.17

[1] Seow (2011, 64–65) omits this example from his list of orthographic discrepancies between 4QPalaeoJob^c and MT Job.

Admitting that the fragmentary character of 4QPaleoJob^c (4Q101) leaves a great deal unknown, in the extant material it consistently presents more defective spelling than the relevant MT material.

See further on 4QSamuel^b (4Q52) in §2.0, below.

1.2. Proto-Tiberian Orthography

Along with evidence of pre-Tiberian biblical orthography characterised by comparatively early typological defectiveness, there is also Second Temple and late antique evidence of proto-Tiberian orthography, which is largely consistent with Tiberian orthography proper (as seen in L and A).

1.2.1. 1QIsaiah^b (1Q8)

Ulrich and Flint's (2010, II:200) comparison of MT Isaiah and 1QIsaiah^b (1Q8) determined there to be 161 cases of orthographic deviation and 622 individual textual variants (some consisting of several words). Even so, no diachronically meaningful pattern of distinction was detected. Indeed, most of the variants between these two editions of Isaiah mirror the frequent disagreements among the book's various Masoretic manuscripts, so that 1QIsa^b should be classified, in the words of its editors, "as belonging to the textual group that eventually emerges as the Masoretic family" (Ulrich and Flint 2010, II:200).

1QIsaiah^b (1Q8) 16.1–26 || MT Isaiah 38.11b–40.5^2

אביט אדם עוד עם־יושבי חדל דורי נסע ונגלה מני כאהל רעי קפדתי			1.16
אַבִּיט אָדָם עוֹד עִם־יוֹשְׁבֵי חָדֶל: ^{12} דּוֹרִי נִסַּע וְנִגְלָה מִנִּי כְּאֹהֶל רֹעִי קִפַּדְתִּי			12–11b.38
כארג חיי מדלה יבצעני מיום עד לילה תשלימני כסיס עגור כן אצפצף			2
כָּאֹרֵג חַיַּי מִדַּלָּה יְבַצְּעֵנִי מִיּוֹם עַד־לַיְלָה תַּשְׁלִימֵנִי: ^{14} כְּסוּס עָגוּר כֵּן אֲצַפְצֵף			14, 12
אהגה כיונה דלו עיני למרום יהוה חשקה לי ערבני מה אדבר ואמר לי והוא			3
אֶהְגֶּה כַּיּוֹנָה דַּלּוּ עֵינַי לַמָּרוֹם אֲדֹנָי עָשְׁקָה־לִּי עָרְבֵנִי: ^{15} מָה־אֲדַבֵּר וְאָמַר־לִי וְהוּא			15–14
עשה אדדה כל שנתי על מר נפשי אדני עליהם יחיו ולכל בהן חיי רוחי			4
עָשָׂה אֶדַּדֶּה כָל־שְׁנוֹתַי עַל־מַר נַפְשִׁי: ^{16} אֲדֹנָי עֲלֵיהֶם יִחְיוּ וּלְכָל־בָּהֶן חַיֵּי רוּחִי			15–16
ותחלימני והחיני הנה לשלום מר לי מר ואתה חשקת נפשי משחת ○לי כי השלכת			5
וְתַחֲלִימֵנִי וְהַחֲיֵנִי: ^{17} הִנֵּה לְשָׁלוֹם מַר־לִי מָר וְאַתָּה חָשַׁקְתָּ נַפְשִׁי מִשַּׁחַת בְּלִי כִּי הִשְׁלַכְתָּ			16–17
אחרי גוך כל חטאי כי לא שאול תועד מות יהללך לא ישברו בור אל			6
אַחֲרֵי גֵוְךָ כָּל־חֲטָאָי: ^{18} כִּי לֹא שְׁאוֹל תּוֹדֶךָּ מָוֶת יְהַלְלֶךָּ לֹא־יְשַׂבְּרוּ יוֹרְדֵי־בוֹר אֶל־			18–17
אמתך חי חי הוא יודך היום כמוני אב לבנים יודע אלה אמתך יהוה להשיעני			7
אֲמִתֶּךָ: ^{19} חַי חַי הוּא יוֹדֶךָ כָּמוֹנִי הַיּוֹם אָב לְבָנִים יוֹדִיעַ אֶל־ אֲמִתֶּךָ: ^{20} יְהוָה לְהוֹשִׁיעֵנִי			20–18
ונגנותי ננגן כל ימי חיינו על בית יהוה ויאמר ישעיהו ישאו דבלת תאנים			8
וּנְגִנוֹתַי נְנַגֵּן כָּל־יְמֵי חַיֵּינוּ עַל־בֵּית יְהוָה: ^{21} וַיֹּאמֶר יְשַׁעְיָהוּ יִשְׂאוּ דְּבֶלֶת תְּאֵנִים			21–20
וימרחו אל השחין ויחי ויאמר חזקיהו מה אות כי אעלה בית יהוה			9
וְיִמְרְחוּ עַל־הַשְּׁחִין וֶיֶחִי: ^{22} וַיֹּאמֶר חִזְקִיָּהוּ מָה אוֹת כִּי אֶעֱלֶה בֵּית יְהוָה: ס			22–21
			10
בעת ההוא שלח מרדך בלאדן בן בלאדן מלך בבל ספרים ומנחה אל חזקיהו			11
^{1} בָּעֵת הַהִוא שָׁלַח מְרֹדַךְ בַּלְאֲדָן בֶּן־בַּלְאֲדָן מֶלֶךְ־בָּבֶל סְפָרִים וּמִנְחָה אֶל־חִזְקִיָּהוּ			1
וישמע כי חלה ויחזק וישמח עליהם חזקיהו ויראם את בית נכתה את הכסף			12
וַיִּשְׁמַע כִּי חָלָה וַיֶּחֱזָק: ^{2} וַיִּשְׂמַח עֲלֵיהֶם חִזְקִיָּהוּ וַיַּרְאֵם אֶת־בֵּית נְכֹתוֹ [נכתה] אֶת־הַכֶּסֶף			2–1.39
ואת הזהב ואת הבשמים ואת השמן הטוב ואת כל בית כליו ואת כל אשר נמצא			13
וְאֶת־הַזָּהָב וְאֶת־הַבְּשָׂמִים וְאֵת הַשֶּׁמֶן הַטּוֹב וְאֵת כָּל־בֵּית כֵּלָיו וְאֵת כָּל־אֲשֶׁר נִמְצָא			2
באצרתיו לא היה דבר אשר לא הראם חזקיהו בביתו ובכל ממשלתו			14
בְּאֹצְרֹתָיו לֹא־הָיָה דָבָר אֲשֶׁר לֹא־הֶרְאָם חִזְקִיָּהוּ בְּבֵיתוֹ וּבְכָל־מֶמְשַׁלְתּוֹ:			2
ויבוא ישעיהו הנביא אל המלך חזקיהו ויאמר אליו מה אמרו האנשים			15
^{3} וַיָּבֹא יְשַׁעְיָהוּ הַנָּבִיא אֶל־הַמֶּלֶךְ חִזְקִיָּהוּ וַיֹּאמֶר אֵלָיו מָה אָמְרוּ ׀ הָאֲנָשִׁים			3
האלה ומאין יבאו אליך ויאמר חזקיהו מארץ רחוקה באו אלי מבבל ויאמר			16
הָאֵלֶּה וּמֵאַיִן יָבֹאוּ אֵלֶיךָ וַיֹּאמֶר חִזְקִיָּהוּ מֵאֶרֶץ רְחוֹקָה בָּאוּ אֵלַי מִבָּבֶל: ^{4} וַיֹּאמֶר			4–3
מה ראו בביתך ויאמר חזקיהו את כל אשר בביתי ראו לא היה דבר אשר לא			17
מָה רָאוּ בְּבֵיתֶךָ וַיֹּאמֶר חִזְקִיָּהוּ אֵת כָּל־אֲשֶׁר בְּבֵיתִי רָאוּ לֹא־הָיָה דָבָר אֲשֶׁר לֹא־			4
הראיתם באצר○○○○ ○○ ישעיהו אל חזקיהו שמע דבר יהוה צבאות הנה			18
הִרְאִיתִים בְּאוֹצְרֹתָי: ^{5} וַיֹּאמֶר יְשַׁעְיָהוּ אֶל־חִזְקִיָּהוּ שְׁמַע דְּבַר־יְהוָה צְבָאוֹת: ^{6} הִנֵּה			6–4
ימים באים ונשא כל אשר בביתך ואשר אצרו אבתיך עד היום הזה בבל			19
יָמִים בָּאִים וְנִשָּׂא ׀ כָּל־אֲשֶׁר בְּבֵיתֶךָ וַאֲשֶׁר אָצְרוּ אֲבֹתֶיךָ עַד־הַיּוֹם הַזֶּה בָּבֶל			6
לא יותר דבר אמר יהוה ומבניך אשר יצאו ממך אשר תוליד יקחו והיו סריסים			20

---

^{2} See Ulrich and Flint (2010, I:127, Plate LXII) for image.

לֹא־יִוָּתֵר דָּבָר אָמַר יְהוָה: 7 וּמִבָּנֶיךָ אֲשֶׁר יֵצְאוּ מִמְּךָ אֲשֶׁר תּוֹלִיד יִקָּחוּ וְהָיוּ סָרִיסִים	7-6	
בְּהֵיכַל מֶלֶךְ בבל וַֽיֹּאמֶר חִזְקִיָּהוּ אֶל יְשַׁעְיָהוּ טוֹב דְּבַר יהוה אשר דברת ויאמר	21	
בְּהֵיכַל מֶלֶךְ בָּבֶל: 8 וַיֹּאמֶר חִזְקִיָּהוּ אֶל־יְשַׁעְיָהוּ טוֹב דְּבַר־יְהוָה אֲשֶׁר דִּבַּרְתָּ וַיֹּאמֶר	8-7	
כי יהיה שלום ואמת בימי	22	
כִּי יִהְיֶה שָׁלוֹם וֶאֱמֶת בְּיָמָי: פ	8	
נחמו נחמו עמו יאמר אלהיכם דברו על לב ירושלם וקראו אליה כי מלא	23	
1 נַחֲמוּ נַחֲמוּ עַמִּי יֹאמַר אֱלֹהֵיכֶם: 2 דַּבְּרוּ עַל־לֵב יְרוּשָׁלִַם וְקִרְאוּ אֵלֶיהָ כִּי מָלְאָה	2-1.40	
צבאה כי נרצה עונה כי לקחה מיד יהוה כפלים בכל חטאתיה קול קורא במדבר	24	
צְבָאָהּ כִּי נִרְצָה עֲוֹנָהּ כִּי לָקְחָה מִיַּד יְהוָה כִּפְלַיִם בְּכָל־חַטֹּאתֶיהָ: ס 3 קוֹל קוֹרֵא בַּמִּדְבָּר	3-2	
פנו דרך יהוה ישרו בערבה מסלה לאלוהינו כל גיא ינשא וכל הר וגבעה ישפלו	25	
פַּנּוּ דֶּרֶךְ יְהוָה יַשְּׁרוּ בָּעֲרָבָה מְסִלָּה לֵאלֹהֵינוּ: 4 כָּל־גֶּיא יִנָּשֵׂא וְכָל־הַר וְגִבְעָה יִשְׁפָּלוּ	4-3	
והיה העקב למישור והרכסים לבקעה ונגלה כבוד יהוה וראו כל בשר יחדיו כי	26	
וְהָיָה הֶעָקֹב לְמִישׁוֹר וְהָרְכָסִים לְבִקְעָה: 5 וְנִגְלָה כְּבוֹד יְהוָה וְרָאוּ כָל־בָּשָׂר יַחְדָּו כִּי	5-4	

Table 3: Summary of *plene* versus defective orthographic discrepancies between 1QIsaiah[b] (1Q8) and MT Isaiah

DSS	MT	Gloss	1QIsaiah[b] (1Q8)	MT Isaiah
יודע	יוֹדִיעַ	'will make known'	16.7	38.19
להשיעני	לְהוֹשִׁיעֵנִי	'to save me'	16.7	38.20
ויבוא	וַיָּבֹא	'and he came'	16.15	39.3
הראיתם	הֶרְאִיתִם	'I have showed them'	16.18	39.4
ב͏אֹצרֹתי	בְּאוֹצְרֹתָי	'in my treasures'	16.18	39.4

Relative to MT Isaiah, 1QIsa[b] col. 16 presents just five orthographic discrepancies. In four of them, MT Isaiah exhibits the more *plene* spelling, while in the one case 1QIsa[b] has the fuller spelling.[3] These few instances of divergence pale in comparison

---

[3] Additional differences are כסוס (1QIsa[b] 16.2) || כְּסוּס (MT Isa. 38.14); יהוה (1QIsa[b] 16.3) || אֲדֹנָי (MT Isa. 38.14); חשקה (1QIsa[b] 16.3) || עָשְׁקָה (MT Isa. 38.14); היום כמוני (1QIsa[b] 16.7) || כָּמוֹנִי הַיּוֹם (MT Isa. 38.19); אלה (1QIsa[b] 16.7) || אֵל (MT Isa. 38.19); אל (1QIsa[b] 16.9) || עַל (MT Isa. 38.21); ההיא (1QIsa[b] 16.11) || הַהוּא (MT Isa. 39.1). The lack in 1QIsa[b] of a parallel to שִׁוִּיתִי עַד־בֹּקֶר כָּאֲרִי כֵּן יְשַׁבֵּר כָּל־עַצְמוֹתָי מִיּוֹם עַד־לַיְלָה תַּשְׁלִימֵנִי (MT Isa. 38.13) is due to parablepsis—the final part of v. 12 is identical to that of v. 13. Returning to his source text after writing out v. 12, the

to the number of cases of orthographic agreement. Considering both pure *matres lectionis* and probable remnants of diphthongs (i.e., historical spellings) in the Tiberian tradition, there are 32 agreements between 1QIsa^b col. 16 and the parallel material in MT Isaiah, along with two further cases of apparent *waw-yod* interchange (assuming correct interpretation on the part of the editor).

It is also worth noting that 1QIsa^b col. 16 evinces paragraph divisions in two of three places where the relevant MT portion has either closed or open spacing markers (the reconstruction of the broken text in the case of the third leaves no space for a division). All of this points to the proto-Tiberian character of 1QIsa^b.

1.2.2. Ein Gedi Burnt Leviticus Scroll

According to preliminary analyses (Segal et al. 2016; Tov et al. 2019), this scroll, found in the remains of the Ein Gedi synagogue, dates to a period ranging from the late 1st century CE to the late 4th century CE. It was damaged by fire between the late 3rd/early 4th centuries CE and ca. 600 CE, and subsequently digitally unrolled and scanned. The first two columns are to date the only columns to have received careful examination.

---

scribe mistook the end of v. 13 for the end of v. 12, resulting in omission of the former between vv. 12 and 14.

12. Orthography

Ein Gedi Burnt Leviticus Scroll col. 1 [link][4] || MT Lev. 1.1–9; 2.1–11

ויקרא אל משה וידבר יהוה אליו מאהל	1
וַיִּקְרָ֖א אֶל־מֹשֶׁ֑ה וַיְדַבֵּ֤ר יְהוָה֙ אֵלָ֔יו מֵאֹ֥הֶל	1
מועד לאמר דבר אל בני ישראל ואמרת	2–1
מוֹעֵ֖ד לֵאמֹֽר׃ דַּבֵּ֞ר אֶל־בְּנֵ֤י יִשְׂרָאֵל֙ וְאָמַרְתָּ֣	2–1
אלהם אדם כי יקריב מכם קרבן ליהוה מן	3
אֲלֵהֶ֔ם אָדָ֗ם כִּֽי־יַקְרִ֥יב מִכֶּ֛ם קָרְבָּ֖ן לַֽיהוָ֑ה מִן־	2
הבהמה מן הבקר ומן הצאן תקריבו את	4
הַבְּהֵמָ֗ה מִן־הַבָּקָר֙ וּמִן־הַצֹּ֔אן תַּקְרִ֖יבוּ אֶת־	
קרבנכם אם עלה קרבנו מן הבקר זכר	5
קָרְבַּנְכֶֽם׃ אִם־עֹלָ֤ה קָרְבָּנוֹ֙ מִן־הַבָּקָ֔ר זָכָ֥ר	3–2
תמים יקריבנו אל פתח אהל מועד יקריב	6
תָּמִ֖ים יַקְרִיבֶ֑נּוּ אֶל־פֶּ֝תַח אֹ֤הֶל מוֹעֵד֙ יַקְרִ֣יב	
אתו לרצנו לפני יהוה וסמך ידו על ראש	7
אֹת֔וֹ לִרְצֹנ֖וֹ לִפְנֵ֥י יְהוָֽה׃ וְסָמַ֤ךְ יָדוֹ֙ עַ֖ל רֹ֣אשׁ	4–3
העלה ונרצה לו לכפר עליו ושחט את בן	8
הָעֹלָ֑ה וְנִרְצָ֥ה ל֖וֹ לְכַפֵּ֥ר עָלָֽיו׃ וְשָׁחַ֛ט אֶת־בֶּ֥ן	5–4
הבקר לפני יהוה והקריבו בני אהרן	9
הַבָּקָ֖ר לִפְנֵ֣י יְהוָ֑ה וְ֠הִקְרִיבוּ בְּנֵ֨י אַהֲרֹ֤ן	
הכהנים את־הדם וזרקו את הדם על המזבח	10
הַכֹּֽהֲנִים֙ אֶת־הַדָּ֔ם וְזָרְק֨וּ אֶת־הַדָּ֤ם עַל־הַמִּזְבֵּ֙חַ֙	
סביב אשר פתח אהל מועד והפשיט את	11
סָבִ֔יב אֲשֶׁר־פֶּ֖תַח אֹ֥הֶל מוֹעֵֽד׃ וְהִפְשִׁ֖יט אֶת־	6–5
העלה ונתח אתה לנתחיה ונתנו בני אהרן	12
הָעֹלָ֑ה וְנִתַּ֥ח אֹתָ֖הּ לִנְתָחֶֽיהָ׃ וְ֠נָתְנוּ בְּנֵ֨י אַהֲרֹ֧ן	7–6
הכהן אש על המזבח וערכו עצים על האש	13
הַכֹּהֵ֛ן אֵ֖שׁ עַל־הַמִּזְבֵּ֑חַ וְעָרְכ֥וּ עֵצִ֖ים עַל־הָאֵֽשׁ׃	
וערכו בני אהרן הכהנים את הנתחים את	14
וְעָרְכ֗וּ בְּנֵ֤י אַהֲרֹן֙ הַכֹּ֣הֲנִ֔ים אֵ֚ת הַנְּתָחִ֔ים אֶת־	8
הראש ואת הפדר על העצים אשר על האש	15
הָרֹ֕אשׁ וְאֶת־הַפָּ֑דֶר עַל־הָעֵצִים֙ אֲשֶׁ֣ר עַל־הָאֵ֔שׁ	
אשר על המזבח וקרבו וכרעיו ירחץ במים	16
אֲשֶׁ֖ר עַל־הַמִּזְבֵּֽחַ׃ וְקִרְבּ֥וֹ וּכְרָעָ֖יו יִרְחַ֣ץ בַּמָּ֑יִם	9–8
והקטיר הכהן את הכל המזבחה עלה אשה	17
וְהִקְטִ֨יר הַכֹּהֵ֤ן אֶת־הַכֹּל֙ הַמִּזְבֵּ֔חָה עֹלָ֛ה אִשֵּׁ֥ה	

---

[4] See also the image and drawing in Segal et al. (2016, 5, 20).

Ein Gedi Burnt Leviticus Scroll col. 2 ‖ Lev. 2.1–11	
ונתן עליה לבנה והביאה אל בני אהרן הכהנים	2
וְנָתַן עָלֶיהָ לְבֹנָה׃ וֶהֱבִיאָהּ אֶל־בְּנֵי אַהֲרֹן הַכֹּהֲנִים֒	2–1
וקמץ משם מלא קמצו מסלתה ומשמנה על כל	3
וְקָמַץ מִשָּׁם מְלֹא קֻמְצוֹ מִסָּלְתָּהּ וּמִשַּׁמְנָהּ עַל כָּל־	
לבנתה והקטיר הכהן את אזכרתה המזבחה	4
לְבֹנָתָהּ וְהִקְטִיר הַכֹּהֵן אֶת־אַזְכָּרָתָהּ הַמִּזְבֵּחָה	
אשה ריח ניחח ליהוה והנותרת מן המנחה	5
אִשֵּׁה רֵיחַ נִיחֹחַ לַיהוָה׃ וְהַנּוֹתֶרֶת מִן־הַמִּנְחָה	3–2
לאהרן ולבניו קדש קדשים מאשי יהוה vac וכי	6
לְאַהֲרֹן וּלְבָנָיו קֹדֶשׁ קָדָשִׁים מֵאִשֵּׁי יְהוָה׃ ס וְכִי	4–3
תקרב קרבן מנחה מאפה תנור סלת חלות מצת	7
תַקְרִב קָרְבַּן מִנְחָה מַאֲפֵה תַנּוּר סֹלֶת חַלּוֹת מַצֹּת	
בלולת בשמן ורקיקי מצות משחים בשמן vac ואם	8
בְּלוּלֹת בַּשֶּׁמֶן וּרְקִיקֵי מַצּוֹת מְשֻׁחִים בַּשָּׁמֶן׃ ס וְאִם־	5–4
מנחה על המחבת קרבנך סלת בלולה בשמן	9
מִנְחָה עַל־הַמַּחֲבַת קָרְבָּנֶךָ סֹלֶת בְּלוּלָה בַשֶּׁמֶן	
מצה תהיה פתות אתה פתים ויצקת עליה	10
מַצָּה תִהְיֶה׃ פָּתוֹת אֹתָהּ פִּתִּים וְיָצַקְתָּ עָלֶיהָ	6–5
שמן מנחה הוא ואם מנחת מרחשת קרבנך	11
שָׁמֶן מִנְחָה הִוא׃ ס וְאִם־מִנְחַת מַרְחֶשֶׁת קָרְבָּנֶךָ	7–6
סלת בשמן תעשה והבאת את המנחה אשר	12
סֹלֶת בַּשֶּׁמֶן תֵּעָשֶׂה׃ וְהֵבֵאתָ אֶת־הַמִּנְחָה אֲשֶׁר	8–7
יעשה מאלה ליהוה והקריבה אל הכהן	13
יֵעָשֶׂה מֵאֵלֶּה לַיהוָה וְהִקְרִיבָהּ אֶל־הַכֹּהֵן	
והגישה אל המזבח והרים הכהן מן המנחה	14
וְהִגִּישָׁהּ אֶל־הַמִּזְבֵּחַ׃ וְהֵרִים הַכֹּהֵן מִן־הַמִּנְחָה	9–8
את אזכרתה והקטיר המזבחה אשה ריח	15
אֶת־אַזְכָּרָתָהּ וְהִקְטִיר הַמִּזְבֵּחָה אִשֵּׁה רֵיחַ	
ניחח ליהוה והנותרת מן המנחה לאהרן	16
נִיחֹחַ לַיהוָה׃ וְהַנּוֹתֶרֶת מִן־הַמִּנְחָה לְאַהֲרֹן	10–9
ולבניו קדש קדשים מאשי יהוה כל המנחה	17
וּלְבָנָיו קֹדֶשׁ קָדָשִׁים מֵאִשֵּׁי יְהוָה׃ כָּל־הַמִּנְחָה	11–10
אשר תקריבו ליהוה לא תעשה חמץ כי כל שאר	18
אֲשֶׁר תַּקְרִיבוּ לַיהוָה לֹא תֵעָשֶׂה חָמֵץ כִּי כָל־שְׂאֹר	

The Ein Gedi burnt Leviticus Scroll is proto-Masoretic in every sense of the term—orthographically, textually, and in terms of content it is identical to MT Leviticus as preserved in L. The agreement extends to paragraph divisions (*parshiyyot*): the closed divisions (*parshiyyot setumot*) in between MT Lev. 2.3 and 4 and between 2.4 and 5 correspond to *vacats* in col. 2 ll. 6 and 8, respectively, while that between MT Lev. 2.6 and 7 may be reconstructed in the lacuna in col. 2 l. 11.

1.3. Inner-Tiberian Orthographic Development

Scholars have also detected diachronically meaningful spelling variation within BH, especially that distinguishing CBH from LBH material. A well-known example is the spelling of the proper name *David*. Freedman (1983) argues that defective דוד is characteristic of CBH, whereas *plene* דויד of LBH and late non-Masoretic biblical and extrabiblical material (see also Gesenius 1815, 30; Kutscher 1974, 5, 99–100; Qimron 1978b, 146; 1986, 91; Greenfield and Naveh 1984, 120–21; Andersen and Forbes 1986, 6–9; Rooker 1990, 68–71; JM §3a, n. 5; Hurvitz 2014, 88–91).

Others downplay the diachronic significance of orthographic variation in the specific case of דו(י)ד and more generally (Rezetko 2003, 223–24; Rezetko and Young 2014, 456–59; cf. Hornkohl 2014b, 654). For such sceptics, orthographic instability carries with it the possibility that the current Masoretic distribution of defective דוד and *plene* דויד, as well as of other spellings cited as diagnostically early or late, is the result of secondary processes, in no way representative of the earliest forms of the relevant texts.

Specialists more optimistic about the diachronic significance of such spellings do not deny the reality of orthographic instability and variation, but merely hold that meaningful patterns have been preserved despite secondary processes. Thus, along with דויד, Hornkohl (2014b, 647–49, 653–67) includes forms (and derivatives) of the numeral שלוש 'three' and the *qal* infinitive construct as *plene* forms especially characteristic of LBH and other Second Temple forms of Hebrew.[5]

In a series of publications, Andersen, Freedman, and Forbes utilise three disparate analysis techniques—clustering, scaling, and seriation—to investigate spelling in the Tiberian tradition of the Hebrew. On the results of seriation, it is worth quoting Andersen and Forbes (2013) in full:

> Seriation uses the characteristics of analyzed objects to order them in terms of some underlying attribute(s), typically *time* in archaeological contexts. Andersen and Forbes' seriated text portions lie along a time gradient, beginning with Exodus, running throughout the other Torah books, proceeding through the Former and Latter Prophets, on to the Writings, ending with Ezra-Nehemiah. The portion positions exhibit scatter, suggesting that time is not the only operative underlying variable.
>
> Andersen and Forbes argue that the data demonstrate that the received spellings of the Hebrew Bible are neither entirely random nor completely rule-governed, but rather contain both 'signal' (remnants of evolving spelling conventions) and 'noise' (random fluctuations introduced during text transmission). When properly analyzed, these perturbed data show that spelling practice was, in fact, dependent on vowel type, on vowel stress level, and on text portion, and that the text portions can be projected onto a

---

[5] Hornkohl (2014b, 648–53) also discusses ירושלים for ירושלם, דרמשק for דמשק, and the theophoric suffix -יה for -יהו, but these written differences reflect distinct phonological realities and are thus not merely orthographic in nature.

time line, with Exodus as the earliest and Ezra-Nehemiah the latest.

2.0. Orthographic Distinctiveness of the Tiberian Torah

Andersen, Freedman, and Forbes also reveal interesting details about the Torah specifically. Their studies involving clustering and scaling demonstrate, among other things, (a) that spelling in the Tiberian Torah, while not homogenous, both unifies the books of the Pentateuch and sets them apart from the rest of the Masoretic Bible; (b) that Torah orthography is conservative, i.e., comparatively defective; and (c) that the Pentateuch's conservative defectiveness, while not untouched by late penetrations of *plene* orthography, correlates meaningfully with typologically early conventions (Andersen and Forbes 1986, 285, 312–314; 2013, 610–11; Freedman 1992, 10–12; see also Cross 1966; 1985).

Intriguingly, when it comes to the historical periodisation of the reputed Pentateuchal sources, orthographic evidence patterns like linguistic evidence. Just as all Pentateuchal sources show CBH constellations of features to the exclusion of LBH alternatives, so the spelling of the Torah is classical across all source material. It is worth quoting Andersen and Forbes (1986, 314) at length:

> So far as spelling is concerned, the most conservative book in the Pentateuch is Exodus, followed by Leviticus, Numbers, Genesis, Deuteronomy. That is, Exodus and Leviticus have by far the most old-fashioned spelling in the entire Bible; and they are dominated by priestly material. There

is a lot of P in Numbers too, and about one quarter of Genesis is P. So, the more P, the older the spelling. This means either that old spellings were still in use in priestly circles well after the Exile, or—more likely—that the P document is actually a pre-exilic composition, and that the whole of the Pentateuch was complete by the time of the onset of the Exile.

Certain claims are more dubious. For example, though Cross reasonably opines that the orthography of the Tiberian Pentateuch is not as developed as that of other parts of the Bible, his use of the term 'pristine' (1966, 86) in reference to the Torah's spelling seems unfortunate. Not only do Andersen and Forbes (1986, 314) note the vagueness of the term, but, as has been demonstrated above (§1.1), certain biblical DSS manuscripts present clear evidence of apparently more pristine pre-Tiberian orthography in the Torah.

It is also worth entertaining the possibility, often raised elsewhere in this volume, that conservative spelling conventions now especially characteristic of the Pentateuch may once have been more broadly typical of what Andersen and Forbes call the 'Primary History' (Torah and Former Prophets). They quote Breuer (1976, XXXII) as saying "The Jewish sages took tremendous pains clarifying the orthographic text of the Torah, but did not exercise the same care with respect to the text of the prophets and hagiographa." Limited evidence of orthographic development in the Former Prophets emerges from a comparison of 4QSam^b (4Q52) and MT Samuel, spelling in the former only slightly more defective than in the latter (Andersen and Freedman 1989). Limited evidence of the preservation of typologically early defective spellings in the Former Prophets may be adduced from MT Kings, presenting orthography nearly as conservative as that of the Torah (Andersen and Forbes 1986, 314–15).

Even so, the fact that the extant orthographic differences between the Torah and Former Prophets in the Tiberian tradition *can* be explained as due to secondary interventions in the latter does not necessarily mean that they *should* be so explained. Such an explanation arguably fits the data in the case of several linguistic features discussed in the preceding chapters, but it is unsuitable in the case of others (see above, Introduction, §7.0), where the specific distributional patterns are better explained on the assumption of sub-chronolects. If simplicity is a priority, and a single comprehensive explanation is preferable to a combination of different explanations, then a hypothesis positing diachronically distinct CBH sub-chronolects explains the most data, with no need to assume that secondary contemporisation, while a reality, is the main factor responsible for the distinction between CBH_1 and CBH_2 language and orthography.

3.0. Summary

In sum, notwithstanding the obscuring effect of secondary features, quantities of primary data sufficient for periodisation are perceptible. These show a distinction between CBH and LBH material, as well as a distinction between the CBH_1 of the Torah and the CBH_2 of the Prophets—though there is some question as to whether the orthographic distinction between the Torah and the Former Prophets is due, at least partially, to secondary developments allowed to affect the Prophets more than the Torah. In any case, it remains possible that the linguistic and orthographic conservatism seen in the Torah is related to the antiquity of the relevant traditions, whenever they were first committed to writing or reached their extant form. It is again worth quoting Andersen and Forbes (1986, 313) at some length:

> The Torah was canonized first and canonized early. The usual critical theories do not place this event earlier than the time of Ezra. If it was a matter of recognizing an old and already fixed text, that would permit an earlier canonization. But if it was a matter of publishing an edition, including post-exilic priestly works (document P), then we have to explain why that work does not display more evidence of the influence of post-exilic spelling; more particularly, why it is so different in its spelling from the contemporary work Ezra-Nehemiah.

Since purported P material, traditionally regarded as among the latest in the Torah, differs conspicuously from LBH in both language and spelling, patterning as typologically earlier than both LBH and TBH, it is more likely substantially to reflect pre-exilic provenance.

While the reality of secondary orthographic developments finds support in the evidence, an argument can be made that such processes were not sufficient to account for all changes. Only the assumption of inner-CBH diachronic development accounts for certain linguistic distinctions, making it likely that this also contributed to the orthographic and linguistic discrepancies that might otherwise be explained solely on the basis of secondary processes.

CONCLUSION

The main question addressed in this book is whether an array of linguistic and orthographic features that distinguish the Tiberian Torah from the non-LBH Prophets and Writings should be interpreted as evidence of inner-CBH diachronic development. While scholars debate the quantity of early and late material in the CBH corpus, there is broad agreement that its composition extended over centuries. According to one common scholarly view, this would have run from approximately 1000 BCE to 600 BCE, though the material might well incorporate far earlier traditions and have undergone modification till the Hellenistic period or beyond. In theory, even the maximal span of four hundred years accorded to CBH in the approach adopted in this volume should have provided ample scope for linguistic evolution, which one might reasonably expect to manifest in chronologically distinct isoglosses.

In practice, however, many factors have contributed to obscuring the effects of inner-CBH diachronic evolution: the possible reduction of oral material to written literature; the semi-opacity and ambiguity of the writing system; such secondary processes as levelling due to scribal convention and deliberate or accidental intervention; the imposition on the written text of a related, but semi-independent oral reading tradition—to name but a few complicating elements. The limited sample size of the Tiberian biblical corpus is also a significant issue, made only slightly less problematic by recourse to a range of helpful evidence: non-Tiberian biblical material, ancient textual witnesses in various languages, extrabiblical Hebrew texts, and cognate sources. According to the approach adopted in this book, such factors complicate, but do not preclude diachronic investigation. Rather than insurmountable barriers, they are hurdles to be taken seriously and overcome by means of judicious use of the evidence, sound methodology, due consideration of alternative explanations, and reasonable and creative interpretation of data, with recognition of the potential implications.

Methodologically, this study confronts two major issues. One, which is raised in every chapter, is the possibility that the extant distinctions between the CBH of the Pentateuch and the CBH of the Prophets and Writings were not representative of the earliest forms of the texts, but developed secondarily, in the course of compositional evolution and transmission. Often considered above is the possibility that a feature once broadly common to all CBH texts was preserved only in the Torah, and superseded in the Prophets and Writings by a variant feature standard in TBH or LBH. Only in the case of a few features, most notably, the onomasticon with and without *yahu* names (ch. 1) and 1st-person *wayyiqtol* morphology (ch. 2), does the nature of the evidence seem to rule out this possibility. The notion of historically deep, rather than secondary, variation seems marginally more appropriate in the case of other features, too.

When it comes to the features discussed in chs 8–11, a second methodological consideration concerns distinguishing between purely orthographic variation and written variation of genuinely linguistic significance. Conscious of the linguistic semi-independence of the written and reading components of the Tiberian biblical tradition, the approach here is deliberately maximal in its interpretation of written diversity. Where spelling differences of potential linguistic significance arise, these are taken seriously, and the possible linguistic import is entertained. While such linguistic interpretations may not convince all, or even most, readers, it is surely advisable to note the features and to weigh alternative explanations. All too often, the distinctiveness of such written features goes unnoticed or is uncritically assumed to be purely orthographic, with little to no consideration of non-orthographic alternatives.

At a more theoretical level, in the context of this study, it was at the outset recognised that the principal research question necessarily carries with it a challenge to specific elements or conceptions of at least two entrenched scholarly paradigms that are regularly cited in discussions on the periodisation of biblical literature, generally, and of the Pentateuch, more specifically—namely, the Documentary Hypothesis and the dichotomous CBH–LBH division of biblical language and literature. No direct challenge to either theory is proposed here, but the results, though mixed, arguably call into question certain rigid versions of each approach.

The late dating of P has been challenged repeatedly by a minority of both language and literary scholars (see Young, Rezetko, and Ehrensvärd 2008, II:13, for a partial list of such scholars), and the findings here largely support the challengers, as material classified as P patterns, like the rest of the Torah, as CBH. Whether the evidence here raises more fundamental questions about the traditional critical division into sources is left for others to evaluate.

It is also worth noting in this connection that there is nothing in the data that marks the author of P (or of any other Pentateuchal source) as an especially gifted post-Restoration writer capable of flawless CBH. P shares thematic concerns with TBH, LBH, and late extrabiblical compositions, but looks like none of them. While sufficiently different in style from other Pentateuchal sources to be identified by experts, P by and large shares with them CBH_1 style. According to the extant evidence, late writers struggled to compose CBH even over short spans. The possibility of an exception to this rule, capable of long stretches of perfect CBH, cannot be definitively excluded, but seems remote and is devoid of solid evidentiary support.

The dichotomous paradigm of pre-exilic and post-exilic BH, while heuristically valid and practically helpful in the case of many features and compositions, has often been modified to comprehend greater nuance. For example, TBH and ABH are today accepted by some. The distribution of features traced in the present monograph tallies with none of the accepted divisions, demanding instead the recognition of diachronic diversity within CBH, which might lead to an overall schema of ABH–CBH_1–CBH_2–TBH–LBH. Given the number and enormity of evidentiary uncertainties, it is tempting to leave the schema unaccompanied by an absolute chronology. But in a study so focused on diachrony and periodisation, such an omission would be unacceptable. So, acknowledging the dearth and problematic nature of pristine evidence in the extant sources, along with the complicating reality of intervening secondary development, one might reasonably, but tentatively and approximatively, associate CBH with

1000–600 BCE, TBH with 600–450 BCE, and LBH with 450 BCE on (the real-world temporal associations of ABH remain unclear). Based primarily on the evidence in chs 1–2 above, one can further divide CBH into CBH_1, substantially representative of the period 1000–800 BCE, albeit possibly preserving some earlier features of pre-monarchic traditions, and CBH_2, reflecting 800–600 BCE.

As to the broader questions of BH diachrony and linguistic periodisation, it will be clear from this study that the author is far more optimistic than many regarding what may be reasonably argued on the basis of the data. It would be preferable to achieve certitude. But given the quantity and nature of the evidence, perhaps the best that can be hoped for is the integration of plausible narratives of high explanatory value. Here the writer seeks to account for apparent inner-CBH variation, in the hopes that the explanations can be usefully integrated into broader understanding of the development of ancient Hebrew and of the composition and transmission of the Hebrew Bible.

REFERENCES

Abegg, Martin G., Jr. 1999–2009. *Qumran Non-biblical Manuscripts (QUMRAN)*. Accordance module version 5.1. Silver Lake, FL: OakTree Software, Inc.

Abraham, Kathleen. 2024. 'Hebrew Names'. In *Personal Names in Cuneiform Texts from Babylonia (c. 750–100 BCE)*, edited by Caroline Waerzeggers and Melanie M. Groß, 139–65. Cambridge: Cambridge University Press.

Andersen, Francis I., and A. Dean Forbes. 1986. *Spelling in the Hebrew Bible*. Biblia et Orientalia. Rome: Biblical Institute Press.

———. 1989. 'Another Look at 4QSam^b'. *Revue de Qumran* 14:7–29.

———. 2013. 'Matres Lectionis: Biblical Hebrew'. In *Encyclopedia of Hebrew Language and Linguistics*, edited by Geoffrey Khan et al., II:607–11. Leiden: Brill.

Anderson, John M. *The Grammar of Names*. Oxford: Oxford University Press.

Arentsen, Niek. 2020. 'לשון ישעיהו השני (יש' מ–סו) ומקומה בתולדות הלשון העברית'. PhD dissertation, The Hebrew University of Jerusalem.

Barr, James. 1981. "A New Look at Kethibh-Qere." *Oudtestamentische Studiën* 21: 19–37.

———. 1989. *The Variable Spellings of the Hebrew Bible*. Schweich Lectures 1986. Oxford: Published for the British Academy by Oxford University Press.

Barth, Jakob. 1890. 'Das passive Qal und seine Participien'. In *Jubelschrift zum Siebzigsten Geburtstag des Dr. Israel Hildesheimer*, 145–53. Berlin: Engel.

BDB = Brown, Francis, Samuel R. Driver, and Charles A. Briggs. 1906. *The Brown-Driver-Briggs Hebrew and English Lexicon*. Boston: Houghton, Mifflin and Company.

Ben-Ḥayyim, Ze'ev. 2000. *A Grammar of Samaritan Hebrew*. Jerusalem: Magnes and Winona Lake, IN: Eisenbrauns.

Blake, Frank R. 1901. 'The Internal Passive in Semitic'. *Journal of the American Oriental Society* 22:45–54.

Blau, Joshua. 1997. 'הרהוריו של ערביסטן על השתלשלות עברית המקרא וסעיפותיה'. *Lešonenu* 60:21–32.

———. 2010. *Phonology and Morphology of Biblical Hebrew*. Linguistic Studies in Ancient West Semitic 2. Winona Lake, IN: Eisenbrauns.

Bloch, Yigal. 2007. 'From Linguistics to Text-Criticism and Back: *Wayyiqṭōl* Constructions with Long Prefixed Verbal Forms in Biblical Hebrew'. *Hebrew Studies* 48:141–70.

Böttcher, J. Freidrich. 1866–1868. *Ausführliches Lehrbuch der hebräischen Sprache*. 2 vols. Leipzig: Barth.

Breuer, Mordekhai. 1976. *The Aleppo Codex and the Accepted Text of the Bible*. Jerusaelm: Mosad Harav Kook.

Carmignac, Jean. 1963. 'La forme poetique du Psaume 151 de la grotte 11'. *Revue de Qumrân* 4:371–78.

Carr, David M. 2011. *The Formation of the Hebrew Bible: A New Reconstruction*. New York: Oxford University Press.

Chomsky, William. 1959. *David Ḳimḥi's Hebrew Grammar (Mikhlol)*. New York: Bloch.

Cohen, Chaim. 'Diachrony in Biblical Hebrew Lexicography and Its Ramifications for Textual Analysis'. In *Diachrony in Biblical Hebrew*, edited by Cynthia L. Miller-Naudé and Ziony Zevit, 361–75. Linguistic Studies in Ancient West Semitic 8. Winona Lake, IN: Eisenbrauns.

Cohen, Maimon. 2007. *The Kethiḇ and Qeri System in the Biblical Text: A Linguistic Analysis of the Various Traditions Based on the Manuscript 'Keter Aram Tsova'*. Publications of the Perry Foundation for Biblical Research in the Hebrew University of Jerusalem. Jerusalem: The Hebrew University Magnes Press.

Cross, Frank Moore. 1966. 'The Contribution of the Qumran Discoveries to the Study of the Biblical Text'. *Israel Exploration Journal* 16:81–95.

———. 1973. *Canaanite Myth and Hebrew Epic*. Cambridge, MA: Harvard University Press.

———. 1985. 'A Literate Soldier: Lachish Letter III'. In *Biblical and Related Studies Presented to Samuel Iwry*, edited by Ann Kort and Scott Morchauser, 41–47. Winona Lake, IN: Eisenbrauns.

———. 1998. 'The Stabilization of the Canon of the Hebrew Bible'. In *From Epic to Canon: History and Literature in Ancient Israel*, 219–29. Baltimore: Johns Hopkins University Press.

Dallaire, Hélène. 2014. *The Syntax of Volitives in Biblical Hebrew and Amarna Canaanite Prose*. Linguistic Studies in Ancient West Semitic 9. Winona Lake, IN: Eisenbrauns.

Delitzsch, Franz. 1877. *Commentary on the Song of Songs and Ecclesiastes*. Translated by M. G. Easton. Edinburgh: T. & T. Clark.

Dobbs-Allsopp, Frederick W. 1998. 'Linguistic Evidence for the Date of Lamentations'. *Journal of the Ancient Near Eastern Society* 26:1–36.

Driver, Samuel Rolles. 1898. *An Introduction to the Literature of the Old Testament*. Revised edition. Edinburgh: T. & T. Clark.

Elitzur, Yoel. 2015. 'The Divine Name ADNY in the Hebrew Bible: Surprising Findings'. *Liber Annuus* 65:87–106.

———. 2018a. 'Diachrony in Standard Biblical Hebrew: The Pentateuch vis-à-vis the Prophets/Writings'. *Journal of Northwest Semitic Languages* 44:81–101.

———. 2018b. 'The Interface between Language and Realia in the Preexilic Books of the Bible'. *Hebrew Studies* 59:129–47.

———. 2019. 'The Names of God and the Dating of the Biblical Corpus'. In *The Believer and the Modern Study of the Bible*, edited by Tova Ganzel, Yehudah Brandes, and Chayuta Deutsch, 428–42. Boston: Academic Studies Press.

———. 2022. 'Emergence and Disappearance of Words and Expressions in Pre-Exilic Biblical Hebrew'. *Revue Biblique* 129:481–504.

Fassberg, Steven E. 2012. 'The Kethiv/Qere הִוא, Diachrony, and Dialectology'. In *Diachrony in Biblical Hebrew*, edited by Cynthia L. Miller-Naudé and Ziony Zevit, 171–80. Linguistic Studies in Ancient West Semitic 8. Winona Lake, IN: Eisenbrauns.

Fernández, Miguel Pérez. 1997. *An Introductory Grammar of Rabbinic Hebrew*. Translated by John F. Elwolde. Leiden: Brill.

Fredericks, Daniel C. 1988. *Qoheleth's Language: Re-evaluating Its Nature and Date*. Ancient Near Eastern Texts and Studies 3. New York: Mellen.

Freedman, David Noel. 1983. 'The Spelling of the Name "David" in the Hebrew Bible'. *Hebrew Annual Review* 7:89–104.

———. 1992. 'The Evolution of Hebrew Orthography'. In *Studies in Hebrew and Aramaic Orthography*, edited by David Noel Freedman, A. Dean Forbes, and Francis I. Andersen, 3–15. Winona Lake, IN: Eisenbrauns.

Friedman, Richard Elliott. 1989. *Who Wrote the Bible?* 2nd edition. San Francisco: HarperSanFrancisco.

———. 2017. *The Exodus: How It Happened and Why It Matters*. New York: HarperCollins.

Garbini, Giovanni. 1960. *Il semitico di nord-ovest*. Naples: Istituto universitario orientale di Napoli.

Gesenius, Wilhelm. 1815. *Geschichte der hebräischen Sprache und Schrift: Eine philologisch-historische Einleitung in die Sprachlehren und Wörterbücher der hebräischen Sprache*. Leipzig: Vogel.

Giesebrecht, Friedrich. 1881. 'Zur Hexateuchkritik: Der Sprachgebrauch des hexateuchischen Elohisten'. *Zeitschrift für die Alttestamentliche Wissenschaft* 1:177–276.

Ginsberg, Harold L. 1929. 'Studies on the Biblical Hebrew Verb'. *American Journal of Semitic Languages and Literatures* 46:53–56.

———. 1934. 'מבעד למסורת'. *Tarbiz* 5:208–23.

———. 1936. '"נוספות ל"מבעד למסורת"'. *Tarbiz* 7:543.

GKC = Emil Kautsch (ed.). 1909. *Gesenius' Hebrew Grammar*. Translated by Arthur E. Cowley. Oxford: Clarendon.

Green, William Henry. 1872. *A Grammar of the Hebrew Language*. 3rd edition. New York: John Wiley & Son.

Greenfield, Jonas, and Joseph Naveh. 1984. 'Hebrew and Aramaic in the Persian Period'. In *The Cambridge History of Judaism*, edited by William D. Davies and Louis Finkelstein, I:115–29. Cambridge: Cambridge University Press.

Grintz, Yehoshua M. 1974–1975. 'Archaic Terms in the Priestly Code'. *Lešonenu* 39:5–30, 163–81; 40:5–32. [Hebrew]

Groves-Wheeler = The J. Alan Groves Center for Advanced Biblical Research. 1991–2016. *Groves-Wheeler Westminster Hebrew Morphology*. Altamonte Springs, FL: OakTree Software, Inc.

Gzella, Holger. 2018. 'Untypical *Wayyiqtol* Forms in Hebrew and Early Linguistic Diversity'. In *The Unfolding of Your Word Gives Light: Studies on Biblical Hebrew in Honor of George L. Klein*, edited by Ethan C. Jones, 21–37. University Park, PA: Eisenbrauns.

Harris, Zellig S. 1939. *Development of the Canaanite Dialects: An Investigation in Linguistic History*. New Haven, CT: American Oriental Society.

Hendel, Ronald. 2000. '"Begetting" and "Being Born" in the Pentateuch: Notes on Historical Linguistics and Source Criticism'. *Vetus Testamentum* 50:38–46.

Hess, Richard S. 1993. *Amarna Personal Names*. American Schools of Oriental Research Dissertation Series 9. Winona Lake, IN: Eisenbrauns.

Hetzron, Robert. 1976. 'Two Principles of Genetic Reconstruction'. *Lingua* 38:89–108.

Hoffmeier, James K. 2005. *Ancient Israel in Sinai: The Evidence for the Authenticity of the Wilderness Tradition*. New York: Oxford University Press.

Hornkohl, Aaron D. 2013. 'Biblical Hebrew: Periodisation'. In *Encyclopedia of Hebrew Language and Linguistics*, edited by Geoffrey Khan et al., I:315–25. Leiden: Brill.

———. 2014a. *Ancient Hebrew Periodization and the Language of the Book of Jeremiah: The Case for a Sixth-century Date of Composition*. Studies in Semitic Languages and Linguistics 74. Leiden: Brill.

———. 2014b. 'Characteristically Late Spellings in the Hebrew Bible: With Special Reference to the *Plene* Spelling of the *o*-Vowel in the *Qal* Infinitive Construct'. *Journal of the American Oriental Society* 134/4:643–71.

———. 2016a. 'Transitional Biblical Hebrew'. In *A Handbook of Biblical Hebrew*, edited by W. Randall Garr and Steven E. Fassberg, I:32–42. Winona Lake, IN: Eisenbrauns.

———. 2016b. 'Hebrew Diachrony and the Linguistic Periodisation of Biblical Texts: Observations from the Perspective of Reworked Pentateuchal Material'. *Journal for Semitics* 25/2:1004–63.

———. 2021a. 'The Linguistic Profile of Select Reworked Bible Material vis-à-vis Masoretic Hebrew and Some Ramifications

Thereof'. In *Hebrew Texts and Language of the Second Temple Period: Proceedings of an Eighth Symposium on the Hebrew of the Dead Sea Scrolls and Ben Sira*, edited by Steven E. Fassberg, 127–52. Studies on the Texts of the Desert of Judah 134. Leiden: Brill.

———. 2021b. 'Niphalisation in Ancient Hebrew: A Perspective from the Samaritan Tradition'. *Journal for Semitics* 30/2:1–17.

———. 2023. *The Historical Depth of the Tiberian Reading Tradition of Biblical Hebrew*. Cambridge Semitic Languages and Cultures 17. Cambridge: Faculty of Asian and Middle Eastern Studies and Open Book Publishers.

Huehnergard, John. 2006. 'Hebrew Verbs I-w/y and a Proto-Semitic Sound Rule'. In *Memoriae Igor M. Diakonoff*, edited by L. Kogan, N. Koslova, S. Loesov, and S. Tishchenko, 457–74. Babel und Bibel 2. Winona Lake, IN: Eisenbrauns.

Hughes, Jeremy. 1994. 'Post-Biblical Features of Biblical Hebrew Vocalization'. In *Language, Theology, and the Bible: Essays in Honour of James Barr*, edited by Samuel E. Balentine and John Barton, 67–80. Oxford: Clarendon.

Hurvitz, Avi. 1967. 'לשונו וזמנו של מזמור קנ"א מקומראן'. *Eretz-Israel* 8:82–87.

———. 1972. *The Transition Period in Biblical Hebrew: A Study in Post-Exilic Hebrew and Its Implications for the Dating of Psalms*. Jerusalem: Bialik. [Hebrew]

———. 1974a. 'The Evidence of Language in Dating the Priestly Code'. *Revue Biblique* 81:24–56.

———. 1974b 'The Date of the Prose-Tale of Job Linguistically Reconsidered'. *Harvard Theological Review* 67:17–34.

———. 1982. *A Linguistic Study of the Relationship Between the Priestly Source and the Book of Ezekiel: A New Approach to an Old Problem.* Cahiers de la Revue Biblique 20. Paris: Gabalda.

———. 1983. 'The Language of the Priestly Source and Its Historical Setting: The Case for an Early Date'. In *Proceedings of the Eighth World Congress of Jewish Studies, Jerusalem, August 16–21, 1981: Panel Sessions: Bible Studies and Hebrew Language*, 83–94. Jerusalem: World Union of Jewish Studies.

———. 1988. 'Dating the Priestly Source in Light of the Historical Study of Biblical Hebrew a Century after Wellhausen'. *Zeitschrift für die Alttestamentliche Wissenschaft* 100 Supplement, 88–99.

———. 1990. Review of Fredericks 1988. *Hebrew Studies* 31:144–54.

———. 2000. 'Once Again: The Linguistic Profile of the Priestly Material in the Pentateuch and Its Historical Age: A Response to J. Blenkinsopp'. *Zeitschrift für die Alttestamentliche Wissenschaft* 112:180–91.

———. 2007. 'The Language of Qoheleth and Its Historical Setting within Biblical Hebrew'. In *The Language of Qohelet in its Context: Essays in Honour of Prof. A. Schoors on the Occasion of his Seventieth Birthday*, edited by A. Berlejung and P. Van Hecke, 23–34. Leuven: Peeters.

———. 2013. 'Biblical Hebrew, Late'. In *Encyclopedia of Hebrew Language and Linguistics*, edited by Geoffrey Khan et al., I:329–38. Leiden: Brill.

———. 2014. *A Concise Lexicon of Late Biblical Hebrew: Linguistic Innovations in the Writings of the Second Temple Period*. Supplements to Vetus Testamentum 160. Leiden: Brill.

JM = Joüon, Paul, and Takamitsu Muraoka. 2008. *A Grammar of Biblical Hebrew*. Subsidia Biblica 27. Rome: Pontifical Biblical Institute Press.

Joosten, Jan. 2013. 'Linguistic Clues as to the Date of the Book of Job: A Mediating Position'. In *Interested Readers: Essays on the Hebrew Bible in Honor of David J. A. Clines*, edited by J. K. Aitken, J. M. S. Clines, and C. M. Maier, 347–57. Atlanta: SBL.

KAI = Donner, Herbert and Wolfgang Röllig. 1968–2002. *Kanaanäische und Aramäische Inschriften*. 4 volumes. Wiesbaden: Harrassowitz.

Khan, Geoffrey. 2013. *A Short Introduction to the Tiberian Masoretic Bible and Its Reading Tradition*. Piscataway, NJ: Gorgias Press.

———. 2020. *The Tiberian Pronunciation Tradition of Biblical Hebrew: Including a Critical Edition and English Translation of the Sections on Consonants and Vowels in the Masoretic Treatise Hidāyat al-Qāri' 'Guide for the Reader'*. 2 vols. Cambridge Semitic Languages and Cultures 1. Cambridge: Open Book Publishers and University of Cambridge Faculty of Asian and Middle Eastern Studies. doi.org/10.11647/OBP.0163

———. 2021. 'The Coding of Discourse Dependency in Biblical Hebrew Consecutive *weqaṭal* and *wayyiqṭol*'. In *New Perspectives in Biblical and Rabbinic Hebrew*, edited by Aaron D. Hornkohl and Geoffrey Khan, 299–354. Cambridge Semitic Languages and Cultures 7. Cambridge: Open Book Publishers and University of Cambridge Faculty of Asian and Middle Eastern Studies. doi.org/10.11647/OBP.0250.12

Kutscher, Eduard Y. 1974. *Language and Linguistic Background of the Isaiah Scroll (1QIsaᵃ)*. Studies on the Texts of the Desert of Judah 6. Leiden: Brill.

———. 1982. *A History of the Hebrew Language*. Jerusalem: Magnes and Leiden: Brill.

Lambert, Mayer. 1900. 'L'emploi du nifal en hébreu'. *Revue des études juives* 41:196–214.

———. 1931. *Traité de Grammaire Hébraïque*. Paris: Presses Universitaires de France.

Mandell, Alice. 2013. 'Archaic Biblical Hebrew'. In *Encyclopedia of Hebrew Language and Linguistics*, edited by Geoffrey Khan et al., I:325–29. Leiden: Brill.

Meek, Theophile J. 1936. *Hebrew Origins*. New York: Harper and Brothers.

———. 1939. 'Moses and the Levites'. *American Journal of Semitic Languages and Literatures* 56:118–20.

Milgrom, Jacob. 1970. *Studies in Levitical Terminology*. Berkeley: University of California Press.

———. 1978. 'Priestly Terminology and the Political and Social Structure of Pre-Monarchic Israel'. *Jerusalem Quarterly Review* 69:65–81.

———. 1991–2001 *Leviticus*. 3 vols. Anchor Bible Commentary. New York: Doubleday.

———. 1992. 'Priestly ("P") Source'. In *Anchor Bible Dictionary*. 5 vols. Edited by David Noel Freedman, V:454–61. New York: Doubleday.

———. 1999. 'The Antiquity of the Priestly Source: A Reply to Joseph Blenkinsopp'. *Zeitschrift für die Alttestamentliche Wissenschaft* 111:10–22.

———. 2007. 'The Case for the Pre-Exilic and Exilic Provenance of the Books of Exodus, Leviticus and Numbers'. In *Reading the Law: Studies in Honour of Gordon J. Wenham*, edited by J. G. McConville and K. Möller, 48–56. New York and London: T. & T. Clark.

Morgenstern, Matthew. 2007. 'The System of Independent Pronouns at Qumran and the History of Hebrew in the Second Temple Period'. In *Shaʻarei Lashon: Studies in Hebrew, Aramaic, and Jewish Languages Presented to Moshe Bar-Asher*, edited by Aharon Maman, Steven E. Fassberg, and Yochanan Breuer, vol. I: 44–63. Jerusalem: Bialik Institute. [Hebrew]

Moshavi, Adina, and Susan Rothstein. 2018. 'Indefinite Numerical Construct Phrases in Biblical Hebrew'. *Journal of Semitic Studies* 63/1:99–123. doi.org/10.1093/jss/fgx038

Noth, Martin. 1968. *Numbers: A Commentary*. The Old Testament Library. Philadelphia: The Westminster Press.

Paran, Menaḥem. 1983. 'Literary Features of the Priestly Code: Stylistic Patterns, Idioms and Structures'. PhD dissertation, The Hebrew University of Jerusalem. [Hebrew]

Paul, Shalom. 2012. 'Signs of Late Biblical Hebrew in Isaiah 40–66'. In *Diachrony in Biblical Hebrew*, edited by Cynthia Miller-Naudé and Ziony Zevit, 293–99. Linguistic Studies in Ancient West Semitic 8. Winona Lake, IN: Eisenbrauns.

Polzin, Robert. 1967. 'Notes on the Dating of the Non-Massoretic Psalms of 11QPsa'. *Harvard Theological Review* 60:468–76.

———. 1976. *Late Biblical Hebrew: Toward an Historical Typology of Biblical Hebrew Prose*. Missoula, MT: Scholars.

Qimron, Elisha. 1978a. 'ללשונה של מגילת המקדש'. *Lešonenu* 42:83–98.

———. 1978b. 'ללשון בית שני בספר תהלים'. *Beit Mikra* 23:139–50.

———. 1980. 'למילונה של מגילת המקדש'. *Šnaton la-Miqra u-l-Ḥeqer ha-Mizraḥ ha-Qadum* 4, edited by Moshe Weinfeld, 39–262. Jerusalem: Neuman.

———. 1986. *The Hebrew of the Dead Sea Scrolls*. Atlanta: Scholars Press.

———. 1997. 'A New Approach to the Use of Forms of the Imperfect without Personal Endings'. In *The Hebrew of the Dead Sea Scrolls and Ben Sira: Proceedings of a Symposium Held at Leiden University, December 1995*, edited by Takamitsu Muraoka and John F. Elwolde, 174–81. Studies on the Texts of the Desert of Judah 26. Leiden: Brill.

———. 2008. 'The Type וְאֶבְנֶה in the Hebrew of the Dead Sea Scrolls'. In *Conservatism and Innovation in the Hebrew Language of the Hellenistic Period: Proceedings of a Fourth International Symposium on the Hebrew of the Dead Sea Scrolls and Ben Sira*, edited by Jan Joosten and Jean-Sébastien Rey,

149–54. Studies on the Tests of the Desert of Judah 73. Leiden: Brill.

———. 2018. *A Grammar of the Hebrew of the Dead Sea Scrolls*. Jerusalem: Ben-Zvi.

Rahkonen, Pauli. 2019. 'Personal Names of the Pentateuch in the Northwest Semitic Context: A Comparative Study'. *Scandinavian Journal of the Old Testament* 33/1:111–35. doi.org/10.1080/09018328.2019.1600259

Rainey, Anson F. 1986. 'The Ancient Hebrew Prefix Conjugation in the Light of Amarnah Canaanite'. *Hebrew Studies* 27:4–19.

Rendsburg, Gary. 1980. 'Late Biblical Hebrew and the Date of "P"'. *Journal of the Ancient Near Eastern Society* 12:65–80.

———. 1982. 'A New Look at Pentateuchal HW"'. *Biblica* 63:351–69.

———. 1990a. *Diglossia in Ancient Hebrew*. American Oriental Series 72. New Haven, CT: American Oriental Society.

———. 1990b. *Linguistic Evidence for the Northern Origin of Selected Psalms*. SBL Monograph Series 43. Atlanta: Scholars Press.

———. 2002a. *Israelian Hebrew in the Book of Kings*. Occasional Publications of the Department of Near Eastern Studies and the Program of Jewish Studies, Cornell University 5. Bethesda, MD: CDL.

———. 2002b. 'Some False Leads in the Identification of Late Biblical Hebrew Texts: The Cases of Genesis 24 and 1 Samuel 2:27–36'. *Journal of Biblical Literature* 121:23–46.

---. 2006. 'Aramaic-Like Features in the Pentateuch'. *Hebrew Studies* 47:163–76.

Revell, E. John. 1988. 'First Person Imperfect Forms with Waw Consecutive'. *Vetus Testamentum* 38:419–26.

Reymond, Eric. 2016. 'The Passive *Qal* in the Hebrew of the Second Temple Period, especially as Found in the Wisdom of Ben Sira'. In *Sibyls, Scriptures, and Scrolls: John Collins at Seventy*, edited by Joel Baden, Hindy Najman, and Eibert J. C. Tigchelaar, 1110–27. Supplements to the Journal for the Study of Judaism 175. Leiden: Brill.

Rezetko, Robert. 2003. 'Dating Biblical Hebrew: Evidence from Samuel–Kings and Chronicles'. In *Biblical Hebrew: Studies in Chronology and Typology*, 215–50. London: T. & T. Clark.

Rezetko, Robert, and Ian Young. 2014. *Historical Linguistics and Biblical Hebrew: Steps toward an Integrated Approach*. Ancient Near Eastern Monographs 9. Atlanta: SBL.

Rooker, Mark F. 1990. *Biblical Hebrew in Transition: The Language of the Book of Ezekiel*. Journal for the Study of the Old Testament Supplement Series 90. Sheffield: Journal for the Study of the Old Testament Press.

Sáenz-Badillos, Angel. 1993. *A History of the Hebrew Language*. Translated by John F. Elwolde. Cambridge: Cambridge University Press.

Schoors, Antoon. 1992–2004. *The Preacher Sought to Find Pleasing Words: A Study in the Language of Qoheleth*. 2 vols. Orientalia Lovaniensia Analecta 41, 143. Leuven: Departement Orientalistiek.

Schuller, Eileen M. 1986. *Non-Canonical Psalms from Qumran: A Pseudepigraphic Collection*. Harvard Semitic Studies/Harvard Semitic Museum Studies 28. Atlanta: Scholars Press.

Segal, Michael, et al. 2016. 'An Early Leviticus Scroll from En-Gedi: Preliminary Publication'. *Textus* 26:1–30.

Segal, Moshe H. 1967. *The Pentateuch: Its Composition and Its Authorship and Other Biblical Studies*. Jerusalem: Magnes.

Seow, Choon L. 1996 'Linguistic Evidence and the Dating of Qohelet'. *Journal of Biblical Literature* 115:643–66.

———. 2011. 'Orthography, Textual Criticism, and the Poetry of Job'. *Journal of Biblical Literature* 130/1:63–85.

Sharvit, Shimon. 2004. פרקים בתולדות הלשון העברית: החטיבה הקלסית—יחידה ג': לשון חז"ל. Tel-Aviv: The Open University of Israel.

Shin, Seoung-Yun. 2007. 'A Lexical Study on the Language of Haggai–Zechariah–Malachi and Its Place in the History of Biblical Hebrew'. PhD dissertation, The Hebrew University of Jerusalem.

Sivan, Daniel. 2009. 'The Internal Passive of G-Stems in Northwest Semitic Languages'. In *Mas'at Aharon: Linguistic Studies Presented to Aron Dotan*, edited by Moshe Bar-Asher and Chaim E. Cohen, 47–56. Jerusalem: Bialik.

Sjörs, Ambjörn. 2021a. 'Notes on the Lengthened Imperfect Consecutive in the Samaritan Pentateuch'. *Journal of Semitic Studies* 66:17–26.

———. 2021b. 'Notes on the Lengthened Imperfect Consecutive in Late Biblical Hebrew'. In *New Perspectives in Biblical and Rabbinic Hebrew*, edited by Aaron D. Hornkohl and Geoffrey

Khan, 275–98. Cambridge Semitic Languages and Cultures 7. Cambridge: Open Book Publishers and University of Cambridge Faculty of Asian and Middle Eastern Studies. doi.org/10.11647/OBP.0250.12

Smith, Mark S. 1997. 'How to Write a Poem: The Case of Psalm 151a (11QPsa 28.3–12)'. In *The Hebrew of the Dead Sea Scrolls and Ben Sira: Proceedings of a Symposium Held at Leiden University, December 1995*, edited by Takamitsu Muraoka and John F. Elwolde, 182–208. Leiden: Brill.

Steiner, Richard C. 2005. 'On the Dating of Hebrew Sound Changes (*H > $Ḥ$ and *$Ġ$ > $ʿ$) and Greek Translations (2 Esdras and Judith)'. *Journal of Biblical Literatures* 124/2: 229–67.

Suchard, Benjamin. 2019. *The Development of the Biblical Hebrew Vowels: Including a Concise Historical Morphology*. Studies in Semitic Languages and Linguistics 99. Leiden and Boston: Brill.

Talshir, David. 1986. 'על ייחודי תחביר בלשון המקרא המאוחרת'. In *Proceedings of the Ninth World Congress of Jewish Studies*, part 4, vol. 1, 5–8. Jerusalem: The World Union of Jewish Studies. [Hebrew]

———. 1987. 'התפתחות מערכת העתיד המהופך בזיקה אל המערכת המודלית'. *Tarbiz* 56:585–91. [Hebrew]

Tov, Emanuel. 2004a. 'The Ketiv-Qere Variations in Light of the Manuscript Finds in the Judean Desert'. In *Text, Theology and Translation: Essays in Honor of Jan de Waard*, edited by Simon Crisp and Manuel Jinbachian, 199–208. Swindon: United Bible Societies.

———. 2004b. *Scribal Practices and Approaches Reflected in the Texts Found in the Judean Desert*. Studies on the Texts of the Desert of Judah 54. Atlanta: Society of Biblical Literature and Leiden: Brill.

———. 2012. *Textual Criticism of the Hebrew Bible*. 3rd revised and expanded edition. Minneapolis, MN: Fortress.

Tov, Emanuel, et al. 2019. 'An Early Leviticus Scroll from En-Gedi: Preliminary Publication'. In *Textual Developments: Collected Essays* 4, 458–69. Supplements to Vetus Testamentum 181. Leiden: Brill.

Tropper, Josef. 2001. 'Das genusindifferente hebräische Pronomen HW' im Pentateuch aus sprachvergleichender Sicht'. *Zeitschrift für die Althebraïstik* 14:159–72.

Ulrich, Eugene, and Peter W. Flint. 2010. *Qumran Cave 1:II—The Isaiah Scrolls*. 2 vols. Discoveries in the Judaean Desert 32. Oxford: Clarendon.

van Soldt, Wilfred H. 2016. 'Divinities in Personal Names at Ugarit'. In *Études ougaritiques* 4, edited by Valérie Matoïan and Michel Al-Maqdissi, 95–107. Ras Shamra–Ougarit 24. Leuven: Peeters.

Wellhausen, Julius. 1885. *Prolegomena to the History of Israel*. Translated by J. S. Black and A. Menzies. Edinburgh: Adam & Charles Black.

WO = Waltke, Bruce K., and Michael O'Connor. 1990. *An Introduction to Biblical Hebrew Syntax*. Winona Lake, IN: Eisenbrauns.

Williams, Ronald J. 1970. 'The Passive Qal Theme in Hebrew'. In *Essays on the Ancient Semitic World*, edited by J. W. Wevers and D. B. Redford, 43–50. Toronto: University of Toronto Press.

Wise, Michael O., Martin G. Abegg, Jr., and Edward M. Cook. 2005. *The Dead Sea Scrolls: A New Translation*. San Francisco: Harper.

Young, Ian. 1993. *Diversity in Pre-Exilic Hebrew*. Forschungen zum Alten Testament 5. Tübingen: Mohr (Paul Siebeck).

Young, Ian, Robert Rezetko, and Martin Ehrensvärd. 2008. *Linguistic Dating of Biblical Texts*. 2 vols. London: Equinox.

———. 2009. 'Is the Prose Tale of Job in Late Biblical Hebrew?" *Vetus Testamentum* 59:606–29.

Zevit, Ziony. 1980. Matres Lectionis *in Ancient Hebrew Epigraphs*. American Schools of Oriental Research Monograph Series 2. Cambridge, MA: American Schools of Oriental Research.

———. 1982. 'Converging Lines of Evidence Bearing on the Date of P'. *Zeitschrift für die Alttestamentliche Wissenschaft* 94:502–9.

PASSAGE INDEX

Hebrew Bible

Genesis

1.9: 118
2.10: 105
2.23: 121
3.7: 164
3.19, 23: 121
4.2: 62, 72, 87
4.10: 138
4.12: 62, 67, 87
4.15: 122
4.18: 119
4.19: 104
4.24: 122
4.26: 119
5.3: 90
5.6: 90, 105
5.11, 15: 105
5.18, 25, 28: 90, 94
6.1: 119
6.10: 104
7.24: 90, 93
8.3: 90, 93
8.5: 117
8.10: 86–87, 105
8.10b: 66
8.12: 57, 63, 85–86, 105
8.12b: 66
8.21: 87
8.22: 86
9.2: 121
9.11: 117
9.14: 117
10.1, 21: 119
10.25: 104, 119
11.10: 90
11.12: 94
11.13: 104
11:14: 94
11.15: 104
11.16, 18–23: 94
11.25: 90
11.32: 94, 105
12.4: 105
12.7: 117–18
12.15: 121
13.8: 142 n. 3
14.2: 152 n. 5
14.9: 105
14.24: 173
17.1: 118
17.12: 105
17.14: 117
17.17: 90, 94, 119
17.24: 96
18.1: 118
18.2: 104
18.4: 121
18.6: 104
18.20–21: 127 n. 1, 137–38
18.29: 86–87
19.8: 104
19.13: 138, 142 n. 3
19.20: 152 n. 5
19.33, 35–36: 164
20.5: 152 n. 5
21.3: 119
21.4: 105
21.5: 90, 92, 119
22.3, 5: 173
22.14: 118
22.19: 173
23.1: 90, 94, 96
24.10: 105
24.14: 168 n. 2
24.15: 119
24.16: 168 n. 2
24.22: 104–5
24.28: 168 n. 2
24.42, 47: 55
24.48: 54 n. 6
24.55, 57: 168 n. 2
24.61: 164, 173
25.1: 86–87

25.7: 90, 96, 105
25.17: 90
25.23: 104
25.27: 173
26.2: 118
26.7: 152 n. 5
26.12: 90, 94
26.24: 118
26.35: 164
27.1: 164
27.9: 104
27.34: 138
29.2: 104
29.4: 142 n. 3
29.16: 104
29.34: 104
30.20: 105
30.24: 72, 87
30.36: 104
30.38–39: 159, 164
31.7: 105
31.14: 164
31.23: 105
31.41: 105
32.4: 54 n. 6
32.8, 11: 104
32.16: 172
33.6: 164
33.13: 172
33.19: 90, 94
34.3, 12: 168 n. 2
35.1: 117
35.9: 118
35.26: 119

35.28: 90, 93, 96
36.5: 119
37.5: 72, 87
37.7: 142 n. 3, 159, 164
37.8: 87
38.5: 87
38.14: 121
38.24: 104
38.25: 152 n. 5
38.26: 85–86
40.10: 104, 152 n. 5
40.12–13, 16, 18–19: 104
41.2–4, 7: 164
41.11: 54 n. 6
41.18, 20–21, 24: 164
41.36: 164, 117
41.50: 104, 119
41.53–54: 164
42.11: 139, 142 n. 3
42.13: 142 n. 3
42.17: 104
42.21, 31–32: 142 n. 3
43.7: 55
43.8, 18: 142 n. 3
43.21: 18, 54 n. 6, 55
43.34: 105
44.9, 16: 142 n. 3

44.23: 62, 72, 87
44.24: 55
45.6, 11, 22: 105
45.23: 105
46.20, 22, 27: 119
46.29: 118
46.34: 142 n. 3
47.2: 105
47.3: 142 n. 3
47.9: 90
47.19: 142 n. 3
47.28: 90, 96
48.3: 117
48.5: 119
48.16: 173
49.26: 161, 164
50.10: 105
50.23: 119

Exodus

1.10: 164
1.16: 152 n. 5
1.17–19: 164
2.2: 104
2.5: 173
2.13: 104
2.16: 164–65
2.18–19: 165
2.23b: 138
3.2: 118
3.13: 28
3.15: 138
3.16: 117
3.18: 104

Passage Index

4.1, 5: 117
5.3: 104
5.7: 65 n. 11, 87
5.16, 18: 121
6.2: 28, 33
6.3: 118
6.16, 18: 90
6.20: 33, 90
7.25: 105
8.5, 7: 165
8.23: 104
8.25: 87
9.28: 87
9.34: 86–87
10.9: 173
10.22–23: 104
10.26: 142 n. 3
10.28–29: 87
11.6: 64, 87
12.15, 19: 105, 117
13.6: 103, 105
13.7: 118
14.10: 138
14.13: 57, 87
14.15: 129, 138
14.25: 181
15.20: 165
15.22: 104
15.24: 129
16.7–8: 142 n. 3
16.10: 117
16.26: 105
16.34: 181

17.9–10, 13–14: 34 n. 5
19.4: 55
19.15: 104
20.9, 11: 105
20.15d: 86
21.20–21: 113, 122
21.37: 105
22.29: 105
23.12: 105
23.14: 104
23.15: 105, 118
23.17: 104, 118
24.5: 173
24.13: 34 n. 5
24.16: 105
25.12: 104
25.16: 181
25.18: 103–4
25.21–22: 181
25.27: 165
25.32: 104–5
25.33: 104
25.34: 105
26.3: 105, 165
26.17: 104
26.19, 21: 104
26.22: 105
26.23: 104
26.25: 104–5
26.27, 32: 105
26.33–34: 181
26.37: 105
27.1: 104–5

27.2: 165
27.18: 105
27.21: 181
28.7, 9, 14: 104
28.17: 105
28.21: 165
28.22: 181
28.23, 26–27: 104
29.30, 35, 37: 105
30.4: 104
30.6, 26: 181
30.33: 117
30.36: 181
30.38: 117
31.7: 181
31.14: 117
31.15, 17: 105
31.18: 181
32.15: 181
32.17: 34 n. 5
33.11: 34 n. 5
33.23: 118
34.1: 104
34.3: 118
34.4: 104
34.12: 118
34.18: 105
34.20: 118
34.21: 105
34.23: 104, 118
34.24: 104, 118 n. 8
34.29: 181
35.2: 105

36.10: 105
36.22, 24, 26: 104
36.27: 105
36.28: 104
36.30: 104–5
36.32, 36, 38: 105
37.3, 7: 104
37.18: 104–5
37.19: 104
37.20: 105
37.27: 104
38.1: 104–5
38.18: 105
38.21: 181
38.25: 90
38.27: 90–91, 95
39.10: 105
39.15: 181
39.16, 19, 20: 104
39.35: 181
40.3, 5, 20, 21: 181

Leviticus

1.1–9: 195
2.1: 196
2.1–11: 195–96
2.3–7: 197
4.2, 13, 22, 27: 165
5.7: 104
5.11: 104, 152 n. 5
5.16: 68, 87
5.17: 165

5.24: 68
7.20–21, 25, 27: 117
7.30: 165
8.33, 35: 105
9.4: 117
9.6, 23: 118
10.14: 121
10.19: 165
11.38: 116, 121
11.39: 152 n. 5
12.2: 105
12.4: 104
12.5: 105
12.8: 104
13.4–5: 105
13.6: 152 n. 5
13.7: 117
13.10: 152 n. 5
13.14, 19: 117
13.21: 105, 152 n. 5
13.26, 31, 33, 50, 54: 105
13.57: 118
14.4: 104
14.8: 105
14.10, 22: 104
14.35: 117
14.38: 105
14.49: 104
15.13: 105
15.14: 104
15.19, 24, 28: 105

15.29: 104
16.2: 118
16.5: 104
16.13: 181
16.31: 152 n. 5
17.4, 9, 14: 117
18.29: 117
19.8: 117
19.20: 121
19.23: 104
19.25: 63–64, 77, 79, 85
20.17–18: 117, 152 n. 5
20.23: 18, 55
20.26: 55
21.9: 152 n. 5
22.3: 117
22.14: 85–86
22.27: 105, 119
23.3, 6, 8: 105
23.13: 104
23.15: 165
23.17: 104, 165
23.18: 105
23.19–20: 104
23.29: 117
23.34, 36, 39–42: 105
24.3: 181
24.5: 104
24.6: 103–4
24.20: 121
25.23, 30: 181

26.13: 55, 181
26.18: 62, 85
26.21: 62, 85–86
26.25: 121
27.5: 105
27.6: 104–5
27.7: 105
27.13, 15, 19, 27: 85–86
27.27b: 66
27.31: 68
27.31b: 66

Numbers

1.8, 10, 13–14: 27 n. 1
1.50, 53: 181
2.5: 27 n. 1
2.9: 90
2.14: 27 n. 1
2.16: 90
2.20: 27 n. 1
2.24: 90–91
2.27: 27 n. 1
2.31: 90
3.24: 27 n. 1
3.47: 105
4.5: 181
5.7: 68, 87
5.13–14: 152 n. 5
6.10: 104
7.14: 105
7.18: 27 n. 1
7.20: 105
7.23: 27 n. 1
7.26, 32, 38: 105
7.42: 27 n. 1
7.44: 105
7.47: 27 n. 1
7.50: 105
7.54: 27 n. 1
7.56: 105
7.59: 27 n. 1
7.62, 68: 105
7.72: 27 n. 1
7.74: 105
7.77: 27 n. 1
7.80: 105
7.89: 181
8.19: 54 n. 6
9.7: 142 n. 3
9.13: 117
9.15: 181
10.2: 104
10.11: 181
10.15, 20, 23, 26: 27 n. 1
10.29: 142 n. 3
10.33: 104
11.19: 105
11.25: 85
11.26: 104
11.28: 34 n. 5
11.32: 105
11.33: 117–18, 118 n. 10
12.14–15: 105
13.8, 16: 34, 34 n. 5
14.6: 34 n. 5
14.10, 14: 117
14.30, 38: 34 n. 5
15.6, 9: 104
15.30, 31: 117
16.19: 118
17.7: 118
17.19, 22–23, 25: 181
18.2: 181
18.16: 105
19.11: 105
19.13: 117
19.14, 16: 105
19.20: 117
20.4: 142 n. 3
20.6: 118
20.16: 142 n. 3
21.30: 54 n. 6, 55
22.15: 86–87
22.19: 68, 71, 87
22.22: 173
22.25–26: 86–87
22.28, 32, 33: 104
23.1, 14, 29: 105
24.7: 179
24.10: 104
25.2: 165
26.54: 110, 121
26.60: 119
26.62: 110, 121
26.65: 34 n. 5
27.1, 2: 165
27.18, 22: 34 n. 5

28.9, 12: 104
28.17, 19: 105
28.20: 104
28.24, 27: 105
28.28: 104
29.3, 9: 104
29.12: 105
29.14: 104
31.19: 105
31.50: 55
32.5: 121
32.12: 34 n. 5
32.14: 59 n. 6, 85
32.15: 85–86
32.17: 142 n. 3
32.28: 34 n. 5
32.32: 139, 142 n. 3
33.8: 104
33.39: 90
34.17: 34 n. 5
34.25, 28: 27 n. 1
35.3–4, 6, 11–12, 14–15: 165

Deuteronomy

1.11: 69 n. 13, 87
1.16, 18: 54 n. 6
1.19: 55
1.28: 142 n. 3
1.38: 34 n. 5
1.41: 142 n. 3
1.44: 165
2.1: 55
2.24–36: 185–86
2.25: 185
2.26–27: 188
2.34: 55
3.14–4.1: 187–88
3.15: 185
3.21: 34 n. 5, 188
3.22, 24–25: 188
3.26: 72, 87, 188
3.27: 185, 187
3.28: 34 n. 5, 188
4.2: 87
4.13, 41: 104
5.3: 142 n. 3
5.13: 105
5.19: 86
5.22: 85–86, 104
5.25: 61, 61 n. 7, 85–86, 142 n. 3
7.1: 105
8.9: 181
9.21: 18, 55
10.1, 3: 104
10.5: 55
12.8: 142 n. 3
13.1: 62–63, 63 n. 10, 68, 87
13.6: 145
13.12: 87
14.6: 104
14.28: 104
15.19: 119
16.3–4: 105, 118
16.8: 103, 105

16.9, 13, 15: 105
16.16: 104, 118
17.6: 103–4
17.16: 63, 87
18.16: 62, 68, 87
19.2, 7: 104
19.9: 58, 62, 104
19.15: 104
19.19: 85
19.20: 63, 87
20.8: 62–63, 85–86
21.15: 104, 165
22.15–16: 168 n. 3
22.19: 90, 93–94, 167 n. 1, 168, 170
22.20–21, 23: 168 n. 3
22.24: 130, 168 n. 3
22.25–26: 168 n. 3
22.27: 130, 168 n. 3
22.28–29: 168 n. 3
23.9: 119
24.1, 3: 181
25.3: 72, 87
28.7, 25: 105
28.68: 87
29.4: 55
29.18: 181
31.3, 7: 34 n. 5
31.11: 118 n. 8
31.14: 34 n. 5

31.15: 118
31.21: 165
31.23: 34 n. 5
32.44: 34, 34 n. 5
34.9: 34 n. 5

Joshua

1.11: 104
2.1: 104
2.16, 22: 104
3.2: 104
3.13: 117, 118 n. 10
3.16: 117
4.7: 117
6.3–4, 6, 14: 105
7.12: 87
9.16: 104
9.23: 117
10.26: 105
14.10: 105
18.2: 105
18.4: 104
18.5–6, 9: 105
22.14: 105
23.13: 87
24.32: 90
24.33: 121

Judges

2.21: 87
3.12: 87
3.16: 104

4.1: 87
5.8: 118
6.12: 118
6.27: 105
6.28: 117
7.16: 104
7.19: 90
8.14: 105
8.28: 85
9.22: 104
9.34: 105
9.37: 87
9.43: 104
10.6: 87
10.10, 12: 127 n. 1
10.13: 87
10.14: 127 n. 1
11.14: 87
11.37–39: 104
11.40: 105
13.1: 87
13.3: 118
13.8: 119
13.10: 117
13.21: 85, 117
14.14: 104
15.7: 122
15.13: 104
16.5: 90
16.7, 8: 105
16.15: 104
16.28: 122
17.2: 90, 121
17.3: 90, 92

17.10: 105
18.2: 105
18.29: 119
19.2: 105
19.4: 104
19.30: 117
20.10: 105
20.22–23, 28: 87
20.35: 90
20.47: 105

1 Samuel

1.2: 104
1.8: 105
1.22: 117
2.21: 104
3.6, 8, 17: 87
3.21: 87, 117
4.11: 121
4.13–14: 127 n. 1
4.17, 19, 21–22: 121
6.1, 4: 105
6.7, 10: 104
9.8: 3.21
10.2–4: 104
10.8: 105
11.3: 105
11.11: 104
13.1, 17, 21: 104
14.24: 122
15.35: 57, 85
16.11: 113
17.12, 17, 40: 105

18.7: 158 n. 2
18.19: 121
18.25: 90, 122
18.29: 65 n. 11, 87–88
19.8, 21: 88
20.13: 87
20.17: 88
20.41: 104
21.4: 105
21.7: 121
22.18: 105
23.4: 88
25.5: 105
25.18: 90, 104–5
25.22: 87
25.27: 121
27.4: 59 n. 6
27.7: 105
28.8: 104
30.12: 104
31.13: 105

2 Samuel

2.10: 104
2.11: 105
2.22: 88
2.23: 130
3.2: 119
3.5: 111, 119
3.9: 87
3.14: 90
3.29: 117
3.35: 87
4.2: 104
4.4: 105
5.5: 105
5.13: 119
6.1: 65 n. 11
6.11: 104
6.13: 105
7.10, 20: 87
8.2: 104
8.4: 90
12.1: 104
13.6: 104
13.38: 104
14.6: 104
14.10: 87
14.27: 104, 119
16.1: 90
17.12: 139 n. 1
17.17: 117
18.11: 105
18.14: 104
18.15: 105
18.22: 88
19.14: 87
20.4: 104
21.1: 104
21.6: 105, 114, 121
21.20: 111, 119
21.22: 119
22.11, 16: 118
24.1: 88
24.3: 88, 90
24.13: 104

1 Kings

2.4: 117
2.21: 121
2.23: 87
2.32, 39: 104
3.5: 117
3.16: 104
5.3: 90, 105
5.28: 104
6.10: 105
6.18: 117, 118 n. 10
6.23: 104
6.24: 105
6.32, 34, 36: 104
7.2: 90, 105
7.4–5, 12: 104
7.16: 104–5
7.18, 24: 104
7.30, 38: 105
7.42: 104
8.8: 118
8.25: 117
8.65: 105
9.2: 117–18
9.5: 117
9.25: 104
10.7: 57, 77 n. 21, 85
10.12: 117
10.17, 19, 22: 104
11.5: 172
11.9: 117
11.16, 31: 105

12.5: 104
12.11, 14: 87
12.28: 104
13.2: 119
14.3: 105
15.2: 104
16.15: 105
16.33: 88
16.34: 6
17.12: 104
17.15: 145
17.21: 104
18.1–2: 117
18.4, 13: 90
18.15: 118
18.23: 104
18.34: 105
20.1: 102 n. 5
20.27: 104
20.29: 90–91, 105
21.10: 104
22.1: 104

2 Kings

2.9–10: 113, 121
2.12, 17: 104
2.24: 102, 104, 172
3.4: 90
3.9: 105
4.43: 90
5.17: 121
5.22–23: 104
6.23b: 66
6.25: 105
6.31a: 66
7.3: 105
7.14: 104
8.17, 26: 104
9.32: 104
10.8: 104
13.7: 105
13.18–19, 25: 104
15.2: 104
15.8: 105
15.27: 104
17.5, 16: 104
18.10: 104
18.30: 121
19.10: 121
19.34: 70
20.6: 85
21.8: 87
21.19: 104
22.7: 121
23.24: 117
23.31: 104
23.33: 90–91
24.1: 104
24.7: 85
24.8: 104
25.17: 104
25.19, 25: 105
25.30: 121

Isaiah

1.5: 87
1.12: 118, 118 n. 8
1.13: 87
1.24: 122
5.10: 105
7.10: 88
7.21: 104
8.5: 88
9.5: 119, 121
10.20: 87
11.11: 87
11.13: 117
11.15: 103, 105
11.17: 172
16.12: 117
16.14: 104
17.6: 104
19.18: 105
20.3: 104
22.25: 117
23.12: 87
24.20: 87
26.15: 85–86
29.1: 66, 85–86
29.12: 121
29.14: 67, 73, 87
29.19: 62, 67, 85
29.20: 117
30.1: 59 n. 6, 85
30.33: 145
31.5: 70
33.7: 130 n. 4
33.16: 121
35.2: 121
36.15: 121
37.10: 121
37.31: 85–86

38.5: 73, 87
38.6: 70
38.11b–40.5: 192–93
38.12–14: 193–94 n. 3
38.19: 193, 193 n. 3
38.20: 193
38.21: 193 n. 3
39.1: 193 n. 3
39.3–4: 193
42.2: 130
46.7: 130
47.1: 87
47.3: 118
47.5: 87
48.19: 117
49.24–25: 121
51.12: 121
51.22: 87
52.1: 87
52.5: 121
53.8: 121
55.13: 117
56.5: 117
60.2: 118
65.14: 127 n. 1, 130
65.19: 127 n. 1
65.20: 90, 92–93
66.8: 119

Jeremiah

2.13: 104
7.21: 85
7.28: 117
8.13: 65 n. 11
13.20: 121
13.26: 117
15.15: 122
20.14–15: 119
21.10: 121
22.26: 119
24.1: 104
25.34–36: 127 n. 1
29.22: 121
31.3: 117
31.12: 87
32.4: 121
32.9: 105
32.24–25, 36, 43: 121
33.17–18: 117
34.3: 121
35.19: 117
36.23: 104
37.17: 121
38.3, 18: 121
39.17: 121
41.1, 8, 15: 105
42.6: 139
42.7: 105
45.3: 85
46.10: 122
46.24: 121
48.3–5, 20, 31, 34: 127 n. 1
48.46: 121
50.15: 122
51.55: 121
52.22, 25: 105
52.34: 121

Ezekiel

1.6: 105
3.15–16: 105
5.16: 68, 87
8.16: 105
9.2: 105
10.1: 117
10.8: 118
10.9, 14, 21: 105
11.1: 105
11.15: 121
15.3–4: 121
16.4: 117
16.34: 121
16.55: 158
19.11: 118
21.19: 117
21.24: 104
23.2: 104
23.14: 88
23.43: 160
25.12, 15: 122
31.14: 121
32.20, 23, 25, 29: 121
33.6, 24: 121

35.12: 121
36.12: 87
37.22: 104
39.12, 14: 105
40.7: 105
40.9: 104
40.19, 23, 27: 90
40.30: 105
40.39–40: 104
40.41–42: 105
40.47: 90
40.48: 104–5
41.2: 105
41.3: 104
41.9, 11–12: 105
41.13–15: 90
41.18, 22: 104
41.23: 103–4
41.24: 104
42.8: 90
42.16: 100
43.14: 104
43.25–26: 105
45.12, 23: 105
46.4, 6: 105
47.11: 121

Hosea

1.6: 87
2.5: 119
8.4: 117
9.15: 68, 87
13.2: 87

Joel

1.5, 16: 117
2.2: 69, 87

Amos

3.12: 104
4.3: 160 n. 5
4.4, 7: 104
4.8: 105
5.2: 58, 87
6.9: 105
7.8, 13: 87
8.2: 87

Obadiah

1.9–10: 117

Jonah

2.1: 104
2.5: 87
3.3: 104

Micah

5.8: 117

Nahum

2.1: 87, 117

Zephaniah

1.2: 65 n. 11
1.11: 117

3.7: 117
3.11: 87

Zechariah

2.3: 105
3.9: 105
4.2: 105
4.3: 104
5.9: 104
8.23: 105
9.10: 117
9.14: 118
9.15: 70
11.7: 104
13.8: 117
14.2: 117

Malachi

3.2: 117

Psalms

10.18: 87
18.16: 118
22.32: 119
37.9, 22, 28, 34, 38: 117
41.9: 87
42.3: 118
61.7: 87
71.14: 61, 79, 85–86
73.16: 145
74.6: 160

77.8: 87
78.6: 119
78.17: 87
84.8: 118
87.4–6: 119
90.2: 119
90.16: 118
102.17: 117
107.6, 13, 19: 127 n. 1
107.28: 127 n. 1, 130
115.14: 88
119: 40 n. 4
120.3: 87

Proverbs

1.5: 88
2.22: 117
3.2: 87
9.9: 88
9.11: 58, 87
10.22, 27: 87
10.31: 117
16.21, 23: 87
17.17: 119
19.4, 19: 87
23.18: 117
23.28, 35: 87
24.14: 117
27.25: 117
30.6: 88
30.15: 104

Job

1–2: 40 n. 4
1.2: 105, 119
1.14: 172
1.17: 104
2.13: 105
3.3: 119
5.7: 119
9.24: 121
11.12: 119
13.18–27: 189
13.24, 26–27: 190
14.7: 117, 118 n. 10
14.13–18: 190
14.14: 189, 190
14.16–17: 190
15.7: 119
15.19: 121
17.9: 87
20.9: 87
27.1: 88
28.2, 15: 121
29.1: 88
31.11: 145
33.21: 117
34.32, 37: 87
36.1: 88
38.11: 87
38.21: 119
40.5: 87
40.32: 88
42.7–17: 40 n. 4
42.8: 105
42.10: 88
42.13, 16: 105

Ruth

1.17: 87
4.2: 105
4.10: 117
4.15: 105
4.17: 119

Song of Songs

2.12: 117
4.5: 104

Lamentations

3.42: 139
4.15–16, 22: 87

Qohelet

1.16: 85
1.18: 87
3.14: 85
4.14: 111 n. 3, 119
5.8: 145
7.1: 111 n. 3, 119
10.6: 121
12.11: 121

Esther

1.1, 4: 90
1.5: 105
2.8: 121

2.12: 105
2.13: 111 n. 3, 121
2.16: 121
3.14: 111 n. 3, 121
3.15: 121
4.8: 121
4.16: 104
5.3, 6: 111 n. 3, 121
6.8: 121
7.2–3: 111 n. 3, 121
8.3: 88
8.9: 90
8.13: 111 n. 3, 121–22
8.14: 121
9.12–14: 111 n. 3, 121
9.30: 90

Daniel

1.13: 118
1.15: 117
4.33: 59
8.1: 117
8.12: 111 n. 3, 121
9.26: 117
10.2–3: 104
10.18: 88
11.2: 104
11.6: 111 n. 3, 121
11.11: 121

Ezra

1.10: 105
6.22: 105
8.26: 90
9.7: 121
10.3: 111 n. 3, 119
10.10: 85

Nehemiah

5.1, 6: 127 n. 1
5.11: 90–91
5.18: 105
6.15: 104
8.17: 6
8.18: 105
9.4, 9, 27–28: 127 n. 1
10.30: 121
12.31: 104
13.10: 121
13.18: 85

1 Chronicles

1.19: 104, 111 n. 3, 119
2.3, 9: 111 n. 3, 119
3.1: 111 n. 3, 119
3.4: 105, 111, 111 n. 3, 119
3.5: 111 n. 3, 119, 119 n. 12
4.5: 104

5.1: 121
5.20: 111 n. 3, 121
5.21: 90
7.21: 111 n. 3, 119
7.26: 6
8.38: 105
9.44: 105
10.12: 105
13.14: 104
14.13: 87
15.26: 105
17.9, 18: 87
18.4: 90
20.6: 111, 111 n. 3, 119
20.8: 111 n. 3, 119, 119 n. 12
21.3: 88, 90
21.5: 90
21.12: 104–5
22.9: 111 n. 3, 119
22.14: 87, 90
26.6: 111 n. 3, 119
29.7: 90
29.16: 145

2 Chronicles

1.7: 117
2.13: 111 n. 3, 121
3.1: 117
4.3, 13: 104
5.9: 118
6.13: 105
6.16: 117

7.8–9: 105
7.12: 118
7.18: 117
8.13: 105
9.6: 57, 77 n. 21, 85
9.11: 118
9.18: 104
9.21: 105
10.5: 104

10.11, 14: 87
13.2: 105
18.14: 111 n. 3
25.6, 9: 90
27.5: 90
28.5: 121
28.13: 85
28.22: 88
30.21, 23: 105

31.16: 105
33.8: 87
33.21: 104
34.16: 121
35.17: 105
36.2: 104
36.3: 90
36.9: 104–5

Iron Age Epigraphy

Arad

2.1: 184
3.1: 184
18.3: 184
18.10, 12: 146 n. 2
24.14–15, 18: 185
40.4: 184
40.7–8: 185
40.9: 184
111.4: 112

Deir ʿAlla

1: 146 n. 2
B.12: 112 n. 5

Ketef Hinnom

1.4: 185

Kuntillet ʿAjrud

9.1: 146 n. 2

Lachish

2.3: 184
3.4: 184
3.21: 112
4.1: 184
4.2: 184–85
4.10–11: 139
21.5: 146

Meshaʿ

3: 44
6: 146 n. 2
7, 9, 11–12, 14: 44
15: 44–45
16–17: 44
18: 44–45
19–20: 44
21: 59 n. 4, 85, 146 n. 2
24: 44
29: 85
30–31: 45

Sefire Treaty Text 1

a.30: 127

Siloam

2: 184–85
3: 184
5: 89, 184
6: 89

Silwan Tomb

1.2: 112

Tell Fekheriye

20: 96–97
21–22: 97

Zakkur

B.4–5: 63, 79, 86

Dead Sea Scrolls

1QH[a]

9.37: 86

1QIsa[a]

11.5: 103 n. 9
20.27–28: 85
23.7: 85
23.29: 62 n. 7, 85
24.7: 85
27.7: 130 n. 4
35.11: 130
39.12: 130 n. 4
52.21: 130 n. 4
55.3: 93

1QIsa[b] (1Q8)

191–94
16.1–26: 192–93
16.2–3: 193 n. 3
16.7: 193, 193 n. 3
16.9, 11: 193 n. 3
16.15, 18: 193
28.4: 93

1QM

9.13: 93

1QpHab

8.12: 86
11.15: 86

1QS

2.11: 86
6.14: 86

1Q14

f8–10.7: 86

2Q29

f1.2: 139

4Q1

f5.9: 93

4Q11

f3–4.4: 130 n. 4

4Q24

f9i+10–17.22: 85

4Q30

f32i+33.4: 103 n. 9

4QDeut[d] (4Q31)

185–88
1.5–17: 186
1.6: 185
1.7–8: 188
2.1–21: 187–88
2.2: 185
2.5, 9, 11, 13, 15–17, 19: 188

4Q37

3.7: 61, 86

4Q41

5.2: 85
5.7: 61

4Q51

9e–i.2: 103 n. 6

4QSam[b] (4Q52)

191, 200

4Q56

f16ii+17–20+20a.11: 85
f22–23.3: 86

4Q64

f1–5.4: 86

4Q73

f2.6: 103 n. 7

4Q83

f9ii.13: 61, 86

4Q88

3.19–21: 130

4QPalaeoJob^c (4Q101)

189–91
f1–2.1–10: 189
f1–2.7, 9–10: 190
f3.1–8: 190
f3.4: 189–90
f3.6–7: 190

4Q129

f1R.13: 61, 61 n. 7, 86

4Q132

f3–4.1: 103 n. 8

4Q135

f1.1: 86
f1.4: 61, 86

4Q136

f1.13: 103 n. 8

4Q137

f1.31: 61, 86

4Q140

f1.14: 103 n. 8

4Q145

f1R.7: 103 n. 8

4QReworked Pentateuch (4Q158; 4Q364–367)

11

4Q159

f1ii.8: 93

4QCommentary Genesis A (4Q252)

11

4Q252

1.7: 93
1.9: 93
1.18: 63
1.19: 86
1.20: 63, 86

4Q265

f4ii.3: 86

4Q266

f10ii.1: 93

4Q286

f7i.8: 86

4Q298

f3–4ii.6–7: 86

4Q299

f30.5: 86

4Q364

f8i.2: 93

4Q365

f5ai.4: 129
f6aii + 6c.10: 129

4Q403

f1i.25: 70 n. 14

4Q405

f3ii.17: 70 n. 14

4Q416

f2iv.7: 86

4Q418

f81 + 81a.17: 86

4Q502

f3.1: 86

4Q503

f15–16.10: 86

4Q525

f1.3: 86

11Q1

5.4: 86
6.2, 4, 9: 86

11Q5

28 (Ps. 151): 11

11QT^a (11Q19)

11
44.6: 93
54.6–7: 63
56.17–18: 63
61.11: 63
65.14: 93
66.2–3, 7–8: 130

XQ2

1.6: 61, 86

Rabbinic Texts

Mishna

Demai

7.7: 95 n. 3

Kilayim

1.3: 86
5.6: 86
7.8: 86

Sheviit

3.2–3: 86

Terumot

4.3–4: 86
4.7, 10: 95 n. 3
5.1–4: 95 n. 3
9.5: 95 n.3

Maasrot

1.1: 86

Maaser Sheni

4.3: 86
5.5: 86

'Orla

1.5: 86

Shabbat

16.3: 95 n. 3

'Eruvin

3.3: 95, 95 n. 3
7.7: 86
8.10: 95, 95 n. 3

Pesaḥim

1.6: 86

Yoma

3.7: 86
4.4: 86
7.5: 86

Sukkah

3.15: 86
5.5: 86

Taʿanit

2.2: 86

Megillah

4.1–2: 86

Ketubbot

3.4: 86
4.3: 95 n. 3
5.1, 5: 86, 95 n. 3
5.7, 9: 86
13.7: 95 n. 3

Nedarim

3.1: 86

Nazir

2.10: 95, 95 n. 3

Soṭa

8.5: 86
9.1: 86
9.5: 63

Qiddushin

4.4: 86

ʿArayot

11: 86

Bava Qamma

4.5: 95 n. 3

Bava Meṣiaʿ

3.8: 95 n.3
4.8: 86
6.5: 86

Bava Batra

9.5: 95 n. 3

Sanhedrin

1.5–6: 86
4.5: 95 n. 3
5.5: 86
11.3: 86

Makkot

3.14: 86

Shevuʿot

2.2: 86

ʿEduyot

2.1: 86
8.1: 86

Zevaḥim

1.3: 86
8.10: 63 n. 10

Menaḥot

13.6: 86

Ḥullin

6.4: 95 n.3

Bekhorot

6.8: 86

ʿArakhin

2.3, 5–6: 86
3.5: 95 n.3
6.2: 86, 95 n.3
8.2–3: 86

Keritot

5.3: 95 n. 3

Tamid

5.1: 87

Middot

3.1: 86
4.7: 95, 95 n. 3
5.1–2: 95, 95 n. 3
3.4: 95, 95 n. 3

ʾOholot

14.3: 95, 95 n. 3
17.1: 95, 95 n. 3

Negaʿim

8.4: 95 n. 3

Makhshirin

1.1–6: 116
2.4: 87

Yadayim

1.1: 87
4.2: 87

Talmud Yerushalmi

Ketubbot 3.9: 167 n. 1
Sanhedrin 7.11: 167 n. 1

Talmud Bavli

Bava Meṣiaʿ 86a: 95
Bekhorot 5a: 95
Ketubbot 40b: 167 n. 1

Other Texts

Sirach

3.27: 86
5.5: 86

Ein Gedi Burnt Leviticus Scroll

194–97

col. 1: 195
col. 2: 196
col. 2. ll. 6, 8, 11: 197

SUBJECT INDEX

1QIsaiah^a, 124
1QIsaiah^b, 191–93
4QDeut^b, 188
4QDeut^d, 185–87
4QPalaeoJob^c, 189–90
4QSamuel^b, 191
ABH (Archaic Biblical Hebrew), 1, 34, 51–52, 134, 179, 206–7
absolute, 15, 17, 22, 66, 70, 89–102–5, 177, 179
accumulation, 7, 10–11, 51, 181
adjective, 172
agreement, 19, 28, 80, 93, 102, 118, 123, 140, 145, 148–49, 162, 169, 172, 194, 196, 203
Akkadian, 36, 139
ʾalef, 140
alternant, 21, 23, 34, 127 n. 1, 142 n. 2, 149, 158–59, 162–63
Amarna, 36
Amos, 30, 58, 75, 87, 104–5, 156, 160
anthroponym, 31
apophonic passive, 107
aqtul, 39, 49
aqtulan[na], 39, 50
aqtulu/a, 39, 49–50

Arabic, 11, 127 n. 1, 139, 149, 155
Arad, 112, 146, 160, 184–85
Aramaic, 4, 6, 20, 29, 36, 63, 70 n. 14, 96–97, 130–31, 137, 139, 178–79
archaic, 12, 72, 77–79, 85, 98, 134, 140–42, 148, 161, 170
archaising, 13, 131, 134
archaism, 96, 180
article (definite), 92
augmented (1st-person *way-yiqtol*), 39–53
BA (Biblical Aramaic), 4, 6, 29, 59 n. 5, 130
BDSS (Biblical Dead Sea Scrolls), 40–45, 47, 61, 85–86, 93, 97, 102–3, 116, 124, 130, 139, 155, 162, 167
Ben Sira, 4, 6, 35 n. 6, 40–41, 43–45, 47, 61–63, 79, 86, 103, 110, 116, 118 n. 11, 131, 162, 167
BH (Biblical Hebrew), 1, 4–5, 7, 9–11, 23, 28–29, 39, 50–51, 54, 61, 69–70, 79, 91, 93, 95–97, 100 n. 4, 102–4, 107, 113–14, 116, 124, 134–35, 139–41, 147–48, 156, 160, 169, 171–72, 179, 185, 197, 206–7

binyan, 107
Canaanite, 36, 53
CBH (Classical Biblical Hebrew), 1–3, 6–8, 11, 14–21, 23, 29, 30 n. 3, 34–35, 37, 39, 40 n. 4, 42–54, 59–60, 63, 65–66, 79, 81–83, 89, 93, 97–99, 104, 108, 110, 112–16, 118–24, 126–27, 131–38, 141–42, 153–54, 163, 167, 170–71, 173–75, 179–80, 183–84, 197, 199, 201–7
CBH_1, 52–53, 99, 136, 152, 201, 206–7
CBH_2, 52–54, 99, 136, 152, 201, 207
Chronicles, 4–5, 13, 19, 27, 30, 31, 33, 40 n. 4, 60, 75, 111, 128–29, 156
chronolect, 1–2, 12–15, 32, 34, 50–51, 53, 83, 89, 99, 113, 115, 134, 136, 174, 201
classical opposition, 5–6
concentration, 4–5, 7, 22, 27, 54, 84, 157, 174
construct, 15, 17, 22, 59, 60, 66, 89–105, 155, 160, 177, 198
contemporisation, 15, 17, 53, 99, 137, 201
copyist, 46
Court History, 19

D(euteronomy), 13, 19, 34 n. 5, 54, 84–85, 87, 142, 158, 165, 181
Daniel, 4, 30–31, 40 n. 4, 75, 156
defective, 17–18, 75–76, 84–85, 87, 146, 150–51, 155, 160, 168–71, 177–78, 180–81, 184–86, 189, 191, 193, 197, 199–201
Deir ʿAlla, 112 n. 5, 146
Deuteronomy, 28, 60, 69, 75, 85, 92, 128, 156–57, 165, 168, 185–86, 188, 199
dialect, 3, 7, 147 n. 3
Documentary Hypothesis, 14, 20, 28, 205
DSSBH (Dead Sea Scrolls Biblical Hebrew), 6
E(lohist), 13, 19, 21–22, 28, 34, 54, 84–85, 87, 90, 92, 117–19, 121–22, 125–26, 142, 158, 164–65, 180–81
Egyptian, 28, 57, 130
Ein Gedi Burnt Leviticus Scroll, 194–96
ending, 22, 30, 31, 133 n. 5, 155 n. 1, 157, 161–62, 168–69, 177–81, 185, 198
epicene, 147–49, 151, 154, 171–73
epigraphy, 4, 7–8, 31, 79, 89, 91, 97–98, 127, 140, 146, 160

Esther, 4, 30, 40 n. 4, 75, 128–29, 156, 170
Ethiopic, 139
Exodus, 22, 75, 128, 156–58, 159 n. 3, 164, 198–99
extrabiblical confirmation, 5–6, 42
Ezekiel, 13, 20, 30, 53, 75, 128, 156–57, 162
Ezra, 4–5, 13, 30–31, 40 n. 4, 60, 75, 85, 90, 105, 111 n. 3, 119, 121, 128, 198–99, 202
Former Prophets, 2, 80, 117, 119, 120–22, 141, 200–201
gender, 147 n. 3, 171–73
Genesis, 8, 11, 15, 22, 36, 60, 63, 75, 128, 152, 156–58, 159 n. 3, 164, 168, 199–200
genre, 2–3, 7, 50, 134
Greek, 4, 16, 171
Habakkuk, 128
Haggai, 20
harmonisation, 94, 102, 133 n. 5, 161, 170
heh, 5, 30 n. 3, 48, 161, 168–70
hifilisation, 64, 71 n. 15, 74, 78–80, 82, 112
hifʿil, 14–15, 17–18, 22, 39, 41, 43–45, 53–55, 57–87, 107, 127 n. 1
historiography, 2, 8, 35, 115, 174
hofʿal, 59 n. 5, 109, 124

Hosea, 30, 34, 75, 128, 156
II-*w/y*, 17, 39, 41, 43–45, 53–55
III-*y*, 17–18, 39–41, 43–45, 47–48, 53, 59 n. 6
infinitive, 59, 60, 64, 66, 70, 112, 155, 160, 198
intransitive, 112
Iron Age II, 1–2, 4, 6–8, 15, 28, 115, 163
Isaiah, 15, 20, 30–31, 53, 60, 75, 128, 156, 191–94
J(ahwist, Yahwist), 13, 19–22, 28–29, 33–34, 36, 54, 84–85, 87, 117–19, 121–22, 125–26, 138, 142, 158–59, 164–65, 168
JDA (Judaean Desert Aramaic), 7
JDH (Judaean Desert Hebrew), 6
Jeremiah, 15, 20, 30–31, 53, 60, 75, 128, 156
Jerome, 162
Job, 40 n. 4, 75, 128, 156, 189–90
Joel, 69, 75, 87, 117, 128, 156
Jonah, 75, 128, 156
Josephus, 35 n. 6
Joshua, 5–6, 8, 29–31, 34–35, 53, 75, 128, 156, 174, 188
Judaean Desert, 4, 16, 185
Judges, 8, 29–31, 35, 53, 60, 75, 128, 156, 170, 174

ketiv, 59 n. 6, 100, 104, 114, 119, 121, 139, 160 n. 4
ketiv-qere, 9, 16, 114, 145 n. 1, 168
Kings, 15, 30–31, 53, 60, 75, 102, 128, 133, 156, 174, 201
Kuntillet ʿAjrud, 146
Lachish, 112, 139, 146, 160, 184–85
Lamentations, 20, 75, 128, 140, 156
late distribution, 5
Latin, 4, 162
Latter Prophets, 2, 80, 117, 119–22, 141, 174, 198
LBH (Late Biblical Hebrew), 1, 3–7, 14–15, 17, 19–21, 29, 30 n. 3, 32, 34–35, 39–40, 49–53, 59–60, 76 n. 19, 77 n. 21, 81, 89, 93, 97–99, 101–3, 110–11, 115–17, 119–23, 126–27, 129, 131–36, 138, 141, 162, 167, 178, 197–99, 201–4, 206–7
LBH+, 40–48, 50–52, 54, 60, 76–80, 82–83
levelling, 2–3, 19, 22–23, 70, 94, 131, 133, 137, 142, 148, 153, 155, 161, 175, 203
Leviticus, 22, 60, 75, 156–58, 159 n. 3, 163, 165, 194–96, 199
lexeme, 22, 127 n. 1, 171–72, 177–80

lexicon, 5
long (1st-person *wayyiqtol*), 18, 39–49, 50, 52–55
LXX (Septuagint), 7, 65 n. 11
Malachi, 20, 30, 156
matres lectionis, 9, 17, 22–23, 58–59, 65, 76, 183, 186, 194
Meshaʿ Stele, 44–45, 51, 53, 61
methodology, 3–5, 178, 204
Micah, 30, 128, 156
Middle Akkadian, 139
Mishna, 61–63, 86, 94–95, 102, 155
Moabite, 44, 54, 59 n. 4, 61
monarchic period, 2, 29, 31, 35–36, 115
morphology, 5, 14–15, 17–18, 21–22, 39–47, 49–55, 59 n. 6, 60, 63–64, 67, 69, 71–73, 76–77, 79, 81, 83–85, 93, 107–9, 111–14, 116, 118, 120, 123–26, 147–49, 151–52, 158, 160–63, 172, 179–80, 204
Mosaic, 12, 27, 174
Murabbaʿat, 160
Nahum, 75
NBDSS (Non-biblical Dead Sea Scrolls), 32, 40–45, 47, 61–62, 86, 93, 97, 102–3, 116, 139, 162

Nehemiah, 4–5, 13, 30–31, 40 n. 4, 60, 75, 128–29, 156, 198–99, 202
NENA (North-eastern Neo-Aramaic), 147 n. 3
Neo-Assyrian, 139
Neo-Babylonian, 139
nifalisation, 107 n. 1, 112–13, 115, 123
nifʿal, 15, 17, 21, 107–26, 127 n. 1
Northwest Semitic, 28
noun, 15, 70 n. 14, 89–90, 94, 100, 127 n. 1, 160, 167, 177–79, 181
NT (New Testament), 7
Numbers, 22, 27–28, 33, 60, 75, 128, 152, 156–58, 163, 165, 199–200
numeral, 89, 94, 100–4, 198
nun, 6, 177
OA (Old Aramaic), 63, 96–97, 127 n. 2
Obadiah, 30, 156
onomasticon, 8, 15, 27–29, 31, 33, 35–37, 54, 175, 204
P(riestly Code/source), 12–14, 19–22, 27–28, 32–34, 54, 84–85, 87, 90, 92–93, 117–19, 121, 125–26, 138, 142, 158, 159 n. 3, 164–65, 180–81, 199–200, 202, 205–6
paradigm, 1, 51–52, 58–59, 65–66, 82, 109, 134, 205–6

participle, 59–60, 61 n. 7, 66, 69 n. 13, 70 n. 14, 73, 83, 109, 160, 172
passive, 15, 17, 21, 59, 107–26
Patriarchal, 174
Pentateuch, 3, 8, 11–12, 14, 16–17, 21, 28–29, 31–32, 34–36, 45–46, 54, 60, 62–63, 67, 76–82, 84, 89, 92, 94, 102, 104, 122–23, 125, 131–32, 134–35, 137, 140–41, 145–47, 149–54, 157, 158 n. 2, 163–64, 167–68, 170, 174–75, 177–80, 183–84, 199–200, 204–5
Persian Period, 14, 21, 27, 76
Peshiṭta, 4, 97
pielisation, 62 n. 8, 111
piʿʿel, 62, 107
plene, 17–18, 64, 74–78, 80, 82, 84, 85, 87, 148, 167 n. 1, 168, 170–71, 177–81, 184–86, 193, 197–99
poetry, 1, 34, 43, 50, 121, 134, 161
pre-monarchic, 2, 7–8, 15, 29, 31–32, 34–37, 115, 125, 136, 174–75, 207
prefix, 29, 31, 58, 59, 62, 64, 67, 70–73, 75–76, 84–85, 87, 108–9, 112, 120, 155–58, 161–64
preposition, 160

pronunciation, 9, 17–19, 22–23, 41, 54, 58, 64, 65 n. 11, 108, 115, 124, 145, 152, 155–57, 160–61, 167–68, 180, 183
proto-Masoretic, 16, 196
PS (proto-Semitic), 39 n. 1, 49–50, 67, 71 n. 16, 149, 155, 162
Proverbs, 30, 75, 128, 156
Psalms, 50, 60, 75, 128, 156
pseudo-cohortative (1st-person *wayyiqtol*), 39
pu‘‘al, 108–9
QA (Qumran Aramaic), 41, 130
qal, 14–15, 17–18, 20–22, 39, 41, 43–45, 53–55, 57–85, 87, 107–26, 127 n. 1, 198
qatal, 62, 66, 83
qere, 59 n. 6, 100, 104, 114, 119, 121, 139, 160 n. 4
qere perpetuum, 145, 168–69
QH (Qumran Hebrew), 6, 63, 70 n. 14, 110, 118 n. 11, 139, 155, 162, 167
Qohelet, 40 n. 4, 60, 75, 128–29
redaction, 16, 34, 123, 158, 175
regional variation, 3
register, 2–3, 7, 17, 139
Reworked Pentateuch, 11, 63
Rewritten Bible, 11, 63
RH (Rabbinic Hebrew), 32, 70, 79, 94–97, 102–3, 110, 116, 118 n. 11, 131–32, 139–40, 162, 167, 179
root, 57, 116, 119, 125, 127–30, 132, 137, 167
Ruth, 29, 75, 87, 105, 117, 119, 156
Samuel, 8, 15, 29–31, 35–36, 53, 57, 60, 75, 111, 128, 156–57, 162, 174, 200
scribe, 11, 46, 48–49, 98, 123, 129 n. 3, 137, 151, 194 n. 3
Second Isaiah, 20
Seder ‘Olam Rabba, 96
SH (Samaritan Hebrew), 62, 110, 131, 139
short (1st-person *wayyiqtol*), 14, 17–18, 39, 41, 43–46, 48–49, 51–55
Song of Songs, 156
SP (Samaritan Pentateuch), 40–41, 43–45, 61–62, 65 n. 11, 67–68, 79, 86, 90–91, 94, 97–98, 102–3, 116, 124, 131, 135, 137, 155
spelling, 17–19, 64–67, 72, 74, 77–78, 80–83, 112, 145–46, 148–51, 153, 156–57, 160–61, 168–71, 177, 180, 184–86, 189, 191, 193–94, 197–202, 205
stative, 69–70
stem, 58–59, 61, 65–66, 69, 70 n. 14, 71, 74, 87, 107–9, 111, 112 n. 5

Subject Index

stem shift, 15, 65, 71, 78–79, 110, 112 n. 4, 120, 122
sub-chronolect, 1, 14, 53, 83, 99, 136, 201
suffix, 29–31, 59–60, 62 n. 7, 64, 71–73, 83, 108, 133 n. 5, 140, 155, 160, 167, 171, 178–79, 183, 198 n. 5
suppletion, 66, 81–82, 108–9
synonymy, 57, 112–14, 127 n. 1
Syriac, 4, 7, 65 n. 11, 130
TA (Targumic Aramaic), 131
Talmud, 95
Targum, 97
TBH (Transitional Biblical Hebrew), 1, 19–20, 34, 51–54, 99, 134, 138, 140, 162, 202, 204, 206–7
Tetragrammaton, 28–29, 33–34
theophoric (name), 8, 29–32, 36, 133 n. 5, 198 n. 5
Torah, 2, 8, 14–16, 21, 29–30, 33, 35, 37, 39–41, 43–55, 63, 80, 82–83, 91, 94, 97–98, 102, 104, 117, 119–24, 126, 131, 133, 135–38, 141–42, 145–54, 157, 159, 162–63, 167–71, 173–75, 177–81, 183–84, 198–205
transitive, 112 n. 4
Ugaritic, 36
variant, 18–19, 22–23, 51, 139, 148, 184, 191, 204

verb, 17–18, 21, 39–41, 43–45, 53, 57, 61–62, 69, 70–71, 107–9, 111–12, 115, 116 n. 7, 118, 120, 123–26, 127 n. 1, 159–60
Vulgate, 7, 65 n. 11
waw, 62 n. 7, 64, 82, 146–47, 177, 194
wayyiqtol, 14, 17–18, 39–49, 51–55, 58–59, 59 n. 3, 62, 64, 72, 155, 204
Wellhausen, 12–13, 27–28, 32, 174
weqatal, 62 n. 7, 70, 139 n. 1
Writings, 2–3, 14, 16, 18, 40–41, 43–48, 50, 52, 54, 60, 76, 80, 98, 117, 119–24, 126, 132–38, 141, 145, 151–54, 163, 167, 170, 173–75, 177, 180, 198, 203–4
yafʿil, 69–72
yahu, 8, 15, 17, 21, 27, 29, 33, 35 n. 6, 204
yaqtel, 62
Yhwh, 28–33, 35
yiqtol, 64, 87
yod, 64, 72, 74, 77–78, 82–83, 146, 194
Zechariah, 20, 30, 75, 128, 156–57, 162
Zephaniah, 30, 128

About the Team

Geoffrey Khan and Alessandra Tosi were the managing editors for this book.

Anne Burberry performed the copyediting of the book in Word. The fonts used in this volume are Charis SIL, SBL Hebrew, SBL Greek, Estrangelo Edessa and Scheherazade New.

Cameron Craig created all of the editions—paperback, hardback, and PDF. Conversion was performed with open source software freely available on our GitHub page at https://github.com/OpenBookPublishers.

Jeevanjot Kaur Nagpal designed the cover of this book. The cover was produced in InDesign using Fontin and Calibri fonts.

www.ingramcontent.com/pod-product-compliance
Lightning Source LLC
Chambersburg PA
CBHW061251230426
43664CB00025B/2929